Microsoft® Access VBA Programming for the Absolute Beginner
Second Edition

MICHAEL VINE

THOMSON

™

COURSE TECHNOLOGY

Professional ■ Trade ■ Reference

ISBN: 1-59200-723-6

Library of Congress Catalog Card Number: 2004114910

Printed in the United States of America

05 06 07 08 09 BH 10 9 8 7 6 5 4 3 2 1

Publisher and GM of Course PTR:
Stacy L. Hiquet

Associate Director of Marketing:
Sarah O'Donnell

Marketing Manager:
Heather Hurley

Manager of Editorial Services:
Heather Talbot

Acquisitions Editor:
Mitzi Koontz

Senior Editor:
Mark Garvey

Marketing Coordinator:
Jordan Casey

Project Editor:
Scott Harris/Argosy Publishing

Technical Reviewer:
Eric Olson

PTR Editorial Services Coordinator:
Elizabeth Furbish

Copy Editor:
Tonya Cupp

Interior Layout Tech:
Shawn Morningstar

Cover Designer:
Mike Tanamachi

CD-ROM Producer:
Keith Davenport

Indexer:
Nancy Fulton

Proofreader:
Jan Cocker

THOMSON

COURSE TECHNOLOGY

Professional ■ Trade ■ Reference

Thomson Course Technology PTR,
a division of Thomson Course Technology
25 Thomson Place
Boston, MA 02210
http://www.courseptr.com

To Sheila: 143

ACKNOWLEDGMENTS

Writing any book is not easy, especially a technical programming book. It takes many great, patient, and talented people to write, edit, design, market, finance, and produce a book and accompanying CD-ROM. Without the publishing assistance of Mitzi Koontz, Scott Harris, and Tonya Cupp, it would be impossible for me to share with you my knowledge of programming in such a professional and fun manner.

I'd like to thank a good friend, Eric Olson, who ensured the technical accuracy of this book. Thanks Eric! Now that the book is done, let's go fishing!

Beyond the technical and business workings of creating a book, the Author must be fed, loved, and encouraged. Without the support of my beautiful wife Sheila, this would never have happened. Thanks baby: I love you!

ABOUT THE AUTHOR

Michael Vine has taught computer programming, Web design, and database classes at Indiana University/Purdue University in Indianapolis, IN, and at MTI College of Business and Technology in Sacramento, CA. Michael has over 13 years of experience in the information technology profession. He currently works full time at a Fortune 100 company as an IT Project Manager overseeing the development of enterprise data warehouses.

CONTENTS

Chapter 6   CODE REUSE AND DATA STRUCTURES 147

INTRODUCTION

I ntroduced in the early 1990s, Microsoft Access has become one of the most powerful and popular applications in the Microsoft Office suite of applications. Part of Microsoft Office Professional Edition 2003, Microsoft Access 2003 allows database developers and programmers to build dynamic and easily portable databases. Access comes with many easy-to-use features such as graphical forms, report designers, and SQL query builders, as well as a subset of the Visual Basic language known as VBA for building data-driven applications.

Microsoft Access VBA Programming for the Absolute Beginner, Second Edition, is not a guide on how to use Access and its many wizards. There are already many books that do that! Instead, *Microsoft Access VBA Programming for the Absolute Beginner* concentrates on VBA programming concepts including variables, conditions, loops, data structures, procedures, file I/O, and object-oriented programming with special topics including Microsoft Jet SQL, database programming with ADO, Microsoft Office objects, and data access pages.

Using Premier Press's *Absolute Beginner* series guidelines' professional insight, clear explanations, examples, and pictures, you learn to program in Access VBA. Each chapter contains programming challenges, a chapter review, and a complete program that uses chapter-based concepts to construct a fun and easily built application.

To work through this book in its entirety, you should have access to a computer with Microsoft Access installed. The programs in this book were written in Microsoft Office 2003, specifically Access 2003. Those readers using older versions of Microsoft Access, such as Access 2002 or Access 2000, will find that many of the VBA programming concepts still apply.

WHAT YOU'LL FIND IN THIS BOOK

To learn how to program a computer, you must acquire a complex progression of skills. If you have never programmed at all, you will probably find it easiest to go through the chapters in order. Of course, if you are already an experienced programmer, it might not be necessary to do any more than skim the earliest chapters. In either case, programming is not a skill you can learn by reading. You'll have to write programs to learn. This book has been designed to make the process reasonably painless.

Each chapter begins with a brief introduction to chapter-based concepts. Once inside the chapter, you'll look at a series of programming concepts and small programs that illustrate each of the major points of the chapter. Finally, you'll put these concepts together to build a complete program at the end of the chapter. All of the programs are short enough that you can type them in yourself (which is a great way to look closely at code), but they are also available on the accompanying CD-ROM. Located at the end of every chapter is a summary that outlines key concepts learned. Use the summaries to refresh your memory on the important concepts. In addition to summaries, each chapter contains programming challenges that will help you learn and cement chapter-based concepts. Throughout the book, I'll throw in a few other tidbits, notably the following:

 These are good ideas that experienced programmers like to pass on.

 There are a few areas where it's easy to make a mistake. I'll point them out to you as we go.

 Pay special attention to these areas for clarification or emphasis on chapter concepts.

IN THE REAL WORLD

As you examine concepts in this book, I'll show you how the concepts are used beyond beginning programming.

WHO THIS BOOK IS FOR

Microsoft Access VBA Programming for the Absolute Beginner, Second Edition, is designed for the beginning Access VBA programmer. Persons with backgrounds in other programming languages and databases will find this book to be a good tutorial and desk reference for Access VBA. Specifically, this book is for the following groups:

- High school or college students enrolling or enrolled in an Access programming class
- Programming hobbyists and enthusiasts
- Office personnel with beginning database programming responsibilities
- Professional database developers wanting to learn the Microsoft Access VBA language
- Home users wanting to learn more about Access and VBA

ACCESS ESSENTIALS

I ntroduced over a decade ago, Microsoft Access is a fully functional *RDBMS (Relational Database Management System)* that has become one of the most powerful programs in the Microsoft Office suite of applications.

Part of the Microsoft Office Professional Edition 2003, Access 2003 provides both beginning and professional database developers alike a cost effective way to leverage key database functionality with an easy-to-use graphical interface.

In this chapter I get you started using the Access 2003 application by showing you Access essentials such as files, databases, tables, fields, relationships, forms, controls, and queries. You learn these Access essentials by building a simple database to manage students and homework assignments.

GETTING STARTED WITH ACCESS 2003

Microsoft has done a great job making Access 2003 intuitive and easy to learn by providing a simple interface and an excellent help system. If you're already familiar with previous versions of Access databases, you'll appreciate the new and updated functionality for

- Viewing object dependencies
- Enabling automatic error checking in forms and reports
- Propagating control property changes to bound fields
- Smart Tags with Access objects

- Database backups
- XML support
- Improved Microsoft Office online help
- Collaborate development efforts with friends and colleagues using Microsoft SharePoint Services
- Improved macro and function security
- Context-based help for SQL view
- Manage SQL Server databases with Access projects
- Updated Microsoft Office 2003 Object Model
- New Visual Basic objects, properties, and methods

System Requirements

System requirements for installing and using Microsoft Access 2003 are straightforward, as depicted in Table 1.1.

TABLE 1.1   ACCESS 2003 SYSTEM REQUIREMENTS

Component	Requirements
Processor	Pentium 233 MHz or faster processor
Memory	128 MB or RAM or greater
Hard Disk	180 MB minimum, an additional 200 MB for optional files
Drive	CD-ROM or DVD
Display	600×800 or higher resolution monitor
Operating System	Windows 2000 with sp3, Windows XP or later

Once installed, you can harness many of the great features of Access 2003 on your local PC by building databases with tables and queries, and creating user interfaces with forms, reports, and Data Access Pages.

If you wish to deploy Data Access Pages over the Internet, you also need access to a web server such as IIS (Internet Information Services). For more information please visit Microsoft's IIS web site at http://www.microsoft.com/WindowsServer2003/iis/default.mspx.

Microsoft SharePoint Services is also recommended for professional Access developers collaborating with other colleagues on development activities such as versioning, check-in/check-out processes, and approval workflows. For more information, see Microsoft's SharePoint Services web site at `http://www.microsoft.com/windowsserver2003/technologies/sharepoint/default.mspx`.

Migrating to Access 2003

Depending on which previous Access version you were leveraging, migration woes range from none to minor. In fact, migrating from Access 2002 is real easy. In most cases you simply need to open your previously created Access 2002 database in Access 2003 once installed. Your Data Access Pages and VBA code from Access 2002 should also open in Access 2003 with no problems.

If you're migrating from Access 2000, it is also easy to upgrade as Access 2003 supports the same file format. Like previous versions of Access 2002 databases, Access 2003 should import your Access 2000 databases with no problems, including your Access 2000 VBA code. However, you need to convert any Data Access Pages built in Access 2000 by simply opening the Data Access Page in Design view with an Access 2002 or higher database. Microsoft Access should then prompt you to convert the Data Access Page.

For versions older than 2000, such as Access 97, you must convert the Access files first. Microsoft provides step-by-step procedures and toolkits for converting older Access files in this situation.

For more information on converting older Access files, simply use the key phrase "converting an Access file" in the Microsoft Office online help in Access 2003 or on the web at `http://office.microsoft.com`.

YOUR FIRST ACCESS DATABASE

IT professionals, teachers, students, accountants, managers, scientists, computer enthusiasts, and many more people just like you have a need to collect and manage data. Data that is complex or changes frequently is best stored and managed in a database such as Access.

Let's say you are a school teacher who has a list of students, attendance, grades, tests, quizzes, and homework. You could keep track of your students, their attendance, grades, and such in a notebook or in an electronic document. But suppose one of your students has a name change in the middle of the school year. To solve this record-keeping issue, you need to update all occurrences of this student's name in your lists, whether paper or electronic. In a well-designed Access database, you only need to make this change once.

Databases allow you to ask questions of your data. For example, you could group your students by their grade point average, find out which students missed fewer than 3 school days, and which students have failed to turn in 10 or more homework assignments and have a grade point average less than 2.0.

Access implements a relational database to link information such as homework results to one or more students. Looking at Figure 1.1, you can easily see how Access links a student to one or more homework assignments using tables and keys.

 A *relational database* stores data in separate tables by subject matter and provides a system or user-defined link (key) between the tables to produce useful information through the relationship.

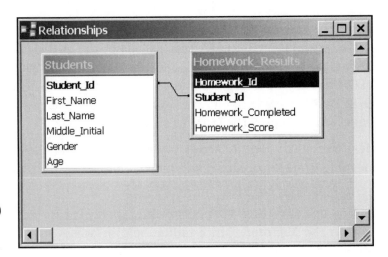

FIGURE 1.1

Relational data in
Microsoft Access.

The two sets of tables in Figure 1.1 are relational in that the HomeWork_Results table maintains a student key (in other words, a relationship) back to the Students table.

Creating an Access Database

One of the most important database professional jobs is the up-front requirement gathering and data analysis of your database project. For example, you should consider answers to the following questions before creating your database:

- What is the purpose of my database?
- Who will use my database and how will they access it?

- What types of data will my database contain?
- What are the relationships between my data?
- What types of user interfaces to my database will I need?
- What types of reports does my database need to produce?
- What types of queries (questions) does my database need to answer?

Many of the beforementioned questions require a fair amount of analysis and design. Good analysis prior to creating a database is essential to creating an effective database that requires minor maintenance, yet is extendable and robust.

The remainder of this chapter assists you in understanding how many of these questions can be answered from an analysis, design, and construction point of view. Specifically, I show you how to create a simple database that can manage and report students and their homework scores.

For now, simply launch the Access program icon by choosing Start, Programs, or from any other shortcut you may have created during or after the Microsoft Office installation.

Once opened, you should see an Access window similar to the one depicted in Figure 1.2.

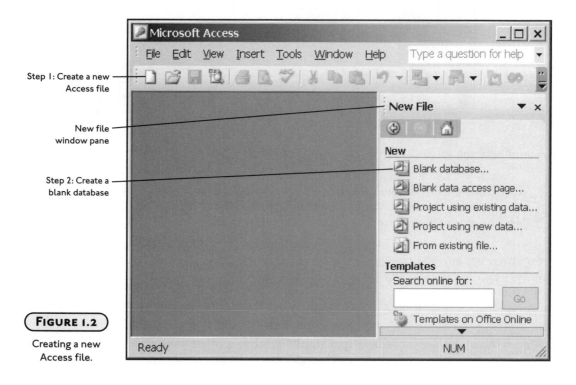

FIGURE 1.2

Creating a new Access file.

If you do not see the New File pane shown in Figure 1.2, simply click the New File icon on the Access toolbar or select it from the File, New menu item. Once you see the New File window pane, click the Blank Database link depicted in Figure 1.2. The Blank Database link opens another window, allowing you to select where your database is initially created and saved. Finish creating your database by simply typing a filename for your database and click Create as seen in Figure 1.3.

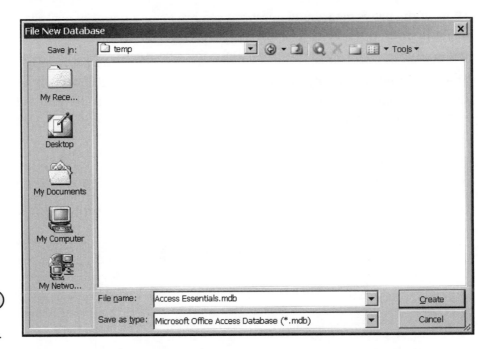

FIGURE 1.3

Creating a new
Access database.

You should now see an Access window similar to that in Figure 1.4.

 Microsoft Access databases are always stored in binary files with the file extension .mdb. These files store relevant information about your Access database, including tables, fields, reports queries, and much more.

You can also open an existing Access file by clicking the Open icon on the Access toolbar or by choosing File, Open (both depicted in Figure 1.5).

If you're looking for sample databases to learn, work, or play with, Microsoft has been providing the Northwind database for many Access versions now. You can find the Microsoft sample Northwind database by clicking the Help, Sample Databases menu item seen in Figure 1.5.

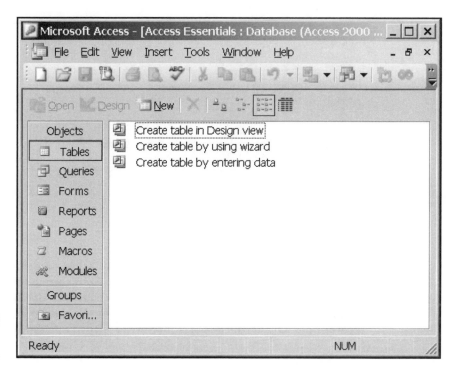

FIGURE 1.4

New Access
Database window.

You may have to install the sample database feature, which Access prompts you to do if the Northwind database is not already installed. I recommend installing the sample Northwind database if you have not already done so, as I use its tables and records periodically during this book.

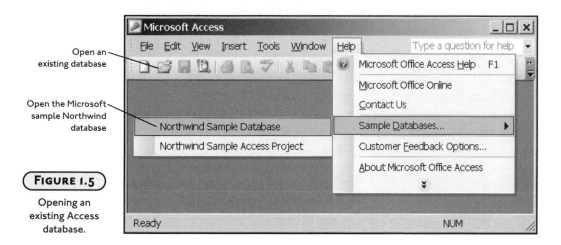

Open an existing database

Open the Microsoft sample Northwind database

FIGURE 1.5

Opening an existing Access database.

When opening an existing Access database, you may get an unsafe expression or macro security warning such as the one seen in Figure 1.6.

FIGURE 1.6

Access macro security warning.

In short, you get this security message because your macro security is set to Medium and Access cannot verify this is a trusted source (digitally signed, for instance) or that someone has not tampered with your database since you last opened it. You can, however, disable this warning by changing the macro security level to Low, which is accessed from the Security menu item in the Tools, Macro menu.

Tables and Fields

After creating your Access database file, you are now ready to begin defining how your data is stored. Access groups data by subject matter in entities called *tables*. Tables have *fields*, which describe the subject matter. For example, a Student table may have fields called Student_Id, First_Name, Last_Name, Middle_Initial, Gender, and Age. Each field has a definition that tells Access how the field values should be stored. For example, the Student_Id field is stored as a number as opposed to the First_Name field, which is stored as text.

Each Access table must contain at least one or more fields. Together the fields comprise a row of data also known as a *record*. Generally speaking, tables should be assigned a *primary key*, which identifies each row of information in the table as unique. For example, the Student_Id field in the Students table is an excellent candidate for the primary key. The notion of primary keys is essential for creating relationships between tables in Access.

To create a table in Access, simply double click the Create table in Design view link as seen in Figure 1.7.

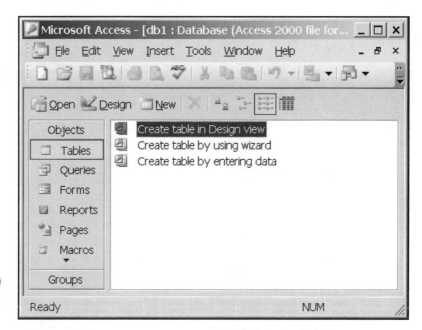

FIGURE 1.7

Creating tables in
Access.

Access puts you in Design mode when first creating a table. Design mode allows you to define your table's field and field definitions as seen in Figure 1.8.

FIGURE 1.8

Defining fields
and field
definitions.

There are a number of common data types for storing information in fields. The most common of these data types are seen in Table 1.2.

TABLE 1.2 COMMON ACCESS DATA TYPES

Data Type	Description
AutoNumber	An autogenerated number whose values can be incremented or randomly generated. Often used as the table's primary key.
Currency	Stores numbers and prevents rounding off during calculations.
Date/Time	Can store dates and times in a multitude of formats.
Memo	Used for storing nonnumeric data such as strings. The Memo data field can store up to 65,536 characters.
Number	Stores numbers such as Integers, Singles, and Doubles. Also a good candidate for primary keys.
Text	Used for storing nonnumeric data such as strings. The Text data field can store up to 255 characters.
Yes/No	Stores Boolean values such as Yes/No, True/False, or On/Off.

TRAP The Text data type is by default set to a maximum size of 50 characters. Trying to insert data greater than the maximum size allowed in a Text field type generates a database error. If your Text field storage needs require greater length, you need to increase its field size attribute during table design. If you require a number of characters greater than 255 (the maximum size allowed in a Text field), use the Memo field type.

To better understand data types and their use, database developers must understand the data they are working with and how it can be logically grouped into tables and then separated into appropriate fields or data types. This type of database work is commonly referred to as *normalization* or *data modeling*. See if you can model some data by matching an Access data type (seen in Table 1.2) with the data that needs represented in the following numbered list.

1 An employee's social security number.

2 The start time of a test.

3 The number of employees in a company.

4 A varying bonus percentage applied to employee salaries.

5 Determines if a user is currently logged into a system.

6   Stores the address of homes.

7   The textual contents of a sample chapter.

8   An ID generated each time a new user is created.

9   The cost of a book.

10   A computer's serial number.

The correct data types for the previous storage needs are listed here:

1   Text (If dashes are used when entering data)

2   Date/Time

3   Number

4   Number

5   Yes/No

6   Text

7   Memo

8   AutoNumber

9   Currency

10   Text (If dashes are used when entering data)

Once an Access table has been created, you enter data directly into the fields by opening the table's name from the main window. As seen in Figure 1.9, Access provides a built-in graphical interface for managing data in a table directly.

From a developer's point of view, using the built-in table interface to manage data directly is sufficient while designing or maintaining a database, but is not adequate or friendly to most users.

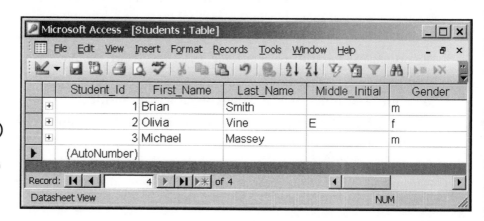

FIGURE 1.9

Managing table data directly with the Access table graphical interface.

Relationships

As mentioned before, Access implements a relational database, allowing database developers to link one or more tables using keys or relationships. To demonstrate, follow the next sequence of steps to link two tables called Students and HomeWork_Results.

1. Create and save a new Access file and database.

2. Create two new tables called Students and HomeWork_Results.

3. The Students table should have the following fields: Student_Id (AutoNumber), First_Name (Text), Last_Name (Text), Middle_Initial (Text), Gender (Text), and Age (Number).

4. Set the Student_Id in the Students table as the primary key by right-clicking the Student_Id field in Design view and right-clicking the Primary Key menu option.

5. The HomeWork_Results table should have the following fields: Homework_Id (Number), Student_Id (Number), Homework_Completed (Yes/No), and Homework_Score (Number).

6. Set two fields as the primary key in the HomeWork_Results table by holding down your Shift or Ctrl key and clicking both the Homework_Id and Student_Id fields.

7. While both fields are highlighted and still holding the Shift or Ctrl key, right-click in the gray column to the left of one of the highlighted fields and select the Primary Key menu option. This is known as a *multifield key*!

8. Ensure both tables are saved and named then select Tools, Relationships from the Access menu. An interim window is displayed from where you will add both tables to the relationship window. After which, the relationship window displays your two new tables. Note the primary keys in both tables are highlighted in black as seen in Figure 1.10.

9. Drag and drop the Student_Id field from the Students table onto the Student_Id field in the HomeWork_Results table. A new window appears, as depicted in Figure 1.11.

10. Click the Create New button and you have created a *one-to-many relationship*, which means for every student in the Students table, there are many occurrences of that student in the HomeWork_Results table.

The primary key in the Students table, Student_Id, has also now become a foreign key in the HomeWork_Results table.

You must make other considerations about a relationship:

- Enforce *referential integrity*, which means values entered into the foreign key must match values in the primary key.

- Enforce *cascading updates* between one or more tables, which means related updates from one table's fields are cascaded to the other table or tables in the relationship.

- Enforce *cascading deletes* between the two tables. In short, this means any relevant deletions from one table cascade in the other table(s).
- Both cascading updates and deletes help enforce referential integrity.

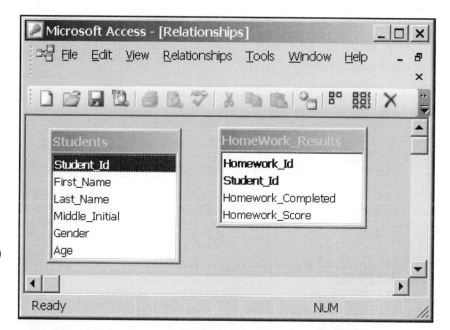

FIGURE 1.10

Viewing relationships between two tables.

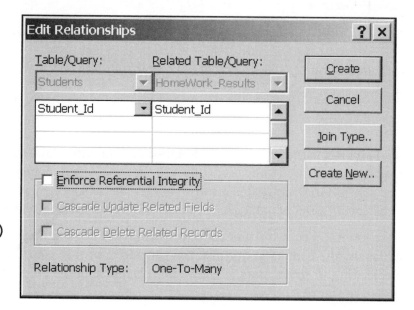

FIGURE 1.11

Editing a relationship between two tables.

To better visualize the relationship, enter a few records into the Students and HomeWork_Results tables by double-clicking each table, one at a time, from the main Access window. Remember, opening a table from the main Access window allows you to manage field values directly!

11. After you've entered data in both tables, open the Students table again and you should see a plus sign (+) to the left of each Student_Id.

Click the plus sign and you should see the related HomeWork_Results record for the student, as depicted in Figure 1.12.

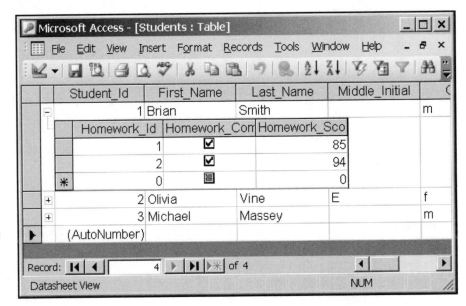

FIGURE 1.12

Viewing related table information after creating a table relationship.

The book's accompanying CD has a copy of the database discussed in this section titled Chapter1.mdb.

Forms

Though careful analysis is the key to a well-designed and adaptive database, end users are more likely to appreciate a well-built user interface time and again. A good interface leverages forms and controls in a way that is intuitive to users for managing data. User interfaces should hide the complexities of a database, such as business rules and relationships.

Access *forms* are graphical controls that act as containers for other graphical controls such as text boxes, labels, and command buttons. You can add a form to your database by clicking the Form object in the Access main window and then clicking the Create form in Design view item as seen in Figure 1.13.

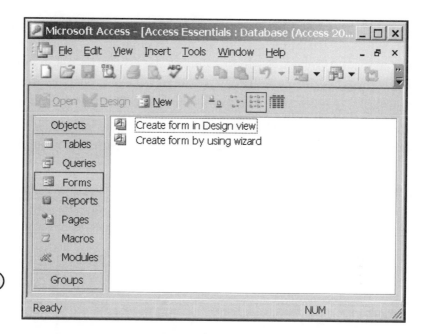

FIGURE 1.13

Creating a new form in Access.

After creating a form in design view, you should see an empty form as demonstrated in Figure 1.14.

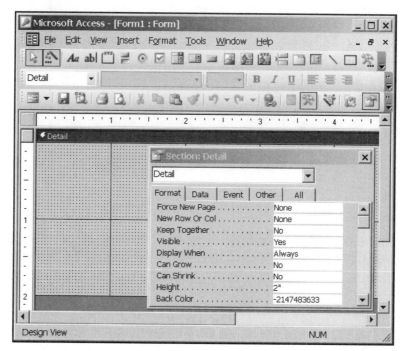

FIGURE 1.14

Viewing a new form and the form Properties window in Access.

Both forms and controls have properties that describe how they look and behave (*attributes*). You can manage these attributes directly in design time using the Properties window. If you're unable to see the Properties window, choose the Properties menu item from the View menu or simply press F4. Using the list box at the top of the Properties window (seen in Figure 1.14) you can easily switch between available control properties during design time.

Not all control properties are accessible or available with the Properties window in design time. This means other properties are available only during runtime through VBA statements.

Common Controls

Controls can be accessed and placed onto your form by clicking the control in the Toolbox window and clicking the form revealed in Figure 1.15.

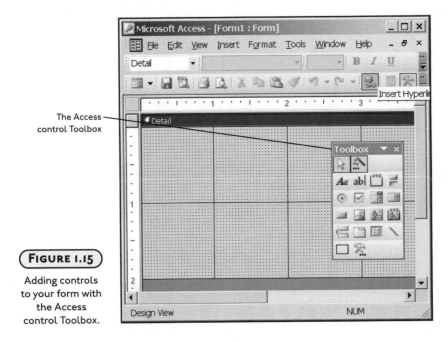

The Access control Toolbox

FIGURE 1.15

Adding controls to your form with the Access control Toolbox.

If your Toolbox window does not appear, simply select View, Toolbox.

Access places the control on your form in a predetermined shape and size. You can resize controls using your left mouse button, or clicking the control and then using the Ctrl and arrows key simultaneously to resize the control. Use the Shift and arrows keys simultaneously to move the control.

Just like data fields, controls have properties that determine the control's various attributes or settings. A control's properties can be accessed by right-clicking the control and selecting Properties from the menu. A sample control property window is shown in Figure 1.16.

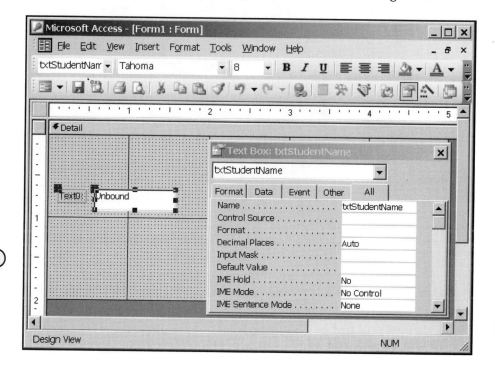

FIGURE 1.16

Displaying a control's properties through the Properties window.

Both the Properties window and control Toolbox can be moved in and out of the main Access window. Both windows can also be docked in and around the main Access window by grabbing the top portions of either window and dragging them to the top, bottom, or sides of the main Access window.

In this section I specifically look at four common controls: text boxes, labels, images, and command buttons. You can see in Figure 1.17 a visual depiction of where these common controls are located in the Access Toolbox.

To get started, I create a new form called Manage Students, after which I place one label control at the top of the form and set the following label property values:

- Name: lblManageStudents
- Caption: Manage Students
- Font Size: 14

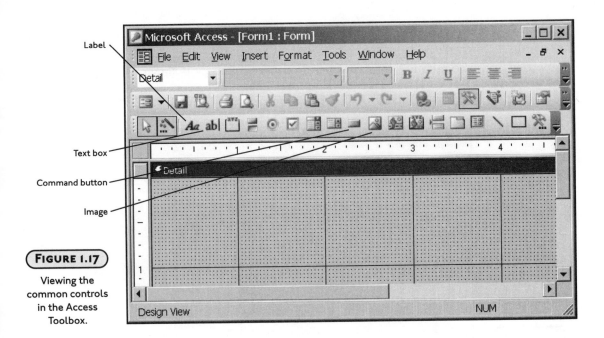

Label

Text box

Command button

Image

FIGURE 1.17

Viewing the
common controls
in the Access
Toolbox.

Below the label, I add six text boxes and align them on the form, one below the other. Notice after adding a text box control that you actually get two controls for the price of one. Specifically, you get one text box and one label control just to the left. Both controls have their own, distinct properties and can be moved and deleted independently of each other.

Assign the following properties to each respective text box:

- Name: txtStudentId
- Name: txtFirstName
- Name: txtLastName
- Name: txtMiddleInitial
- Name: txtGender
- Name: txtAge

Assign the following properties to each respective text box labels:

- Name: lblStudentId
- Caption: Student Id:
- Name: lblFirstName
- Caption: First Name:

- Name: lblLastName
- Caption: Last Name:

- Name: lblMiddleInitial
- Caption: Middle Initial:

- Name: lblGender
- Caption: Gender:

- Name: lblAge
- Caption: Age:

Next, I add one image control to the upper-right corner of the form and assign the following property values. I've copied the image used in this control to the book's accompanying CD for your convenience.

- Name: imgTeacher
- Picture: teacher.WMF
- Size Mode: Stretch

Last but not least, I add a command button to my new form that exits the user from the application. When you add a command button to any form, Access launches a Command Button Wizard that can aid you in assigning various built-in actions to your command button's click event. Though I typically shy away from wizards in this book, this is a good example of when using one is helpful in assigning a simple action to a control.

As seen in Figure 1.18, select the Application Category and Quit Application Action from the Command Button Wizard and click Finish.

Your form in Design view should now look similar to the one in Figure 1.19.

After saving the form, open it and click the command button. What result did you get after clicking the command button? If the entire Access application exited, you got the effect intended by the Command Button Wizard quit application action. In a later section, I show you how to create a dashboard, which you can exit back to instead of quitting the entire Access application.

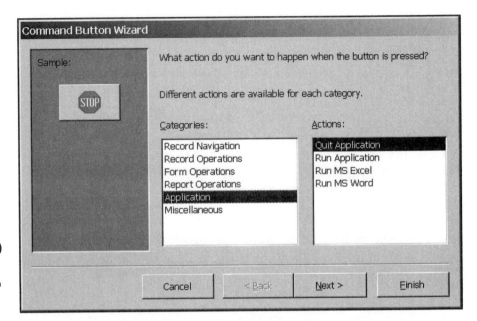

FIGURE 1.18

Using the
Command Button
Wizard to assign
an action.

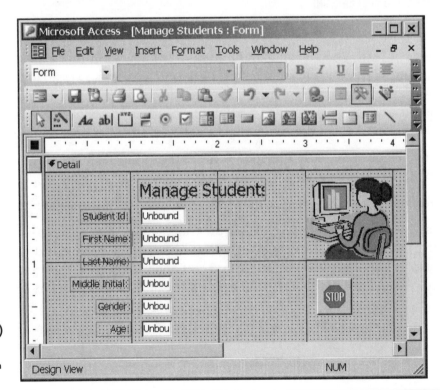

FIGURE 1.19

The Manage
Students form in
Design view.

Hungarian Notation

You may have noticed the naming convention I used to assign control names in the previous section. I recommend using a naming convention to provide readability and consistency throughout your database and code.

The naming convention I use and recommend is called *Hungarian Notation* (named after a computer scientist). To apply this notation, simply modify the Name property of each control to use a three-letter prefix (all in lowercase) that indicates the control type followed by a meaningful description. Each word that describes the control (not the prefix) should have its first letter capitalized.

Table 1.3 shows some sample naming conventions for controls discussed in this chapter and throughout this book.

TABLE 1.3 COMMON CONTROL-NAMING CONVENTIONS

Control	Prefix	Example
Check Box	chk	chkRed
Combo Box	cbo	cboStates
Command Button	cmd	cmdQuit
Form	frm	frmMain
Image	img	imgLogo
Label	lbl	FirstName
List Box	lst	lstFruits
Option Button	opt	optMale
Text Box	txt	txtFirstName

Bound Controls

Besides exiting the Access application, the Manage Students form has no other functionality as of yet, but that is about to change! You can easily bind controls to tables and fields. This binding is the essence of forms and hence, of graphical interfaces in general.

To begin the binding, first bind your Manage Students form to the Students table by setting the form's Record Source property (in the Properties window) to the Students table seen in Figure 1.20.

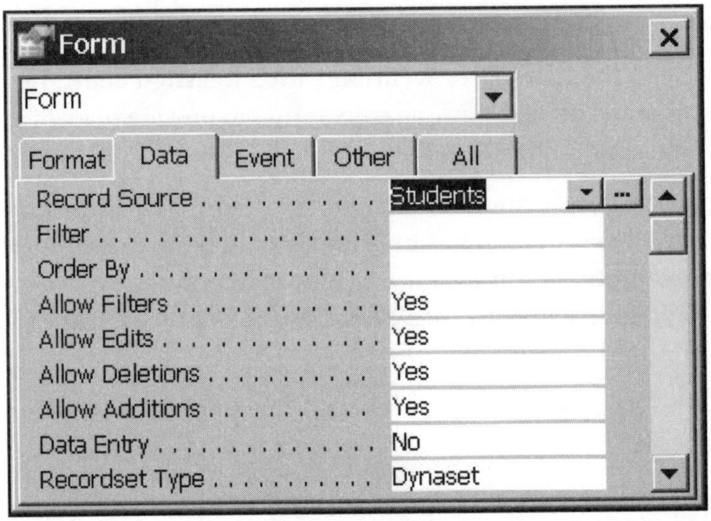

FIGURE 1.20

Binding the
Manage
Students form
to the Students
table.

Next, bind all of the text box fields to the appropriate Students table fields as described in these bulleted lists:

- Name: txtStudentId
- Control Source: Student_Id
- Locked: Yes

- Name: txtFirstName
- Control Source: First_Name
- Locked: No

- Name: txtLastName
- Control Source: Last_Name
- Locked: No

- Name: txtMiddleInitial
- Control Source: Middle_Initial
- Locked: No

- Name: txtGender
- Control Source: Gender
- Locked: No

- Name: txtAge
- Control Source: Age
- Locked: No

Note that I've set the txtStudentId Locked property value to Yes. I did this because this field is a primary key with a data type of AutoNumber. Since an AutoNumber is generated automatically by the Access system, it is neither necessary nor advisable to let users manage this field manually.

Now that the controls have been bound to the Students table, users can view, update, and add student records using the form's built-in navigation bar seen in Figure 1.21.

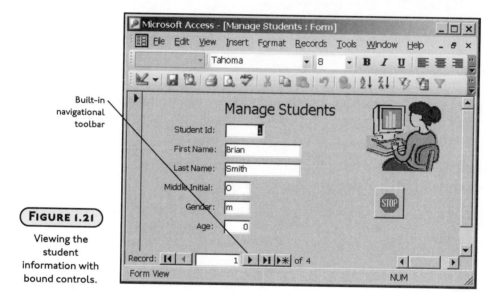

FIGURE 1.21

Viewing the student information with bound controls.

In future chapters I show you how to further control the relationship between controls, tables, and fields by harnessing the power of the Access VBA language.

Startup Forms and Dashboards

For a better user experience, you can customize your form as the startup object by selecting Tools, Startup and changing the Display Form/Page option as revealed in Figure 1.22.

In addition to changing the startup form in the Startup dialog window, you can choose not to have the database window or status bar displayed at program startup by deselecting the respective check boxes also in the Startup window. (These check boxes can be seen in Figure 1.22.)

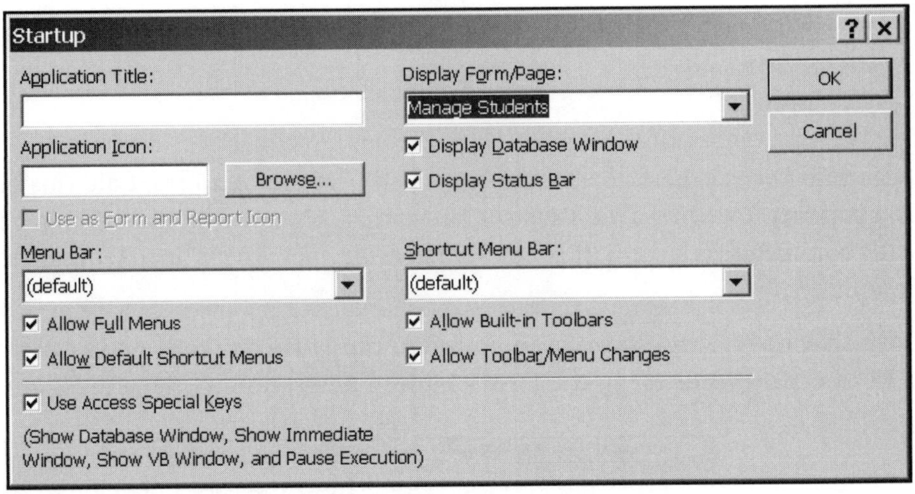

FIGURE 1.22

Customizing
startup
properties with
the Startup dialog
window.

Since users will probably do more in your application than manage students (they can manage grades, homework, and attendance), you should probably create a dashboard for them that displays at application startup. Users can leverage this dashboard to navigate between forms in your application.

To create a navigational dashboard, I simply create a new form called `Dashboard` and set it as the startup object in the Startup dialog window.

Next, I add one label and two command button controls. I set their respective properties like this:

- Name: `lblMainDashboard`
- Caption: `Main Dashboard`
- Font Size: `14`
- Name: `cmdManageStudents`
- Caption: `Manage Students`
- Picture: `None`
- Use the Command Button Wizard to select the Form Operations Category and Open Form Action, and then select the `Manage Students` form.
- Name: `cmdQuitApplication`
- Caption: `Quit Application`
- Picture: `None`
- Use the Command Button Wizard to select the Application Category, then select the Quit Application Action, and then click Finish.

My new dashboard form looks similar to the one in Figure 1.23.

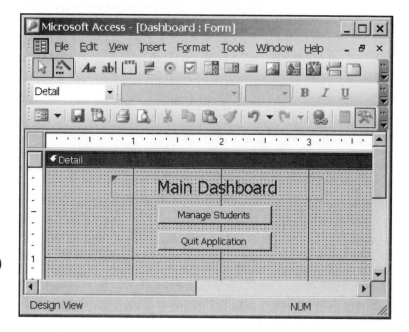

FIGURE 1.23

Creating a
dashboard form
in Design view.

TRAP
If you change the name of a control after creating it in an Access wizard (such as the Command Button Wizard), the events associated with that control may no longer work. This happens because Access automatically creates VBA code inside the event procedures for the control's previous name (whatever name the wizard gave it) prior to you changing the control name's property value.

More specifically, if you change the control name manually after creating it in the wizard, you must go into the VBA code and change the control's name for each event procedure that Access put VBA code into.

You can access the VBA code created by the wizard by right-clicking the control in design time and selecting the Build Event menu item. Once the Visual Basic Environment window is opened, you can manually change the control name in each event procedure.

In chapters to come, you learn how to manage event procedures and assign actions to controls via the Visual Basic for Applications (VBA) language.

Next, I add another command button to the Manage Students form so users can navigate back to my dashboard. Properties and settings of the new command button on the Manage Students form are shown next:

- Name: cmdBacktoDashboard
- Caption: Back to Dashboard
- Picture: None
- Use the Command Button Wizard to select the Form Operations Category and Open Form Action, and then select the Dashboard form.

Ensure you have set the Dashboard form as the startup object in the Startup dialog window. Save and test your work.

> **TRICK** Access provides a wizard for creating dashboard forms (also known as *switchboards*). To access the Switchboard Wizard, simply select the Switchboard Manager item from the Tools, Database Utilities menu.

Queries

Database queries provide the mechanism by which people can question their data and get responses. Database queries are typically written using a database language called SQL (Structured Query Language), which I discuss later in the book. Nevertheless, I show you how to create queries using Microsoft's built-in query designer, which is sufficient for most database queries in Access.

To get started, ask your database for the first and last names of all students in your Students table. Create a new query in Access by clicking the Query object in the Access main window. Double-click Create Query in Design View as shown in Figure 1.24.

A new window allows you to select tables, other queries, or both for your new query. For this exercise, select the Students table by clicking the Add command button, then clicking the Close button (seen in Figure 1.25).

With the Students table available for your query, select both last- and first-name fields, displaying them in ascending order. This can be accomplished in one of two ways: Either double-click one or more fields in the Students table or select one field at a time in each Fields drop-down list box in the matrix at the bottom of the window. After selecting the Last_Name and First_Name fields, your query should look like Figure 1.26.

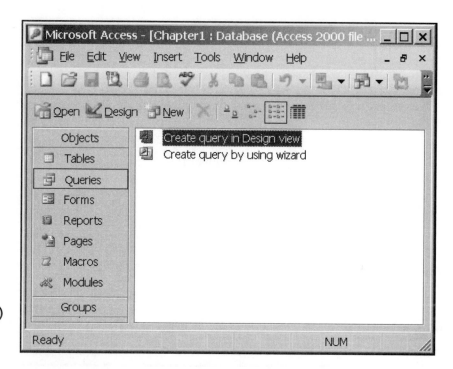

FIGURE 1.24

Creating a new
query in Access.

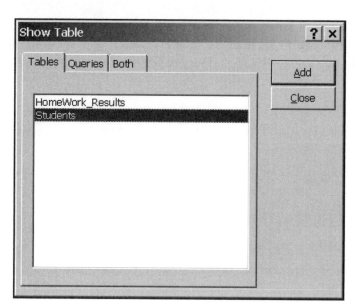

FIGURE 1.25

Selecting the
Students table
for a new query.

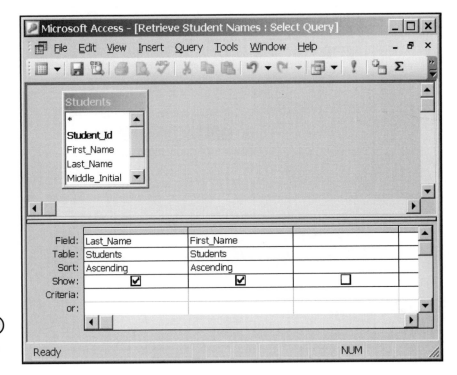

FIGURE 1.26

Selecting fields
for a query.

You can easily select all fields in a table for a query by simply selecting the
asterisk (*) character at the top of a table.

Access allows you to verify the underlying SQL query generated by the Access query designer
by selecting the SQL View item from the View menu. The SQL query generated for my students
query looks like this:

```
SELECT Students.First_Name, Students.Last_Name
FROM Students
ORDER BY Students.First_Name, Students.Last_Name;
```

Save your query and name it Retrieve Student Names.

You can now verify the results of your query by running or executing it. To run a query from
the Access query designer, simply select Query, Run from the menu, or click the exclamation mark (!) on the Access toolbar. Results from my Retrieve Student Names query are seen
in Figure 1.27.

FIGURE 1.27

Viewing the results of the Retrieve Student Names query.

Let's create a new query—one that asks a more pointed question of your data. Specifically, the new query should say "Give me a list of all student names and their grades for homework assignment number 2." You can accomplish this by creating a new query called Homework #2 Results and selecting both Students and HomeWork_Results tables. Your new query should look similar to the one in Figure 1.28.

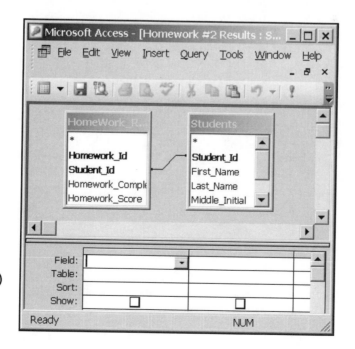

FIGURE 1.28

Creating a new query using multiple tables.

Notice in Figure 1.28 that Access displays the relationship between both tables by displaying a graphical link between the Student_Id primary and foreign keys.

To build the query, select the following fields in the following order by double-clicking each field from the corresponding table in the query designer.

- Last_Name (ascending order)
- First_Name (ascending order)
- Homework_Score
- Homework_Id

The query is almost done, but not yet—you still need to tell the query to limit the query results to show only homework scores for homework assignment number 2. You can accomplish this by specifying criteria (or a condition) of =2. Moreover, since the criteria is applied against the Homework_Id field, which you don't want displayed in your query results, tell the query designer to not show the field un-checking the Show check box. The finished query is depicted in Figure 1.29.

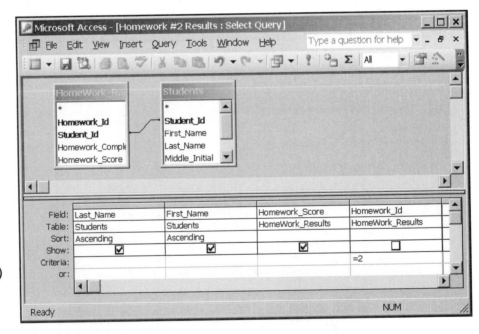

FIGURE 1.29

Using criteria to build an Access query.

Save your query as Homework #2 Results and run it to view results, which are revealed in Figure 1.30.

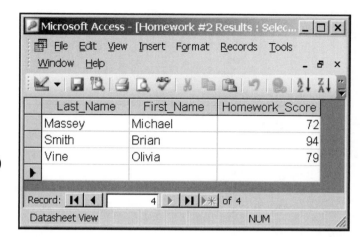

FIGURE 1.30

Viewing the
Homework #2
Results query
outputs.

As seen in Figure 1.30, Access has limited query results based upon my criteria to show all students and their scores for homework assignment 2. What you don't see is that Access created a join behind the scenes using SQL statements to display field values from both tables.

I discuss joins and SQL statements later in the book, but for now you can appreciate what happened behind the scenes by looking at the following SQL statements Access created for the Homework #2 Results query.

```
SELECT Students.Last_Name, Students.First_Name, HomeWork_Results.Homework_Score
FROM Students INNER JOIN HomeWork_Results
ON Students.Student_Id = HomeWork_Results.Student_Id
WHERE (((HomeWork_Results.Homework_Id)=2))
ORDER BY Students.Last_Name, Students.First_Name;
```

As you can see from the previous SQL query, Access has done a lot of work behind the scenes in creating the necessary joins and SQL conditions.

GETTING HELP WITH ACCESS 2003

Though the remainder of this book concentrates on Access VBA programming, the Access 2003 application contains many more great features, which I encourage you to learn more about.

If you'd like to find more about Access 2003 features and functionality, Microsoft provides a wealth of knowledge in both the application's help system and via the Internet. I recommend starting with the built-in Access 2003 help system, which can be accessed via the Help menu seen in Figure 1.31.

Search for help
using the Access
help system

View the Access
help table of
contents

Find more Access
information online
via the Internet

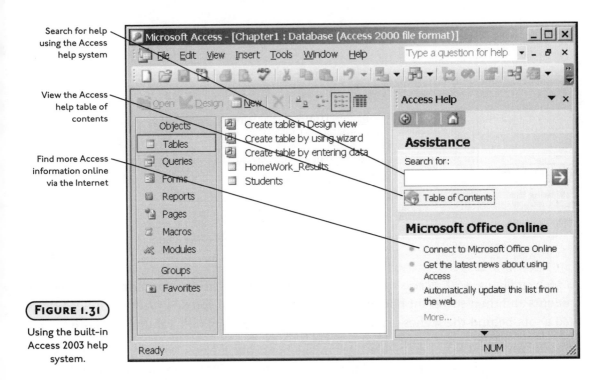

FIGURE 1.31

Using the built-in
Access 2003 help
system.

You can find additional information about the Access 2003 application via Microsoft's Access 2003 product page at `http://office.microsoft.com/en-us/FX010857911033.aspx` or by searching Microsoft's free developer's network (MSDN) knowledge base and library at `http://msdn.microsoft.com/`.

CHAPTER SUMMARY

- Relational databases store data in separate tables by subject matter and provide a link (key) between the tables to produce useful information through the relationship.

- Access databases are stored in binary files with the file extension `.mdb`. These files store relevant information about your Access database including tables, fields, reports queries, and much more.

- Microsoft provides a sample database, called `Northwind`, that you can use for learning.

- Access tables must contain at least one or more fields.

- Opening a table from the main Access window allows you to manage field values directly.

- The `AutoNumber` data type is an autogenerated number whose values can be incremented or randomly generated. It is often used as the table's primary key.

- If you require a number of characters greater than 255 (the maximum size allowed in a Text field), you need to use the Memo field type.
- Referential integrity means values entered into the foreign key must match values in the primary key.
- Access forms are graphical controls that act as containers for other graphical controls such as text boxes, labels, and command buttons.
- Controls have properties that determine various control attributes or settings.
- Access allows you to bind controls to tables and fields.
- You can assign a form as the startup object.
- Database queries provide the mechanism by which people can ask their data questions and get responses.
- You can limit the result set of a query using criteria, also known as conditions.

PROGRAMMING CHALLENGES

1. Create a new table called Homework and add the following fields: Homework_Id (AutoNumber), Homework_Title (Text), and Point_Possible (Number).

2. Create a new relationship between the Homework and HomeWork_Results table using the Homework_Id fields.

3. Add another command button to the Manage Students form that allows a user to delete a record from the Students table.

4. Create a new form called Manage Homework that allows a user to manage the Homework table.

5. Add another command button to the Dashboard form that allows a user to navigate to the Manage Homework form.

6. Create a new query called Homework #1 Not Complete. This new query should list all student names that did not complete homework assignment number 1.

INTRODUCTION TO ACCESS VBA

L ike many professional *RDBMS (Relational Database Management Systems)*, Microsoft Access comes with its own programming language called VBA. VBA, or Visual Basic for Applications, is a subset of Microsoft's popular enterprise programming language Visual Basic. VBA follows the Visual Basic language syntax and comes with many of its common features such as an *integrated development environment (IDE)* and many common controls for building professional event-driven and data-driven applications.

Though VBA supports the look and feel of Visual Basic, it is not Visual Basic. A main difference being that Visual Basic allows for creation of executable programs, whereas VBA does not. Moreover, VBA for Access is specifically designed for Microsoft Access. Meaning, it has knowledge of and support for the Microsoft Access object model. The concept of an object model is different for each Microsoft Office application. For example, both Microsoft Excel and Microsoft Word support VBA, but each has its own object model.

THE EVENT-DRIVEN PARADIGM

The *event-driven paradigm* is a powerful programming model that allows programmers to build applications that respond to actions initiated by the user or system. Access VBA includes a number of events that are categorized by the objects they represent. VBA programmers write code in event procedures to respond to user actions (such as clicking a command button) or system actions (such as a form loading).

To demonstrate the event-driven model, consider a form, which has a corresponding Form object that contains many events such as Click, Load, and MouseUp. As seen next, both Click and MouseUp events are triggered by the user performing an action with the mouse on the form.

```
Private Sub Form_Click()
    'write code in here to respond to the user clicking the form
End Sub

Private Sub Form_MouseUp(Button As Integer, _
    Shift As Integer, X As Single, Y As Single)
    'write code in here to respond to the user releasing a mouse button
End Sub
```

I discuss the details of these event procedures soon enough. For now, understand that objects have related events, which can be triggered by users. You, the VBA programmer, write code in these event procedures to respond to user actions. Moreover, events can be triggered by the system or the program itself. For example, the Load event seen next is triggered when a form's Form object is first loaded into memory.

```
Private Sub Form_Load()
    'write code in here to respond to the form loading into memory
End Sub
```

If you're new to event-driven programming, this may seem a bit awkward at first. I promise you, however, it is really not that difficult. In fact, VBA does a great job of providing much of the detail for you. By the end of this chapter, you will be writing your first Access VBA event-driven programs with ease.

OBJECT-BASED PROGRAMMING

The key to programming in VBA is using objects. Objects have properties that describe the object and methods, which perform actions. For example, say I have an object called Person. The Person object contains properties called HairColor, Weight, Height, and Age that describe the object. The Person object also contains methods that describe an action the object can perform such as Run, Walk, Sleep, and Eat. As you can see, understanding the concept of objects is really quite simple!

Many Access VBA objects also contain data structures called collections. In a nutshell, *collections* are groupings of objects, which you are introduced to in this chapter.

Access VBA supports many objects such as the Form object, which is simply a window or dialog box. The Form object contains many properties such as Caption, Moveable, and Visible. Each of these properties describes the Form object and allows VBA programmers to set characteristics of a user's interface. Like the object Person, the Form object contains methods such as Move and Refresh.

Many objects share common characteristics such as properties and methods. To demonstrate, the Label object (which implements a label control) shares many of the Form properties such as Caption and Visible.

Properties and methods of objects are accessed using the dot operator (.) as demonstrated in the next two VBA statements.

```
Label1.ForeColor = vbBlue
```

```
Label1.Caption = "Hello World"
```

Don't worry about the details in the previous statements for now, but do realize that properties such as ForeColor and Caption belong to the Label1 object and they are accessed using the dot operator. I discuss this in more detail in sections to come.

THE VBA IDE

If you've written programs in Visual Basic before, the VBA *integrated development environment (IDE)* should feel very familiar to you. If not, don't worry—the VBA IDE is user friendly and easy to learn. For ease of use, I refer to the VBA integrated development environment as the *Visual Basic Editor*, or *VBE*, from now on.

The VBE contains a suite of windows, toolbars, and menu items that provide support for text editing, debugging, file management, and help. Two common ways for accessing the VBE is with forms and code modules.

After adding a form to your database, make sure your form is highlighted (selected) in Design view and then select View, Code. If your Code menu item is not selectable, make sure you've created and selected (highlighted) a form first.

 TRICK An easy shortcut to opening the VBE and alternating between Access and the VBE is by simultaneously pressing Alt+F ll.

After selecting the Code menu item, the VBA IDE should open up in a separate window similar to the one shown in Figure 2.1.

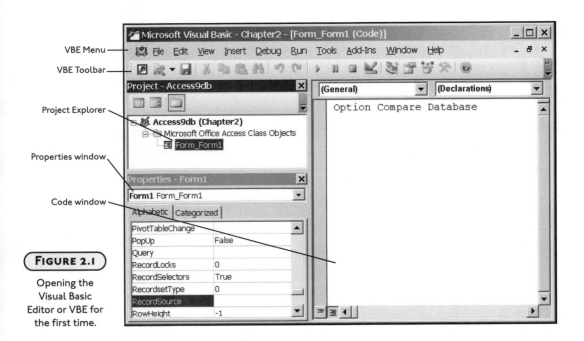

VBE Menu
VBE Toolbar
Project Explorer
Properties window
Code window

FIGURE 2.1

Opening the
Visual Basic
Editor or VBE for
the first time.

The first time you open the VBE, certain windows such as Project Explorer and Properties windows may not be visible, but can be accessed from the View menu.

There are a few VBE components you should familiarize yourself with right away. Each is described here and seen in Figure 2.1.

- Toolbars: Toolbars contain shortcuts to many common functions used throughout your VBA development, such as saving, inserting modules, and running your program code. Additional Toolbars can be added from the View menu item.

- Menus: Menus in the VBE provide you with many development features, such as file management, editing, debugging, and help.

- Project Explorer window: The Project Explorer window provides you with a bird's-eye view of all files and components that build your Access VBA programming environment. Notice in Figure 2.1 that my form's name (Form_Form1) appears under the Microsoft Office Access Class Objects heading. If I had multiple forms in my database, there would be multiple form names in this folder. Remember, Microsoft Access stores all components including forms, queries, reports, modules in single .mdb file.

- Properties window: The Properties window shows all available properties for the object selected in the list box above. Most importantly, the Properties window allows you to change the values of an object's property during design-time development.

- Code window: The Code window is where you enter your VBA code and find procedures and event procedures for objects using the two list boxes at the top of the Code window.

If you haven't done so yet, explore each of the previously mentioned components and windows so that you are comfortable navigating the VBE environment.

Introduction to Event Procedures

Procedures are simply containers for VBA code. Access VBA contains four types of procedures:

- Subprocedures
- Function procedures
- Property procedures
- Event procedures

Each type of procedure is designed to accomplish specific tasks. For example, event procedures are designed to catch and respond to user initiated events such as a mouse click on a command button or system initiated event such as a form loading. In this section I concentrate an event procedure, as they are the foundation for an event-driven language such as VBA. In subsequent chapters, you learn about other types of procedures in detail.

As mentioned, objects such as the `Form` object contain methods and properties. They also contain specialized events that are automatically provided after the object has been added to your database. VBA takes care of naming your object's events for you. Their naming convention follows.

ObjectName_EventName

For example, a form added to your Access database called `Form1` has a number of events, including the following.

```
Private Sub Form_Load()

End Sub


Private Sub Form_Unload(Cancel As Integer)

End Sub
```

Notice the naming convention used for each event procedure: object name followed by the event name with an underscore in between. The objects and their events in Figure 2.2 are accessed from the VBE Code window.

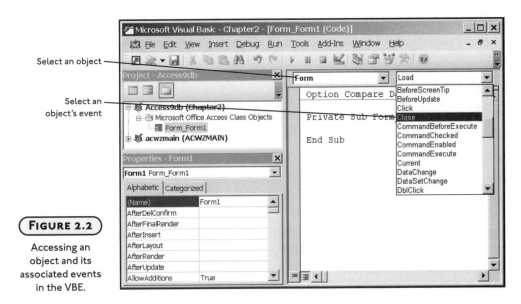

Select an object

Select an object's event

FIGURE 2.2

Accessing an object and its associated events in the VBE.

The leftmost list box in the Code window identifies available objects. The rightmost list box contains all available events for the object selected in the left list box. Each time you select an event, VBA creates the event shell for you automatically. This saves you from having to manually type each event's beginning and ending procedure statements.

TRICK   Each procedure in the VBE code window is separated by a horizontal line.

Empty event procedures serve no purpose until you write code in them using VBA statements.

Introduction to VBA Statements

VBA *statements* are comprised of variables, keywords, operators, and expressions that build a complete instruction to the computer. Every VBA statement falls into one of three categories:

- Declaration statements: Creates variables, data types, and procedures.
- Assignment statements: Assigns data or values to variables or properties.
- Executable statements: Initiates an action such as a method or function.

Most VBA statements fit onto one line, but sometime it is appropriate to continue a VBA statement onto a second or more lines for readability. To split a single VBA statement into multiple lines, VBA programmers use the concatenation character (&) and the line continuation character (_) separated by a space. To demonstrate, the following assignment statement uses the concatenation and continuation characters to extend a statement across two lines.

```
Private Sub Label3_Click()

Label3.Caption = "This is a single VBA assignment " & _
    " statement split onto two lines."

End Sub
```

 The term *concatenation* means to glue or put one or more items together.

One of the best ways to provide understandable VBA statements is with comments. Comments provide you and other programmers a brief description of how and why your program code does something. In Access VBA, comments are created by placing a single quote (') , sometimes called a *tick mark*, to the left side of a statement. Comments are also created by placing the keyword REM (short for remark) at the left side of a statement. The following statements demonstrate both ways of creating VBA comments.

```
' This is a VBA comment using the single quote character.
REM This is a VBA comment using the REM keyword.
```

When a computer encounters a comment, it is ignored and not processed as a VBA statement.

ACCESSING OBJECTS AND THEIR PROPERTIES

Besides the Properties window, Microsoft Access provides a number of ways for accessing objects and their properties. Each way provides a level of intricacy and detail while providing specific performance characteristics. In its simplest form, programmers can directly call the name of an object (such as the Form object) or the name of a control (such as a command button). This is only applicable when accessing objects and controls that belong to the current scope of a code module. For example, the next VBA assignment statement updates the form's Caption property during the form's Load event.

```
Private Sub Form_Load()
    Form.Caption = "Chapter 1"
End Sub
```

In addition to forms, controls belonging to the current form and scope can be referenced by simply calling their name.

```
Private Sub Form_Load()
    lblSalary.Caption = "Enter Salary"
    txtSalary.Value = "50000.00"
    cmdIncrease.Caption = "Increase Salary"
End Sub
```

There are times, however, when you need to go beyond the current scope and access forms and controls that do not belong to the current object. There are a number of other reasons for being more specific about what controls you are referencing, including performance considerations and advanced control access techniques such as enumerating. To accomplish these goals, I show you how to access forms and controls using common VBA techniques with the Me keyword prefix and collections such as the Forms collection.

The Forms Collection

Properties of the Form object can be accessed in the VBE code window by simply supplying the form's Access class name.

```
Form_Form1.Caption = "updating the form's caption property"
```

Notice the naming convention used in the keyword Form_Form1. When an Access form in created and saved, Microsoft Access refers to it in the VBE as a Microsoft Office Access Class Object with the name Form representing the standard object name with a trailing underscore (_) followed by the individual form's name. Moreover, you can use the form's Access class name to not only access its own properties, but controls contained on the form. For example, the following VBA assignment statement uses the Access form class name to modify a label's caption property.

```
Form_Form1.Label1.Caption = "update the label's caption property"
```

TRAP If your form name contains spaces, you must surround the Access form class name using brackets.

```
[Form_Light Switch].Label1.Caption = "Light Switch"
```

This approach is convenient when working with small VBA projects. At times, however, you want to use a more advanced feature (such as the Forms collection) when working with multiple forms or with multiple controls on a form. Access provides the Forms collection for specifying which form's Caption property you are referencing.

The Forms collection contains all open forms in your Access database. To access individual forms in the Forms collection, simply supply the Forms collection an index or form name as seen in the next statements.

```
'   Using an index to refer to a form in the collection.
Forms(0).Caption = "Chapter 1"


'   Using a form name to reference a form in the collection.
Forms("Form1").Caption = "Chapter 1"
```

 TRICK Because form indexes can change, it is considered safer to use the form name when accessing forms in the Forms collection.

Notice when passing the name of the form to the Forms collection, you must surround the form name in double quotes. If the form's name contains one or more spaces, you must use brackets ([]) to surround the name. After specifying a form in the Forms collection, you can use the dot operator to reference the individual form's properties, such as Caption.

The Me Keyword

To make things more interesting, Access provides the Me keyword, which refers to the current object or form within the scope of the VBE code module. More specifically, I can use the Me keyword in place of the Access form class name to access the current form's properties, methods, and controls.

```
Me.Caption = "updating the form's caption property"

Me.lblSalary.Caption = "updating the label's caption property"
```

The Me keyword provides a self-documenting feature for VBA programmers in that it explicitly tells the reader what object, property, or form you are referring to.

In addition to the dot operator (.), Microsoft VBA provides the exclamation point (!) identifier for identifying what type of item or object immediately follows.

```
Me!lblSalary.Caption = "updating the label's caption property"
```

VBA supports two operators, the dot and exclamation mark, for accessing object properties and collection items. Because the dot and exclamation mark operators can often be interchanged, it can be confusing to remember which serves what purpose and when to use what. As a general rule of thumb, use the exclamation mark operator prior to accessing an item in a collection, and use the dot operator when referencing a property of a form or control. To keep things simple however, I use the dot operator to reference both items in collections and properties of forms and controls.

Assignment Statements

You can assign data to object properties, such as the form's `Caption` property, using an assignment operator in a VBA assignment statement. The *assignment operator* is really a fancy term for the equals (=) sign. However, it's really more important, as you soon see. To demonstrate, evaluate the next lines of VBA code, which assign the text "Ouch!" to the `Caption` property of the `Form1` control.

```
Form.Caption = "Chapter 1"
```

Or

```
Forms("Form1").Caption = "Ouch!"
```

Or

```
Forms(0).Caption = "Chapter 1"
```

Or

```
Me.Caption = "Ouch!"
```

Or

```
Form_Form1.Caption = "Ouch!"
```

A core concept in most programming languages is to understand the difference between data assignment and equality testing. This is especially important in programming languages such as VBA, which use the same operator.

Specifically, the following assignment statement reads, "The `Caption` property takes the literal value `Ouch!`" or "The `Caption` property gets the literal value `Ouch!`"

```
Me.Caption = "Ouch!"
```

Either way, the equals sign in an assignment statement is not testing for equality. In other words, you never want to read the previous assignment as "the `Caption` property equals `Ouch!`"

In the next chapter, I discuss how the equals sign can be used in testing for equality.

Command and Label Objects

I now show you how to put your knowledge of event procedures, VBA statements, objects, and their properties to work by building two small programs with VBA.

Let's start by building a program that allows a user to turn off and on a light switch. Begin by adding a new form to an Access database and naming it `Light Switch`. Next, add one label control to the form and assign the following property values to it:

- Name: `lblCaption`
- Caption: `Lights are on`
- Font Size: `10`

Now I add three image controls to the form, but only one of them is visible during the form's runtime. (You see why shortly.) Add the following property values to the image controls:

- Name: `imgMain`
- Picture: `LIGHTON.ICO` (Image located on accompanying CD)
- Visible: `Yes`

- Name: `imgOn`
- Picture: `LIGHTON.ICO` (Image located on accompanying CD)
- Visible: `No`

- Name: `imgOff`
- Picture: `LIGHTOFF.ICO` (Image located on accompanying CD)
- Visible: `No`

Now add two command buttons to the form, which allows the user to turn off and on the light switch. Do not use the wizard while adding these command buttons.

- Name: `cmdOn`
- Caption: `On`

- Name: `cmdOff`
- Caption: `Off`

 TRICK You can turn off the control wizards (command button control wizard) by clicking the Control Wizards button on the Access Toolbar seen in Figure 2.3.

Turn off and on
Control Wizards

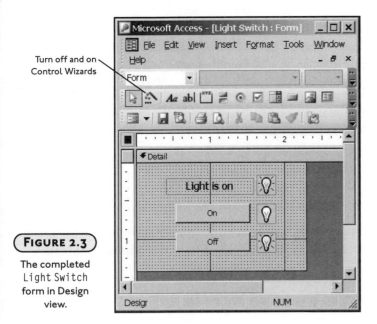

FIGURE 2.3

The completed
Light Switch
form in Design
view.

When a graphic's path and file name is assigned to an Image control's Picture property, Microsoft Access does not include the image as part of its .mdb file. To use the light switch program located in this book's accompanying CD ROM, you must first change in Design time the Picture property's value to a location on your PC. This applies to all programs on the accompanying CD-ROM that have references to images.

A depiction of my completed form in Design view is revealed in Figure 2.3. Sample code from the Light Switch form is shown next.

```
Private Sub cmdOff_Click()
   Me.lblCaption.Caption = "Light is off"
   Me.imgMain.Picture = Me.imgOff.Picture
End Sub
```

```
Private Sub cmdOn_Click()
   Me.lblCaption.Caption = "Light is on"
   Me.imgMain.Picture = Me.imgOn.Picture
End Sub
```

I use only one image control (imgMain) to display one or the other light bulb image. This is why I set the other two image control's Visible property to No. The final output of my Light Switch form in runtime mode is seen in Figure 2.4.

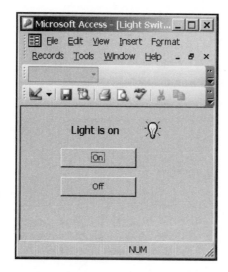

FIGURE 2.4

The completed Light Switch form in Design view.

TRICK You can get rid of the lines and scrollbars on a form in runtime by setting the following form property values to No:

- DividingLines: Used to separate sections on a form.
- NavigationButtons: Provides access to navigation buttons and a record number box.
- RecordSelectors: Record selectors display the unsaved record indicator when a record is being edited in Form view.

I now create a Colors program that allows a user to change the color of a label control and exit the Access application without the assistance of a control wizard. First, I create my Colors form and set the following form properties:

- Caption: Off
- Dividing Lines: No
- Navigation Buttons: No
- Record Selectors: No

I add four command buttons (three to change colors and one to exit the application) and one label control that displays the color selected by the user:

- Name: cmdExit
- Caption: E&xit

- Name: cmdRed
- Caption: Red

- Name: cmdWhite
- Caption: White

- Name: cmdBlue
- Caption: Blue

- Name: lblDisplay
- Caption: colors
- Font Weight: Bold
- Back Style: Normal

TRAP The label's BackColor property cannot be changed unless the corresponding label's BackStyle property is set to Normal.

A picture of the Colors form in design time should look similar to that in Figure 2.5.

```
Private Sub cmdBlue_Click()
   Me.lblDisplay.BackColor = vbBlue
End Sub
```

```
Private Sub cmdRed_Click()
   Me.lblDisplay.BackColor = vbRed
End Sub
```

```
Private Sub cmdWhite_Click()
   Me.lblDisplay.BackColor = vbWhite
End Sub
```

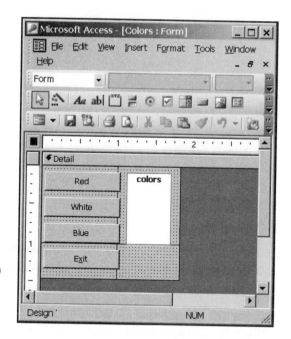

FIGURE 2.5

The completed
Colors form in
Design view.

The way I used the Me keyword to access the label and its corresponding properties should not be new to you. What should have caught your attention were the values I used in assigning BackColor properties. Specifically, VBA provides you access to eight color constants:

- vbBlack
- vbRed
- vbGreen
- vbYellow
- vbBlue
- vbMagenta
- vbCyan
- vbWhite

It's important to note that BackColor and ForeColor properties actually take a number value, which each color constant stores representatively. In addition to using VBA color constants, you can assign numbers representing a multitude of colors using either the RGB function or by viewing the BackColor or ForeColor properties in design time using the Properties window.

To terminate an Access application, use the DoCmd object and access its built-in Quit method as shown in the next command button Click event procedure.

```
Private Sub cmdExit_Click()
    DoCmd.Quit
End Sub
```

The VBA code in `cmdExit_Click()` event procedure is similar to the code generated by the Access control wizard to quit an Access application using the `DoCmd` object and its `Quit` method.

TRICK   The ampersand (&) character creates keyboard shortcuts with the Alt key when placed in the `caption` property of certain controls such as command buttons.

Getting User Input with Text Boxes

Text box controls receive all types of input from users such as dates, time, text, and numbers. VBA programmers (that's you) write code in procedures to collect the user input and process it. This may seem trivial, but it's not.

Consider a simple application that requests a user enter two numbers, after which the user clicks a command button to add the two numbers. After adding the numbers, the program should display its output in a label control.

```
Private Sub cmdAdd_Click()
    Me.lblOutput.Caption = Me.txtNum1.Value + Me.txtNum2.Value
End Sub
```

I can use a VBA assignment statement to add the value of both text boxes and assign the result to the label control's `Caption` property. Given this fact, why is the output of this VBA statement 55, as revealed in Figure 2.6, instead of 10?

This is an excellent question and best answered by examining the `Value` property of a text box. The text box's `Value` property returns or sets the text box's `Text` property (more on this in a moment). Because the `Text` property returns a *string* (a textual description of what's inside the text box), the output seen in Figure 2.6 is generated because I've added two strings together (`"5"` and `"5"` makes `"55"`). In other words, I concatenated them.

To accurately process numbers retrieved from text boxes, you use a built-in VBA function called `Val`. The `Val` function is simple to use. It takes a string as input and returns a numeric value. The next set of VBA code uses the `Val` function to correct the previous program's output.

```
Private Sub cmdAdd_Click()
    Me.lblOutput.Caption = Val(Me.txtNum1.Value) + _
        Val(Me.txtNum2.Value)
End Sub
```

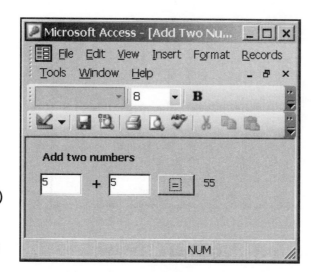

FIGURE 2.6

Concatenating
two numbers
instead of adding
them.

Notice in this example that each Val function takes a string as input. Specifically, I use two separate Val functions to convert each text box's Value property, one at a time, on both sides of the addition operation. The strings contained in the Value property are converted to numeric values prior to performing mathematical operations.

Now back to the relationship between the text box's Value and Text properties. If the Text property already contains the contents of the text box, then why use the Value property? Another excellent question. Before I answer, look at the following updated code that uses the Text property to add two numbers with output seen in Figure 2.7.

```
Private Sub cmdAdd_Click()
    Me.lblOutput.Caption = Val(Me.txtNum1.Text) + _
        Val(Me.txtNum2.Text)
End Sub
```

As Figure 2.7 depicts, VBA does not like this approach. Why? The Text property of a text box is only accessible once the text box has focus. In other words, the Text property is only current or valid once the text box has the focus. The Value property however, is the saved value of the text box control regardless of its focus.

To clear the text box of all contents, simply assign an empty string, also known as *empty quotes*, to the text box's Value property.

```
Me.Text1.Value = ""
```

In subsequent chapters I show you how to validate user input with validation programming patterns and text box events.

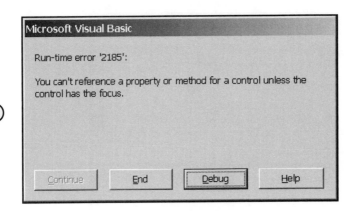

FIGURE 2.7

Attempting to
use the Text
property to
retrieve user
input from
text boxes.

VARIABLES AND BEGINNING DATA TYPES

Paramount in any programming language is the concept of variables. In a nutshell, *variables* are pointers to storage locations in memory that contain data. You often hear variables referred to as *containers* for data. In reality they are pointers that represent a memory address pointing to a memory location.

Though every variable created is unique (unique memory address), all variables share some common characteristics:

- Every variable has a name.
- Each variable has an associated memory address (hidden in high-level languages such as VBA).
- Variables have a data type such as `String`, `Integer`, or `Boolean`.

Variables in Access VBA must begin with a letter and cannot be longer than 255 characters, nor can they contain periods or spaces. When created, variable names point to a location in memory that can be managed during the execution of your program.

Demonstrated next, VBA programmers use the `Dim` keyword (short for dimension) to declare a new variable in what's called a *declaration statement*:

```
Dim myVariable
```

Once a variable has been declared, VBA reserves space in memory so you can store and retrieve data from its memory location using VBA statements. Simply declaring variables is not the end of the road. It is good programming practice to tell VBA what kind of variable, the *data type*, you are creating. When creating variables, you should ask yourself whether your variable stores strings, numbers, Boolean, dates, or object type data.

VBA provides a number of data types for declaring variables. The more common are listed in Table 2.1.

TABLE 2.1 COMMON DATA TYPES IN VBA

Data Type	Storage Size	Range
Boolean	2 bytes	True/False
Currency	8 bytes	−922,337,203,685,477.5808 to 922,337,203,685,477.5807
Date	8 bytes	I January 100 to 3I December 9999
Double	8 bytes	−1.79769313486231 E308 to −4.94065645841247E-324 for negative values and from 4.94065645841247E-324 to 1.79769313486232E308 for positive values
Integer	2 bytes	−32,768 to 32,767
Long	4 bytes	−2,147,483,648 to 2,147,483,647
Single	4 bytes	−3.402823E38 to −1.401298E-45 for negative values and from 1.401298E-45 to 3.402823E38 for positive values
String (variable length)	10 bytes + string length	up to approximately 2 billion (2^31) characters
String (fixed length)	length of string	I to approximately 64K (2^16) characters
Variant (with numbers)	16 bytes	up to range of Double data type
Variant (with characters)	22 bytes + string length	same as variable-length string

By default, VBA initializes your declared variables for you. Specifically, all number-based variables are initialized to zero (0), strings are initialized to empty string (""), and Boolean variables are initialized to False. This may seem trivial, but it is a nice feature that is not offered in every programming language.

To assign a data type to a variable, simply supply a data type name in the variable declaration using the As clause.

```
Dim myName As String
```

With this declaration statement, I've created one variable of String data type called myName. I can now use the myName variable in VBA statements to get and set data inside reserved memory, to which the variable myName points. This concept is demonstrated in the following statement.

```
myName = "Emily Elizabeth"
```

Notice when assigning data to string variables that the data on the right side must be enclosed with double quotes. Moreover, VBA programmers can use the concatenation operator (&) to glue two or more strings together. The next few VBA statements reveal VBA string concatenation.

```
Dim myTitle As String
myTitle = "Access VBA " & "Programming for the " & "Absolute Beginner"
Me.Caption = myTitle
```

In the preceding example, I successfully assigned the contents of the myTitle variable to the Caption property of the form, which works because both the String variable and Caption property store string data types.

Numbers however, do not require double quotes when used in assignment statements.

```
Dim mySalary As Double
mySalary = 50000.55
myBalance = -457.23
```

 Understanding the difference between string data and string variables is an important concept in beginning programming. Beginning programmers often forget to surround text with double quotes when assigning data to string based variables or properties. Forgetting to do so can cause compile-time errors.

Study the next program statement and see if anything strikes you as weird.

```
Dim mySalary As Double
Me.Caption = mySalary
```

It's intriguing that I can assign the variable mySalary (a Double) to a property such as Caption, which holds String data types. After executing, the value in the Caption property is now "50000.55" and not 50000.55.

Many languages such as C language, would not like the proceeding assignment statement one bit. This is because many languages require you to convert or cast data of one data type prior to assigning the value to a container of different data type.

IN THE REAL WORLD

At the lowest computer architecture level, data is represented by electrical states in digital circuits. These states can be translated into binary representations of 0s and 1s, which modern day computing systems can understand as machine language. Understanding how data is converted to and from binary codes is beyond the scope of this book. But, it is worth noting that depending on interpretation, binary codes can represent both a character and an Integer number. To demonstrate this concept, study Table 2.2.

TABLE 2.2 EXAMPLE BINARY REPRESENTATIONS

Binary Code	Integer Equivalent	Character Equivalent
01100001	97	a
01100010	98	b
01100011	99	c
01100100	100	d

Wow! The information in Table 2.2 should trigger an interesting question in your head, which goes something like this. "If binary codes can represent both characters and numbers how do I know what type of data I'm working with?" The notion and application of variables help to answer this question. Variables provide a storage mechanism that accurately manage the binary representations for us. For example, if I store data in an Integer variable, I can feel pretty good VBA will give me back an Integer number. And, if I store data in a String variable, I feel pretty good VBA will give me back characters and not a number. Using built-in VBA functions, it is possible to convert numbers to strings (characters) and strings to numbers.

With the knowledge of how data is represented, it's time to find where and how data is stored. Data can be stored in varying types of media such as volatile memory (also known as random access memory or RAM) and nonvolatile areas such as disk drives. Programmers can easily manage volatile memory areas using variables with languages like VBA. Nonvolatile memory areas such as hard drives are generally managed (stored) in systems such as files or databases like Microsoft Access.

Do not count on VBA to always convert data successfully for you. In fact, it is good programming practice to always use the Val function to convert strings to numbers when performing numeric calculations on string variables or properties.

In addition to variables most programming languages, including VBA, provide support for constants. Unlike variables, constants retain their data values throughout their scope or lifetime.

Constants are useful for declaring and holding data values that will not change during the life of your application. Unless they are declared in a standard code module using the `Public` keyword, constants cannot be changed once declared.

In VBA, you must use the `Const` statement to declare a constant as revealed in the next statement, which creates a constant to hold the value of `PI`.

```
Const PI = 3.14
```

For readability, I like to capitalize the entire constant name when declaring constants in my VBA code. This way, they really stick out for you and other programmers when seeing their name amongst other variable names in program code.

Variable Naming Conventions

Depending on the programmer and programming language, there are a number of popular naming conventions for variables. I like to use a single prefix that denotes data type, followed by a meaningful name with first letters capitalized for each word comprising the variable name. Table 2.3 lists some common data types with a sample variable name and purpose.

TABLE 2.3 SAMPLE NAMING CONVENTIONS

Data Type	Purpose	Sample Variable Name
Boolean	Determines if a user is logged in	bLoggedIn
Currency	Specifies an employee's salary	cSalary
Date	Employee's hire date	dHireDate
Double	Result of calculation	dResult
Integer	Tracks a player's score	iScore
Long	Current temperature	lTemperature
Single	Miles traveled on vacation	sMilesTraveled
String	Employee's last name	sLastName
Const	A constant, which holds the current tax rate	TAXRATE

As you program more and see more programming, you will notice many other popular naming conventions. The important note is to use a naming convention and stick with it.

Variable Scope

Variable scope is a fancy way of describing how long a variable will hold its data, or in other words its lifetime. VBA supports three types of variable scope.

- Procedure-level scope
- Module-level scope
- Public scope

To create a variable with procedure-level scope, simply declare a variable inside of a procedure.

```
Private Sub Form_Load()

    Dim dProfit As Double
    dProfit = 700.21


End Sub
```

In the preceding form Load event procedure, I declared a Double variable called dProfit that will hold its value so long as the current scope of execution is inside the procedure. More specifically, once program execution has left the form Load procedure, the dProfit variable is initialized back to 0.

If you need to maintain the value of dProfit for a longer period of time, consider using a module-level or public variable. Module level variables are only available to the current module from where they are declared, but are available to all procedures contained within the same module. Moreover, module-level variables are considered private and can either be declared with the keyword Dim or Private in the general declarations area as demonstrated next.

```
Dim dRunningTotal As Double ' module-level variable

Private iScore As Integer ' module-level variable
```

You can create public variables that are available to the entire project (all code modules) by declaring a variable using the Public keyword in the general declarations area of a code module.

```
Public bLoggedIn As Boolean
```

> The general declarations area is located at the top of a code module and is considered an area, which is outside of any procedure.

Determining variable scope is part of application development. During which, you define all needed variables, their storage type and scope.

Option Statements

VBA has a few module level utility statements known as options that are used for naming conventions, string comparisons and other internal settings. First off, you may have already noticed the `Option Compare Database` statement located in the general declarations area of the VBE code window.

Per Microsoft Access Help, `Option Compare Database` is defined as "this statement results in string comparisons based on the sort order determined by the locale ID of the database where the string comparisons occur." This statement can be modified to either `Option Compare Binary` or `Option Compare Text` instead of `Option Compare Database`. If your VBE code module does not include an `Option Compare` statement, VBA will default to `Option Compare Binary`, which results in string comparisons based on a character's internal binary representation.

The next option statement, `Option Explicit`, is more important to beginning VBA programmers as it forces you to explicitly declare all variables before you can use them. This is a huge; I mean HUGE service to even seasoned VBA programmers. By forcing the explicit declaration of variables, you are saved an often painful process of misspelling or misrepresenting variables that ultimately lead to program or compile error.

Unless you tell Microsoft Access to make it so, the `Option Explicit` statement may not appear by default in your VBE code module. To have this statement provided in each of your code modules, simply access the Options window from the VBE Tools menu and select the `Require Variable Declaration` setting as demonstrated in Figure 2.8.

The next option clause is the `Option Base` statement, which is manually typed into the general declarations area of each code module. In a nutshell, the `Option Base` statement defines the lower bounds for arrays. VBA arrays are by default 0-based arrays, but can start at 1 using an `Option Base` statement as seen next.

```
Option Base 1
```

I discuss arrays and their upper and lower bounds in more detail in subsequent chapters.

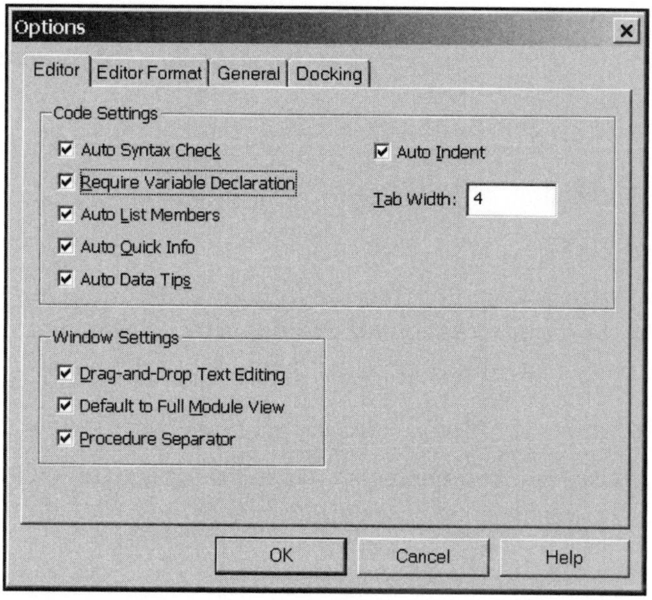

FIGURE 2.8

Requiring variable
declaration in the
Options window.

VBA ARITHMETIC AND ORDER OF OPERATIONS

It's no secret programming in any language involves some level of math. Though it's not
necessary to be a mathematical wiz in calculus, algebra or trigonometry, it is useful to
understand the essential arithmetic operators and order of precedence offered in a given
programming language. For basic mathematical operations, VBA supports the operators
seen in Table 2.4.

TABLE 2.4 COMMON MATHEMATICAL OPERATORS

Operator	Purpose	Example	Result
+	Addition	dSalary = 521.9 + 204	725.9
–	Subtraction	iPoints = 100 – 20	80
*	Multiplication	dResult = 5 * 213.78	1068.9
/	Division	iResult = 21 / 3	7
^	Exponentiation	iResult = 2 ^ 3	8

In addition to basic math operations, VBA supports what's known as order of operations using parenthesis. Without parentheses, VBA determines order of operations in the following order.

1. Exponents
2. Multiplication and division
3. Addition and subtraction

When VBA encounters a tie between operators, it performs calculations starting from the leftmost operation. To get a better handle of the importance of operator precedence and order of operations, consider the following equation, which calculates a profit.

```
Profit = (price * quantity) - (fixed cost + total variable cost)
```

The next VBA assignment statement implements the preceding equation without parentheses: In other words, without a well-defined order of operations.

```
dProfit = 19.99 * 704 - 406.21 + 203.85
```

The result of this calculation is 13870.6. Now study the next VBA statement which implements the same equation, this time using parentheses to build a well-defined order of operations.

```
dProfit = (19.99 * 704) - (406.21 + 203.85)
```

Using parentheses to guide my order of operations, my new profit is 13462.9. That's a difference of $407.70 that might have been recorded as inflated profits!

CHAPTER PROGRAM: FRUIT STAND

Fruit Stand is a simplified data entry system for a small fruit vendor. It implements many chapter based concepts such as variables, constants, and VBA statements.

To build the Fruit Stand program, you'll need to create a form in design view as seen in Figure 2.9.

Controls and properties of the Fruit Stand program are described in Table 2.5.

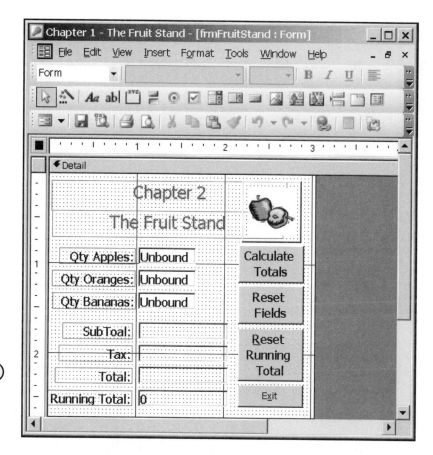

FIGURE 2.9

Building the
Fruit Stand
program in
Design view.

TABLE 2.5 CONTROLS AND PROPERTIES OF THE FRUIT STAND PROGRAM

Control	Property	Property Value
Form	Name	Fruit Stand
	Caption	Fruit Stand
	Record Selectors	No
	Navigation Buttons	No
	Dividing Lines	No
Label	Name	lblTitle1
	Caption	Chapter 2

(continues)

TABLE 2.5 CONTROLS AND PROPERTIES OF THE FRUIT STAND PROGRAM *(continued)*

Control	Property	Property Value
Label	Name	lblTitle2
	Caption	The Fruit Stand
Label	Name	lblQtyApples
	Caption	Qty Apples:
Label	Name	lblQtyOranges
	Caption	Qty Oranges:
Label	Name	lblBananas
	Caption	Qty Bananas:
Label	Name	lblSubTotalCaption
	Caption	Sub Total:
Label	Name	lblTaxCaption
	Caption	Tax:
Label	Name	lblTotalCaption
	Caption	Total:
Label	Name	lblRunningTotalCaption
	Caption	Running Total:
Text Box	Name	txtApples
Text Box	Name	txtOranges
Text Box	Name	txtBananas
Label	Name	lblSubTotal
	Caption	(empty)
	Special Effect	Sunken
Label	Name	lblTax
	Caption	(empty)
	Special Effect	Sunken
Label	Name	lblTotal
	Caption	(empty)
	Special Effect	Sunken

TABLE 2.5 CONTROLS AND PROPERTIES OF THE FRUIT STAND PROGRAM (continued)

Control	Property	Property Value
Label	Name	lblRunningTotal
	Caption	(empty)
	Special Effect	Sunken
Command Button	Name	cmdCalculateTotals
	Caption	Calculate Totals
Command Button	Name	cmdResetFields
	Caption	Reset Fields
Command Button	Name	cmdResetRunningTotal
	Caption	Reset Running Total
Command Button	Name	cmdExit
	Caption	E&xit
Image	Name	imgFruit
	Picture	apples.gif (located on the CD)

All of the code required to build the Fruit Stand program is shown here.

```
Option Compare Database
Option Explicit

' declare module level variable and constants
Dim dRunningTotal As Double
Const TAXRATE = 0.07
Const dPricePerApple = 0.1
Const dPricePerOrange = 0.2
Const dPricePerBanana = 0.3
```

```
Private Sub cmdCalculateTotals_Click()
    ' declare procedure-level variables
    Dim dSubTotal As Double
```

```
    Dim dTotal As Double
    Dim dTax As Double

    ' calculate and apply sub total
    dSubTotal = (dPricePerApple * Val(Me.txtApples.Value)) + _
        (dPricePerOrange * Val(Me.txtOranges.Value)) + _
        (dPricePerBanana * Val(txtBananas.Value))

    Me.lblSubTotal.Caption = "$" & dSubTotal

    ' calculate and apply tax
    dTax = (TAXRATE * dSubTotal)
    Me.lblTax.Caption = "$" & dTax

    ' calculate and apply total cost
    dTotal = dTax + dSubTotal
    Me.lblTotal.Caption = "$" & dTotal

    ' build and apply runnning total using module-level variable
    dRunningTotal = dRunningTotal + dTotal
    Me.lblRunningTotal.Caption = "$" & dRunningTotal
End Sub


Private Sub cmdExit_Click()
  DoCmd.Quit   ' terminates the application
End Sub


Private Sub cmdResetFields_Click()
    ' reset application fields
    Me.txtApples.Value = "0"
    Me.txtOranges.Value = "0"
    Me.txtBananas.Value = "0"
    Me.lblSubTotal.Caption = "$0.00"
    Me.lblTax.Caption = "$0.00"
    Me.lblTotal.Caption = "$0.00"
End Sub
```

```
Private Sub cmdResetRunningTotal_Click()
    ' reset running total variable and application field
    dRunningTotal = 0
    Me.lblRunningTotal.Caption = "$0.00"
End Sub
```

```
Private Sub Form_Load()
    ' set focus to first text box
    Me.txtApples.SetFocus
    'set default quantities when the form first loads
    Me.txtApples.Value = 0
    Me.txtBananas.Value = 0
    Me.txtOranges.Value = 0
End Sub
```

Chapter Summary

- The event-driven paradigm allows programmers to build applications that respond to actions initiated by the user or system.
- Access VBA includes a number of events that are categorized by the objects they represent.
- Objects are nouns such as a person, place, or thing.
- Objects have properties that describe the object and methods, which perform actions.
- Properties and methods of objects are accessed using the dot operator (period).
- The VBE (Visual Basic Environment) contains a suite of windows, toolbars, and menu items that provide support for text editing, debugging, file management, and help.
- Procedures are containers for VBA code.
- VBA statements are comprised of variables, keywords, operators, and expressions that build a complete instruction to the computer.
- Comment statements are ignored and not processed as a VBA statement by the computer.
- The Forms collection contains all open forms in an Access database.
- The Me keyword refers to the current object or form within the scope of the VBE code module.

- Use the `Val` function to accurately process numbers retrieved from text boxes.
- Variables are declared using the keyword `Dim`.
- Variables are pointers to storage locations in memory that contain data.
- All number-based variables are initialized to zero (0), string variables are initialized to empty string ("") and Boolean variables are initialized to `False`.
- Constants are useful for declaring and holding data values that will not change during the life of your application.
- The `Option Explicit` statement forces an explicit declaration before a variable can be used.
- VBA supports order of operations using parentheses.

PROGRAMMING CHALLENGES

1. Create a simple word processor that allows a user to enter text into a large text box. (Hint: Set the `Enter Key Behavior` property of a text box to `New Line in Field`.) The user should be able to change the foreground and background colors of the text box using three command buttons representing three different colors. Also, the user should be able to change the font size of the text box using up to three command buttons representing three different font sizes.

2. Build a simple calculator program with an Access form that allows a user to enter numbers in two separate text boxes. The Access form should have four separate command buttons for adding, subtracting, multiplying, and dividing. Write code in each command button's click event to output the result in a label control.

3. Create a discount book program that allows a user to enter an initial book price, a discount rate, and a sales tax percentage. The program should display, in labels, a discount price, sales tax amount, and a final cost.

   `((Initial book price - Discount price) + Tax amount)`

CONDITIONS

In this chapter I show you how to implement *conditions*, which allow programmers to build decision-making abilities into their applications using If blocks and Select Case structures. In addition, I show you how to leverage VBA's built-in dialog boxes and additional controls to enhance your graphical interface and your system's intelligence.

IF BLOCKS

A basic component of a high-level language is the ability to construct a condition. Most high-level programming languages offer the If block as a way to evaluate an expression. Before proceeding into If blocks, I discuss what an expression is in terms of computer programming.

In programming terms, expressions are groupings of keywords, operators, and/or variables that produce a variable or object. Expressions are typically used to conduct calculations and manipulate or test data. Moreover, expressions can be used to build conditions, which return a Boolean value of True or False. This is an important concept, so I am repeating it in italics: *Expressions can be used to build conditions that evaluate to* True *or* False.

VBA programmers can use expressions in an If condition.

```
If (number1 = number2) Then
    Me.Label1.Caption = "number1 equals number2"
End If
```

Known as an If block, the preceding code reads "If the variable number1 equals the variable number2, then assign some text to the Caption property of Label1." This means the expression inside of the parentheses must evaluate to true for the VBA statement inside of the If block to execute. Note that the parentheses surrounding the expression is not required, but provide readability.

Also note the inclusion of the Then keyword at the end of the If statement. The Then keyword is required at the end of each If statement.

TRICK   Always indent VBA statements inside of a condition or loop to provide easy-to-read code. A common convention is to indent two or three spaces or to use a single tab. Doing so implies that the VBA assignment statement belongs inside the If block.

But what if the expression does not evaluate to true? To answer this question, VBA includes an Else clause, which catches the program's execution in the event the expression evaluates to false. The If/Else block is demonstrated next.

```
If (number1 = number2) Then
    Me.Label1.Caption = "number1 equals number2"
Else
    Me.Label1.Caption = "number1 does not equal number2"
End If
```

Giving the preceding examples, you might be asking yourself about other possibilities for building simple expressions with operators other than the equals sign. As shown in Table 3.1, VBA supports many common operators to aid in evaluating expressions.

TABLE 3.1 COMMON OPERATORS USED IN EXPRESSIONS

Operator	Description
=	Equals
<>	Not equal
>	Greater than
<	Less than
>=	Greater than or equal to
<=	Less than or equal to

In addition to the Else clause, VBA provides the ElseIf clause as part of a larger expression. The ElseIf clause is one word in VBA and is used for building conditions that may have more than two possible outcomes.

```
If (number1 = number2) Then
    Me.Label1.Caption = "number1 equals number2"
ElseIf (number1 > number2) Then
    Me.Label1.Caption = "number1 is greater than number2"
ElseIf (number1 < number2) Then
    Me.Label1.Caption = "number1 is less than number2"
End If
```

Notice in the preceding example that the ElseIf clause must include an expression followed by the keyword Then, just like an If condition. In addition, you can use the Else clause to act as a concluding clause in the event that none of the conditions evaluates to true, as seen next.

```
If (sColor = "red") Then
    Me.Label1.Caption = "The color is red"
ElseIf (sColor = "white") Then
    Me.Label1.Caption = "The color is white"
ElseIf (sColor = "blue") Then
    Me.Label1.Caption = "The color is blue"
Else
    Me.Label1.Caption = "The color is not red, white or blue"
End If
```

Nested If Blocks

There are times when you may need to provide one or more nested conditions inside of another condition. This concept is known as *nested conditions* and can often require much thought regarding the flow of the program.

To exhibit the concept of nested conditions, I build a nested If block, which implements a simple payroll system.

```
If (sEmployeeType = "salary") Then
    ' Employee is paid a salary.
    cPay = cSalary
Else
    ' Employee paid hourly wages and has worked 40 or less hours
    If (iHoursWorked <= 40) Then
        cPay = cHourlyRate * iHoursWorked
```

```
    Else
        ' Employee earned overtime, which is time and a half
        cOverTime = (iHoursWorked - 40) * (cHourlyRate * 1.5)
        cPay = (cHourlyRate * 40) + cOverTime
    End If
End If
```

Because I used indenting techniques, you can easily see I have a nested If block inside of the Else block. This nested If block is executed only if the first If condition evaluates to false. If the first, or outer, If condition evaluates to true, the employee wage is calculated as a salary, after which program control is sent to the outer, or last, End If statement.

Without indentation, the preceding nested program code is very difficult to read. Always indent program statements that include nested If blocks inside conditions.

Compound If Blocks

So far, you've seen how to build simple and nested conditions using If blocks. There is, however, much more to consider if you plan to build more complex decision-making capabilities such as compound conditions into your VBA applications. To build compound expressions, VBA programmers can use the conditional operators And, Or, and Not.

TRAP
Conditional operators such as And, Or, and Not are considered reserved keywords and must be used in an expression. Otherwise, VBA will generate a compile error.

To get a better understanding of the preceding conditional operators, I use what's known as truth tables to explain possible scenarios and results for each operator. A *truth table* must include inputs and their possible results. Each input can evaluate to either true or false. Using one or more inputs and a corresponding operator, you can build all possible results in a truth table. Regardless of the number of inputs and type of operator, a compound expression ultimately results in either true or false.

Table 3.2 demonstrates the truth table for the And operator. The And operator uses two inputs to determine the result for the entire expression.

TABLE 3.2 TRUTH TABLE FOR THE AND OPERATOR

Input X	Input Y	Result
True	True	True
True	False	False
False	True	False
False	False	False

You can see from the truth table that there is only one occasion when the And operator generates a true result in an expression—when both inputs are true.

The next program block implements a compound condition using the And operator.

```
If (sEmpType = "salary" And sEmpEvalResult <> "poor") Then
   ' Employee is given a 20% bonus.
   cBonusPay = cSalary * .20
End If
```

In the preceding example, the employee is given a 20% bonus only if both conditions are true. If either condition is false, the entire compound condition evaluates to false and the employee is not awarded the bonus.

The Or operator in Table 3.3 has a much different effect based on its inputs. More specifically, the Or operator always generates a true value, providing at least one input is true. The only time a compound condition using the Or keyword results in a false result is when both inputs are false.

TABLE 3.3 TRUTH TABLE FOR THE OR OPERATOR

Input X	Input Y	Result
True	True	True
True	False	True
False	True	True
False	False	False

The next block of code demonstrates a compound condition using the Or keyword programmatically.

```
If (sMonth = "June" Or sMonth = "July") Then
    sSeason = "Summer"
End If
```

So long as the variable sMonth is either June or July, the variable sSeason is set to Summer. Only one side of the expression needs to be true for the entire condition to be true.

The truth table for the Not operator (seen in Table 3.4) contains only one input. In a nutshell, the Not operator reverses the value of its input value such that Not true results in false and Not false results in true.

TABLE 3.4 TRUTH TABLE FOR NOT OPERATOR

Input X	Result
True	False
False	True

The Not operator is implemented in VBA, as seen in the next program block.

```
If Not(5 = 5) Then
    Me.lblResult.Caption = "true"
Else
    Me.lblResult.Caption = "false"
End If
```

Given the preceding code, what do you think the value of the label's Caption property will be? If you said false, you would be correct. Why? To understand, you must look at the result of the inner expression (5=5) first, which evaluates to True. The outer expression, Not(True) or Not(5=5) evaluates to False, which means the statement inside the If condition does not execute. Instead, the statement inside the Else condition executes.

SELECT CASE STRUCTURES

The Select Case structure is another tool for VBA programmers to build conditions. Specifically, the Select Case structure evaluates an expression only once. It's useful for comparing a single expression to multiple values.

```
Select Case sDay
    Case "Monday"
        Me.lblDay.Caption = "Weekday"
    Case "Tuesday"
        Me.lblDay.Caption = "Weekday"
    Case "Wednesday"
        Me.lblDay.Caption = "Weekday"
    Case "Thursday"
        Me.lblDay.Caption = "Weekday"
    Case "Friday"
        Me.lblDay.Caption = "Weekday"
    Case Else
        Me.lblDay.Caption = "Weekend!"
End Select
```

In this case (excuse the pun) the Select Case structure evaluates a string-based variable and uses five Case statements to define possible expression values. The Case Else statement catches a value in the top expression that is not defined in a Case statement.

The Case Else statement is not required in a Select Case structure. After code within a Case or Case Else block is executed, program control is then moved to the End Select statement, which is required.

The Select Case structure is very flexible. For example, I can simplify the preceding structure by using Select Case's ability to place multiple items in a single statement separated by commas.

```
Select Case sDay
    Case "Monday", "Tuesday", "Wednesday", "Thursday", "Friday"
        Me.lblDay.Caption = "Weekday"
    Case Else
        Me.lblDay.Caption = "Weekend!"
End Select
```

In the following code, the Select Case structure also allows you to check for a range of values using the Is and To keywords.

```
Select Case dTemperature
    Case Is < 32
        Me.lblTemperature.Caption = "Freezing"
```

```
    Case 32 To 45
        Me.lblTemperature.Caption = "Cold"
    Case 46 To 69
        Me.lblTemperature.Caption = "Cool"
    Case 70 To 89
        Me.lblTemperature.Caption = "Warm"
    Case Is > 90
        Me.lblTemperature.Caption = "Hot"
End Select
```

Using ranges of values and comparison operators, I can easily build logic into my `Case` statements to determine temperature ranges.

DIALOG BOXES

Dialog boxes are generally small windows that prompt the user for a response. Dialog boxes can be configured to include one to three command buttons, which provide the user with various options for interaction. In this section you learn about two common VBA dialog boxes: the message box and the input box.

Message Box

VBA's `MsgBox` function is a built-in function that can generate a dialog box. The `MsgBox` function takes five parameters, separated by commas, as input:

```
MsgBox Prompt, Buttons, Title, HelpFile, Context
```

The only argument required by the `MsgBox` function is the `Prompt` parameter, which is displayed on the dialog box to the user. Though not required, the `Buttons` parameter is very useful. You can specify various VBA constants to customize the available buttons. The most common of these constants are shown in Table 3.5.

Another useful but unrequired parameter is the `Title` argument, which displays text in the title bar area of the message box. Using these parameters, I can create and display a simple dialog box in the `Click` event of a command button:

```
Private Sub Command1_Click()
    MsgBox "I created a dialog box.", vbInformation, "Chapter 3"
End Sub
```

TABLE 3.5 BUTTON SETTINGS

Constant	Value
vbOKOnly (default)	0
vbOKCancel	1
vbAbortRetryIgnore	2
vbYesNoCancel	3
vbYesNo	4
vbRetryCancel	5
vbCritical	16
vbQuestion	32
vbExclamation	48
vbInformation	64

To successfully use the `Buttons` parameter of the `MsgBox` function, you work with variables and conditions. Specifically, you need to create a variable that holds the user's response when the user selects a button on the dialog box. The variable gets its value from the result of the `MsgBox` function. That's right; the `MsgBox` function not only creates a dialog box, but also returns a value. This is how VBA programmers determine which button on the dialog box was clicked. The possible return values are described in Table 3.6.

TABLE 3.6 MSGBOX FUNCTION RETURN VALUES

Constant	Value
vbOK	1
vbCancel	2
vbAbort	3
vbRetry	4
vbIgnore	5
vbYes	6
vbNo	7

Remember from Chapter 2, "Introduction to Access VBA," that constants are containers for data that cannot be changed. The built-in VBA constants, such as the ones seen in Tables 3.5 and 3.6, hold integer values. This means you can use either the constant name or its value directly. To see how this works, examine the next program. This program uses the MsgBox function, one variable, and a Select Case structure to determine what button the user has pressed.

```
Private Sub Command1_Click()

    Dim iResponse As Integer

    ' Display a message box to the user
    iResponse = MsgBox("Press a button", _
     vbAbortRetryIgnore, "Chapter 3")

    ' Determine which button was selected.
    Select Case iResponse
        Case vbAbort
            Me.lblResponse.Caption = "You pressed abort."
        Case vbRetry
            Me.lblResponse.Caption = "You pressed retry."
        Case vbIgnore
            Me.lblResponse.Caption = "You pressed ignore."
    End Select

End Sub
```

Figure 3.1 demonstrates the message display to the user from the preceding code.

FIGURE 3.1

A multibutton message box.

TRICK Linefeed characters can be added in a message box prompt using the Chr(10) function call.

```
MsgBox    "This prompt demonstrates how to add a" & _

          " line feed character" & Chr(10) & "in a message box."
```

When using the message box function in an expression such as the following, realize that parentheses are required to surround function parameters.

```
iResponse = MsgBox("Press a button", _
    vbAbortRetryIgnore, "Chapter 3")
```

Without parentheses, the VBA compiler complains and prevents further execution. On the other hand, the VBA compiler does not like the use of parentheses when the MsgBox function is used by itself.

```
MsgBox "I created a dialog box.", vbInformation, "Chapter 3"
```

This is standard operating procedure when working with VBA functions, so it's worth repeating again in italics: *Functions in expressions require the use of parentheses for their parameters, whereas functions outside of expressions or by themselves do not.*

Input Box

The *input box* also displays a dialog box, but allows a user to input information (hence the name). Like the message box, the input box is created with a function call but takes seven parameters.

```
InputBox Prompt, Title, Default, XPos, YPos, HelpFile, Context
```

The most common InputBox parameters are Prompt, Title, and Default, where Prompt and Title behave similarly to the same parameters of the message box. The Default argument displays default text in the text box area of the input box. Also note that the InputBox function does not have a Buttons parameter. The only required parameter is Prompt.

The InputBox function returns a string data type, so you need to declare a String variable to capture its return value.

In Figure 3.2, I use an input box to prompt a user with a question.

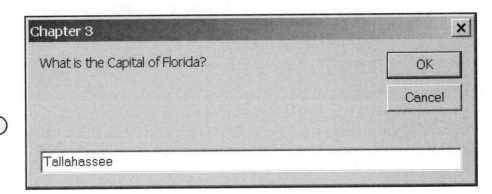

FIGURE 3.2

Using an input
box to prompt
a user for
information.

Sample VBA code for Figure 3.2 would look something like the following.

```
Private Sub cmdAskQuestion_Click()

    Dim sResponse As String

    sResponse = InputBox("What is the Capital of Florida?", _
        "Chapter 3")

    If sResponse = "Tallahassee" Then
        Me.lblResponse.Caption = "That is right!"
    Else
        Me.lblResponse.Caption = "Sorry, that is not correct."
    End If

End Sub
```

I can enhance the previous code to ensure the user has pressed the default OK button on the input box prior to validating the user's response. More specifically, if the user presses the Cancel button, a zero-length string is returned by the InputBox function. To check for this, I can use an outer If block.

```
Private Sub cmdAskQuestion_Click()

    Dim sResponse As String

    sResponse = InputBox("What is the Capitol of Florida?", _
        "Chapter 3")
```

```
' Check to see if the user pressed Cancel.
If sResponse <> "" Then

    If sResponse = "Tallahassee" Then
        Me.lblResponse.Caption = "That is right!"
    Else
        Me.lblResponse.Caption = "Sorry, that is not correct."
    End If

End If

End Sub
```

COMMON CONTROLS CONTINUED

As you've already seen, there are a number of common controls available to you in the Access Toolbox. In this chapter you learn about a few more that can require the use of conditions. Specifically, I discuss the following common controls and you can view them in Figure 3.3:

- Option group
- Option buttons
- Check boxes
- Toggle buttons

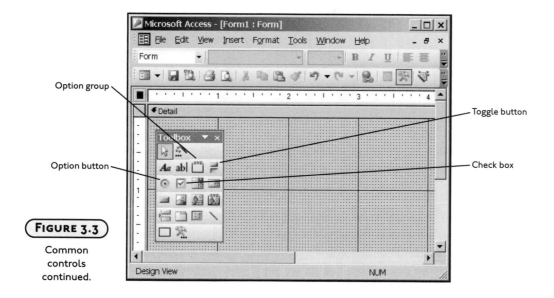

FIGURE 3.3

Common controls continued.

Option Group

The option group control is a container that logically groups controls such as option buttons, check boxes, and toggle buttons. Though not required, the option group provides a very effective wizard for grouping your controls inside the option group's frame.

When first adding an option group to your form, Access initiates the Option Group Wizard. As shown in Figure 3.4, the first step in the wizard is to add label names for each item in your group. At this stage, it doesn't matter what control you're using—you're only adding textual descriptions for each item in the group.

TRAP   The Option Group Wizard does not activate if you've turned off the Control Wizards item in the Access Toolbar.

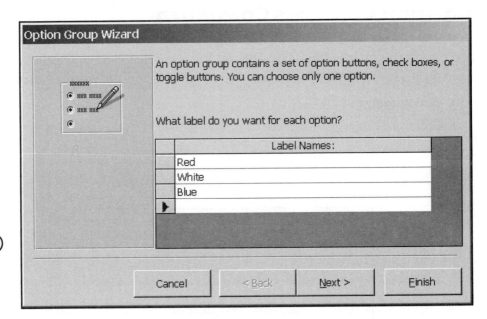

FIGURE 3.4

Adding label names for each control in the option group.

After you've added all label names and clicked next, the wizard asks you to choose a default control if one is desired. In Figure 3.6, I've asked the wizard to make my item, called Red, the default control.

Figure 3.6 depicts the next step in the wizard, where you set values for each option in the group. Option values allow VBA programmers to tell which option the user has selected in the group. The wizard's default values for each option are acceptable.

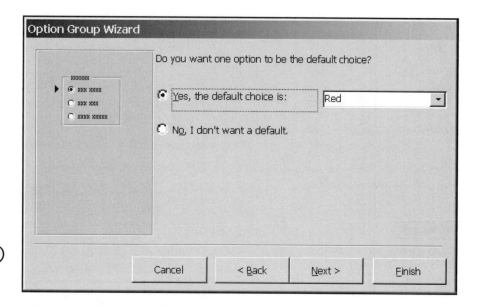

FIGURE 3.5

Selecting a
default control.

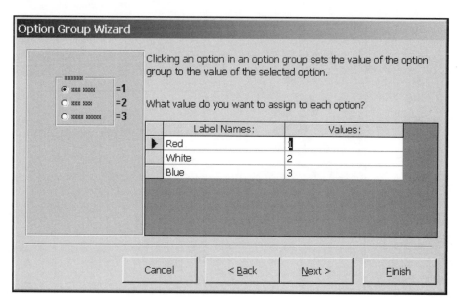

FIGURE 3.6

Providing values
for each option.

The next wizard screen, displayed in Figure 3.7, allows you to select what type of option controls are displayed in your option group.

The last screen in the wizard (see Figure 3.8) prompts you to enter a caption for your option group frame. This caption is actually a property of a label control that automatically sits at the top of the frame.

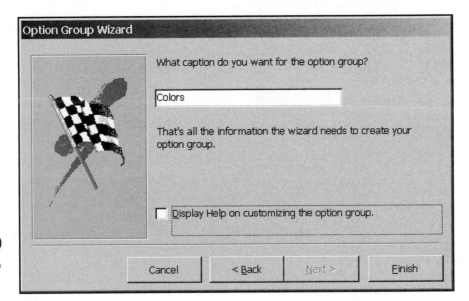

FIGURE 3.7

Choosing an
option control
type for the
option group.

FIGURE 3.8

Entering a caption
for the option
group's label.

In the next three sections I show you specific implementations of option groups.

Option Buttons

Often referred to as *radio buttons*, *option buttons* provide a user with a list of selectable choices. Specifically, the user can select only one option at a time. Individual option buttons comprise two controls, a label, and option button. Each has its own properties and can be managed during design time or runtime.

> **TRICK** After creating an option group either manually or with the Option Group Wizard, you should change the name of each option control to one that contains a meaningful description. This greatly reduces confusion when working with VBA code.

To determine which option button has been selected in a group, you use the option group's `Value` property. For this to work, each option button must have been assigned a valid and unique number in its `OptionValue` property (set by default in the Option Group Wizard). When a user clicks an option button, the `Value` property is set to the same number as the option button's `OptionValue` property. These concepts are demonstrated in the next program code, which implements the *graphical user interface (GUI)* in Figure 3.9.

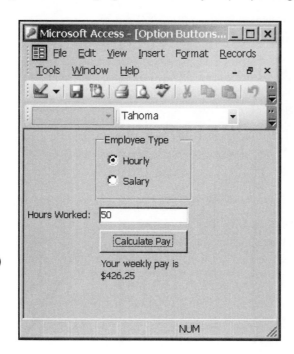

FIGURE 3.9

Using option buttons to determine an employee's pay type.

```
Option Compare Database
Option Explicit

Const SALARY As Double = 350.25
Const HOURLYRATE = 7.75
```

```vba
Private Sub cmdCalculatePay_Click()

Dim dOverTime As Double
Dim dNormalPay As Double

If Me.fraEmployeeType.Value = 2 Then

    ' Employee is paid a salary
    Me.lblPay.Caption = "Your weekly salary is $" & SALARY

Else

    ' Employee is paid by the hour
    ' Find out if the employee has worked overtime
    If Val(Me.txtHoursWorked.Value) > 40 Then

        dOverTime = (Val(Me.txtHoursWorked.Value) - 40) _
          * (HOURLYRATE * 1.5)
        dNormalPay = HOURLYRATE * 40
        Me.lblPay.Caption = "Your weekly pay is $" & _
          dNormalPay + dOverTime

    Else

        Me.lblPay.Caption = "Your weekly pay is $" & _
          HOURLYRATE * Val(Me.txtHoursWorked.Value)

    End If

End If

End Sub
```

```vba
Private Sub optHourly_GotFocus()
    Me.txtHoursWorked.Enabled = True
    Me.lblPay.Caption = ""
End Sub
```

```
Private Sub optSalary_GotFocus()
   Me.txtHoursWorked.Enabled = False
   Me.lblPay.Caption = ""
End Sub
```

The option group is really defined as the name of the frame. (An option group is really a frame control.) Notice that I used the GotFocus method of each option button to disable the Hours Worked text box. The GotFocus event is triggered whenever the option button receives focus.

Check Boxes

When used in an option group, *check boxes* behave much like option buttons. If you have experience in other graphical languages, you might be surprised to learn that a user can select only one check box at a time when it is located in an option group. This is different behavior from VBA's parent language Visual Basic! Remember that an option group provides a single selection for any option-based control such as check boxes, option buttons, and toggle buttons.

To use check boxes in a multiselection facility, you need to add them manually, outside of an option group. In addition, you need to set each check box's DefaultValue property to a unique number during design time.

Implemented in Figure 3.10, the following code demonstrates how one might use check boxes in a multiselection capacity.

```
Option Compare Database
Option Explicit
```

```
Dim dRunningTotal As Double

Private Sub cmdTotal_Click()

   dRunningTotal = 0

   If Me.chkTShirt.Value = True Then
      dRunningTotal = dRunningTotal + 9.99
   End If
```

```
If Me.chkBaseballCap.Value = True Then
    dRunningTotal = dRunningTotal + 12#
End If

If Me.chkSwimmingTrunks.Value = True Then
    dRunningTotal = dRunningTotal + 24.19
End If

If Me.chkSunBlock.Value = True Then
    dRunningTotal = dRunningTotal + 3#
End If

If Me.chkSunGlasses.Value = True Then
    dRunningTotal = dRunningTotal + 6.99
End If

Me.lblTotal.Caption = "Your total is $" & _
    dRunningTotal

End Sub
```

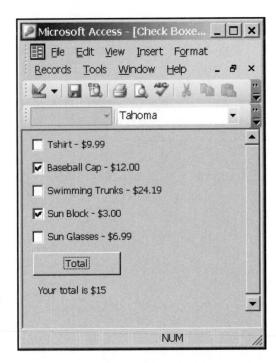

FIGURE 3.10

Selecting more than one check box at a time.

I can use the `Value` property of each check box to determine whether the user has selected it. If the check box has been checked, the `Value` property is set to `True`; if not, it is set to `False`.

Toggle Buttons

When used in an option group, *toggle buttons* serve the same purpose as option buttons and check boxes, which allow a user to select one item at a time.

In the next example (seen below), I use an option group of three toggle buttons to change label properties

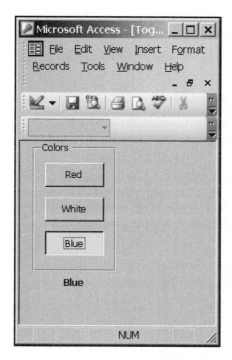

FIGURE 3.11

Using toggle buttons in an option group.

```
Option Compare Database
Option Explicit


Private Sub tglRed_GotFocus()
    lblOutput.ForeColor = vbRed
    lblOutput.Caption = "Red"
End Sub
```

```
Private Sub tglWhite_GotFocus()
    lblOutput.ForeColor = vbWhite
    lblOutput.Caption = "White"
End Sub
```

```
Private Sub tglBlue_GotFocus()
    lblOutput.ForeColor = vbBlue
    lblOutput.Caption = "Blue"
End Sub
```

Toggle buttons, check boxes, and option buttons behave similarly when used in an option group. To use one or the other is simply a preference on your part.

CHAPTER PROGRAM: HANGMAN

Hangman is a game common among school-aged children where a player tries to guess a word or phrase before a figure of a man (in this case a monster) is hanged. Each time the player guesses incorrectly, a portion of a body is shown until the body is complete, at which time the game is over. The player wins by guessing the word or phrase before all body parts are shown.

To build the Hangman program, simply construct the graphical interface as seen in Figure 3.12. The graphic of the monster is really six different graphics files, all of which can be found on the CD.

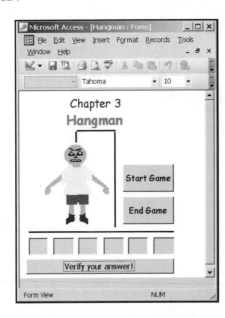

FIGURE 3.12

Using chapter-based concepts to build the Hangman program.

Controls and properties to build the Hangman program are described in Table 3.7.

TABLE 3.7 CONTROLS AND PROPERTIES OF THE HANGMAN PROGRAM

Control	Property	Property Value
Form	Name	Hangman
	Caption	Hangman
	Record Selectors	No
	Navigation Buttons	No
	Dividing Lines	No
Label	Name	lblTitle1
	Caption	Chapter 3
Label	Name	lblTitle2
	Caption	Hangman
Line	Name	Line0
	Border Style	Solid
	Border Color	0
	Border Width	2 pt
Line	Name	Line1
	Border Style	Solid
	Border Color	0
	Border Width	2 pt
Line	Name	Line2
	Border Style	Solid
	Border Color	0
	Border Width	2 pt
Line	Name	Line3
	Border Style	Solid
	Border Color	0
	Border Width	2 pt
Command Button	Name	cmdStart
	Caption	Start Game

(continues)

TABLE 3.7 CONTROLS AND PROPERTIES OF THE HANGMAN PROGRAM (CONTINUED)

Control	Property	Property Value
Command Button	Name	cmdQuit
	Caption	End Game
Command Button	Name	cmdVerify
	Caption	Verify your answer!
Text Box	Name	txtA
Text Box	Name	txtB
Text Box	Name	txtC
Text Box	Name	txtD
Text Box	Name	txtE
Text Box	Name	txtF
Image	Name	imgHead
	Picture	head.gif
	Size Mode	Stretch
Image	Name	imgBody
	Picture	body.gif
	Size Mode	Stretch
Image	Name	imgLeftArm
	Picture	left_arm.gif
	Size Mode	Stretch
Image	Name	imgRightArm
	Picture	right_arm.gif
	Size Mode	Stretch
Image	Name	imgLeftLeg
	Picture	left_leg.gif
	Size Mode	Stretch
Image	Name	imgLeftLeg
	Picture	left_leg.gif
	Size Mode	Stretch

All of the code required to build the Hangman program is seen next.

```
Option Compare Database
Option Explicit
```

```
' Form level variables to track game results.
Dim iCounter As Integer
Dim letter1 As String
Dim letter2 As String
Dim letter3 As String
Dim letter4 As String
Dim letter5 As String
Dim letter6 As String
```

```
Private Sub cmdStart_Click()
    MsgBox "A five letter word for database.", , "Hangman"

    'Reset the game board
    iCounter = 0

    Me.cmdVerify.Enabled = True

    Me.imgHead.Visible = False
    Me.imgBody.Visible = False
    Me.imgLeftArm.Visible = False
    Me.imgRightArm.Visible = False
    Me.imgLeftLeg.Visible = False
    Me.imgRightLeg.Visible = False

    Me.txtA.Enabled = True
    Me.txtB.Enabled = True
    Me.txtC.Enabled = True
    Me.txtD.Enabled = True
    Me.txtE.Enabled = True
    Me.txtF.Enabled = True
```

```vba
        Me.txtA.Value = ""
        Me.txtB.Value = ""
        Me.txtC.Value = ""
        Me.txtD.Value = ""
        Me.txtE.Value = ""
        Me.txtF.Value = ""
End Sub
```

```vba
Private Sub cmdVerify_Click()

    ' Did the user win?
    If (Me.txtA.Value & Me.txtB.Value & Me.txtC.Value & _
        Me.txtD.Value & Me.txtE.Value & Me.txtF.Value) _
        = "Access" Then
            MsgBox "You won!", , "Hangman"
            Me.cmdStart.SetFocus
            Me.cmdVerify.Enabled = False
    Else

            ' User did not guess the correct letter.
            ' Find an available body part to display.
            If Me.imgLeftLeg.Visible = False Then
                Me.imgLeftLeg.Visible = True
                iCounter = iCounter + 1
            ElseIf Me.imgRightLeg.Visible = False Then
                Me.imgRightLeg.Visible = True
                iCounter = iCounter + 1
            ElseIf Me.imgBody.Visible = False Then
                Me.imgBody.Visible = True
                iCounter = iCounter + 1
            ElseIf Me.imgLeftArm.Visible = False Then
                Me.imgLeftArm.Visible = True
                iCounter = iCounter + 1
            ElseIf Me.imgRightArm.Visible = False Then
                Me.imgRightArm.Visible = True
                iCounter = iCounter + 1
```

```
        ElseIf Me.imgHead.Visible = False Then
            Me.imgHead.Visible = True
            iCounter = iCounter + 1
        End If
        ' Find out if the user has lost.
        If iCounter = 6 Then
            MsgBox "Sorry, you lost.", , "Hangman"
            Me.txtA.Enabled = False
            Me.txtB.Enabled = False
            Me.txtC.Enabled = False
            Me.txtD.Enabled = False
            Me.txtE.Enabled = False
            Me.txtF.Enabled = False
        Else
            MsgBox "You have " & 6 - iCounter & _
            " chances left!", , "Hangman"
        End If

    End If

End Sub
```

```
Private Sub Form_Load()

    ' Start the game by calling an event procedure
    cmdStart_Click

End Sub
```

```
Private Sub txtA_LostFocus()
    ' Ensure correct case
    If Me.txtA.Value = "a" Then
        Me.txtA.Value = "A"
    End If
End Sub
```

```vba
Private Sub txtB_LostFocus()
    ' Ensure correct case
    If Me.txtB.Value = "C" Then
        Me.txtB.Value = "c"
    End If
End Sub
```

```vba
Private Sub txtC_LostFocus()
    ' Ensure correct case
    If Me.txtC.Value = "C" Then
        Me.txtC.Value = "c"
    End If
End Sub
```

```vba
Private Sub txtD_LostFocus()
    ' Ensure correct case
    If Me.txtD.Value = "E" Then
        Me.txtD.Value = "e"
    End If
End Sub
```

```vba
Private Sub txtE_LostFocus()
    ' Ensure correct case
    If Me.txtE.Value = "S" Then
        Me.txtE.Value = "s"
    End If
End Sub
```

```vba
Private Sub txtF_LostFocus()
    ' Ensure correct case
    If Me.txtF.Value = "S" Then
        Me.txtF.Value = "s"
    End If
End Sub
```

```
Private Sub cmdQuit_Click()
    DoCmd.Quit
End Sub
```

CHAPTER SUMMARY

- Expressions can be used to build conditions that evaluate to True or False.
- VBA conditions are built with If blocks and Select Case structures.
- Compound conditions have two or more conditions and are built using the operators And, Or, and Not.
- The Select Case structure is useful for checking an expression against a list of values.
- The Case statements in a Select Case structure can check a single value, multiple values, or a range of values.
- VBA contains the built in functions MsgBox and InputBox for building dialog boxes.
- The MsgBox function returns an integer value, whereas the InputBox function returns a string.
- The option group control contains a useful wizard for building groups of option buttons, check boxes, and toggle buttons.
- In an option group, a user can select only one check box, toggle button, or option button at a time.

PROGRAMMING CHALLENGES

1. Construct a simple math quiz that asks a user to answer a math problem of your choice. On the form, place one text box (txtAnswer) and two command buttons (cmdAskQuestion and cmdVerifyAnswer). Store the correct answer as a module-level constant and assign the user's answer in a local or procedure-level variable. Write code in the Click event of one command button to display a math question to the user with a message box. Write code in the other command button's Click event to compare the user's response to the module-level constant and inform the user of the results (correct or incorrect) also using a message box.

(continues)

PROGRAMMING CHALLENGES (CONTINUED)

2. Construct another quiz program, this time using an input box to ask the question and return the user's answer. Reveal the user's result in the form of a message box. Remember to check for an empty string (user presses the Cancel button) before checking the user's response.

3. Enhance the Hangman program to allow the player multiple chances to win. More specifically, display a message box that gives the player a Yes or No option to restart the game only if the game were lost.

4. Create a simple word processor that allows a user to enter text into a large text box. (Hint: Set the Enter Key Behavior property of a text box to New Line in Field.) The user should be able to change the foreground and background colors of the text box using option buttons in an option frame. Also, the user should be able to change the font size of the text box using option buttons in another option frame.

LOOPING STRUCTURES

In this chapter I show you how to build iteration into your programs using VBA looping structures such as Do and For loops. In addition, you learn some new VBA controls for managing groups of items and how to build random numbers into your programs.

INTRODUCTION TO LOOPING STRUCTURES

To *loop*, or iterate, computers need instructions known as *looping structures*, which determine such things as how many times a loop's statements will execute and by what condition the loop exits. Each programming language implements its own version of looping structures, but most languages, including VBA, support some variation of Do and For loops. Though the syntax of looping structures varies from language to language, looping structures share similar characteristics:

- Loops are logical blocks that contain other programming statements.
- Loops can increment a counter.
- Loops implement a condition by which the loop exits.
- Many looping structures support conditions at either the top or bottom of the loop.
- Special statements can cause the loop to exit prematurely.

Before looking at specific VBA implementations, I discuss some possibilities for looping, some of which may not be so apparent at first. Consider the following list of programming scenarios, each of which requires the use of looping structures:

- Displaying a menu
- Running an autopilot system for a jumbo jet
- Finding a person's name in an electronic phone book
- Controlling a laser-guided missile
- Applying a 5% raise to all employees in a company
- Spinning the wheels in an electronic slot machine

Believe it or not, all of the preceding scenarios have already been implemented by programmers using techniques and concepts similar to the ones I show you in this chapter.

Some scenarios require a predefined number of iterations. For example, if I write a software program to apply a 5% raise to all employees in a company, I can be sure there are a limited number of iterations. In other words, the number of times the loop executes is directly related to the number of employees in the company. Displaying a menu, however, can be a much different scenario. Take an ATM (automated teller machine) menu, for example. After a customer withdraws money from the ATM, should the ATM menu display again for the next customer? You know the answer is yes, but then how many times should that same menu display and for how many customers? The answer is indefinitely. It doesn't happen often, but there are times when a loop needs to be infinite.

 TRAP   Infinite loops are created when a loop's terminating condition is never met:

```
Do While 5 = 5
    MsgBox "Infinite loop"
Loop
```

In the previous code example, the loop will never terminate because the expression 5 = 5 will always be True. To break out of an endless loop in VBA, try pressing the Esc key or Ctrl+Break keys simultaneously.

To ensure loops are not endless, each loop has a condition that must be met for the loop to stop iterating. It's important to note that loops use expressions to build conditions, just as an If block or Select Case structure does. Moreover, each loop's condition evaluates to either true or false.

Many times, a loop's exiting condition is determined by a counter that is either incremented or decremented. In VBA, numbers are incremented and decremented using VBA assignment statements. In a nutshell, you must reassign a variable to itself with either an increment or decrement expression.

```
' Increment x by 1
x = x + 1


' Decrement y by 1
y = y - 1
```

After this cursory overview on looping structures, you're now ready to look at some specific VBA implementations. Specifically, you learn about the following VBA looping structures:

- Do While
- Do Until
- Loop While
- Loop Until
- For

Do While

The Do While loop uses a condition at the top of the loop to determine how many times statements inside the loop will execute. Because the loop's condition is checked first, it is possible that the statements inside the loop never execute.

```
Dim x As Integer
Dim y As Integer

Do While x < y

    MsgBox "x is less than y"

Loop
```

In this loop, it's possible that x is less than y, preventing the statement inside the loop from ever executing.

In the Do While loop, the statements are executed so long as the condition evaluates to true. In other words, the loop stops when the condition is false.

In the next example, the Do While loop uses an increment statement to satisfy the condition, which allows the loop to iterate five times.

```
Dim x As Integer
Dim y As Integer

x = 0
y = 5

Do While x < y

    MsgBox "The value of x is " & x
    x = x + 1

Loop
```

Knowing that the loop executes five times, what do you think the value of x is after the last iteration? The value of x is 4 after the last iteration. If you're having trouble seeing this, try placing this code in the Click event of a command button so you can step through it one iteration at a time, with each click of the command button.

Do Until

Similarly to the Do While loop, the Do Until loop uses reverse logic to determine how many times a loop iterates.

```
Dim x As Integer
Dim y As Integer

Do Until x > y

    MsgBox "Infinite loop!"

Loop
```

In the preceding example, the statement inside the loop executes until x is greater than y. Since there is no incrementing of x or decrementing of y, the loop is infinite.

Note that x being equal to y does not satisfy the condition. In other words, the statement still executes inside the loop. Only once x is greater than y does the looping process stop.

Now study the following code and determine how many times the loop iterates and what the value of x is after the loop terminates.

```
Dim x As Integer
Dim y As Integer

x = 0
y = 5

Do Until x > y

    MsgBox "The value of x is " & x
    x = x + 1

Loop
```

This Do Until loop executes six times, and the value of x after the last iteration is 6.

Loop While

Say I wanted to make sure the statements inside a loop execute at least once despite the loop's condition. The Loop While loop solves this dilemma by placing the loop's condition at the bottom of the loop:

```
Dim x As Integer
Dim y As Integer

x = 5
y = 2

Do

    MsgBox "Guaranteed to execute once."

Loop While x < y
```

Because the preceding loop's condition executes last, the statement inside the loop is guaranteed to execute at least once, and in this case, only once.

Loop Until

Using logic combined from the Do Until and Loop While loops, the Loop Until loop uses a reverse logic condition at the end of its looping structure.

```
Dim x As Integer
Dim y As Integer

x = 5
y = 2

Do

    MsgBox "How many times will this execute?"
    y = y + 1

Loop Until x < y
```

Using an increment statement, this loop's statements execute four times. More specifically, the loop iterates until y becomes 6, which meets the loop's exit condition of true.

For

The next and last type of looping structure this chapter investigates is For. The For loop is very common for iterating through a list. It uses a range of numbers to determine how many times the loop iterates.

```
Dim x As Integer

For x = 1 To 5

    MsgBox "The value of x is " & x

Next x
```

Notice that you are not required to increment the counting variable (in this case variable x) yourself. The For loop takes care of this for you with the Next keyword.

 TRICK Though it is common to specify the counting variable after the Next keyword, it is not required. When used by itself, the Next keyword automatically increments the variable used on the left side of the assignment in the For loop.

Using the `For` loop, you can dictate a predetermined range for the number of iterations:

```
Dim x As Integer

For x = 10 To 20

   MsgBox "The value of x is " & x

Next x
```

You can determine how the `For` loop increments your counting variable using the `Step` keyword. By default, the `Step` value is 1.

```
Dim x As Integer

For x = 1 To 10 Step 2

   MsgBox "The value of x is " & x

Next x
```

The preceding `For` loop using the `Step` keyword iterates five times, with the last value of x being 9.

Though it is common to use number literals on both sides of the `To` keyword, you can also use variables or property values:

```
Dim x As Integer

For x = Val(Text1.Value) To Val(Text2.Value)

   MsgBox "The value of x is " & x

Next x
```

Using the value of two text boxes, I can build a dynamic `For` loop that obtains its looping range from a user.

LIST AND COMBO BOXES

Both list and combo boxes store a list of items defined in either design time, in runtime with VBA, or through a linked database form such as Access. Shown in Figure 4.1, list and combo boxes can be added to your forms using the Toolbox.

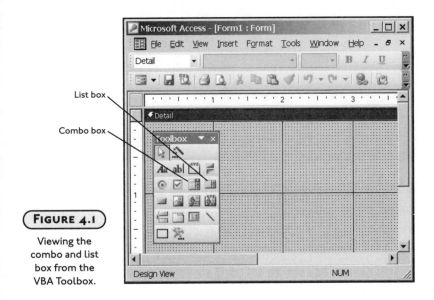

List box

Combo box

FIGURE 4.1

Viewing the combo and list box from the VBA Toolbox.

Whether you are building list and combo boxes manually or through a wizard, you must take into account many properties. The most common properties are listed in Table 4.1.

In addition to common properties, both list and combo boxes share two important methods for adding and removing items. In VBA they are appropriately called AddItem and RemoveItem.

TABLE 4.1 COMMON LIST AND COMBO BOX PROPERTIES

Property	Description
ColumnCount	Specifies the number of columns
ColumnHeads	Determines if the list or combo box has column headings
ColumnWidths	Determines the width of each column, separated by semicolons
ListCount	Determines the number of rows in the list or combo box
ListIndex	Identifies the item selected in the list or combo box
ListRows	Specifies the maximum number of rows to display
MultiSelect	Specifies whether the user can select more than one row at a time
RowSource	Determines the entries in the list, separated by semicolons
RowSourceType	Specifies the type of row: Table/Query, Value List, Field List, or a Visual Basic function

In the next subsections, you learn the most common approaches for managing items in both list and combo boxes.

Adding Items

Depending on the source, adding items with VBA can be a bit different between list and combo boxes. When used in a straightforward manner, however, both list and combo boxes support the AddItem method. Before using the AddItem method, you must set your combo or list box's RowSourceType property to Value List.

TRAP Forgetting to set your list or combo box's RowSourceType property to Value List causes a runtime error when using the AddItem method.

The next program, seen in Figure 4.2, uses the form Load event to execute multiple AddItem methods for both a combo and a list box.

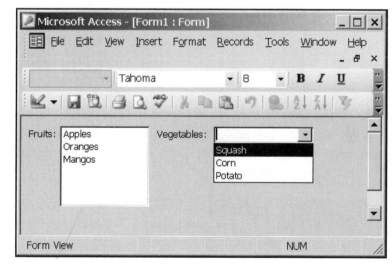

FIGURE 4.2

Using the AddItem method to populate a list box with fruit and a combo box with vegetables.

```
Private Sub Form_Load()

    lstFruits.AddItem "Apples"
    lstFruits.AddItem "Oranges"
    lstFruits.AddItem "Mangos"
```

```
cboVegetables.AddItem "Squash"
cboVegetables.AddItem "Corn"
cboVegetables.AddItem "Potato"

End Sub
```

The AddItem method takes two parameters (Item and Index), the first of which is required.

Many times, loops populate list and combo boxes with static data or table information from a database.

```
Private Sub Form_Load()

    Dim x As Integer

    ' Add 25 items to the list box.
    For x = 1 To 25

        lstFruits.AddItem "The value of x is " & x

    Next x

End Sub
```

So far, adding items has been fairly static. To make things more interesting, you can add items to your list box or combo box based on user input. Before doing so, however, it's fairly common to check for duplicates before adding the item, which the following program and its output in Figure 4.3 demonstrate.

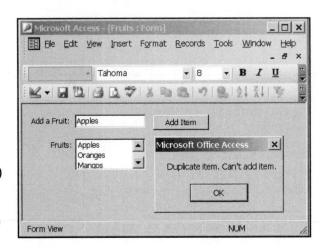

FIGURE 4.3

Checking for a duplicate item before adding the item to a list box.

```
Option Compare Database
Option Explicit
```

```
Private Sub Form_Load()

    ' Add preliminary items to the list box.
    lstFruits.AddItem "Apples"
    lstFruits.AddItem "Oranges"
    lstFruits.AddItem "Mangos"

End Sub
```

```
Private Sub cmdAddItem_Click()

    Dim iCounter As Integer

    ' Search for a duplicate item.
    ' If none is found, add the item.
    For iCounter = 0 To (lstFruits.ListCount - 1)

        If lstFruits.ItemData(iCounter) = txtInput.Value Then

            MsgBox "Duplicate item. Can't add item."
            Exit Sub ' A duplicate was found, exit this procedure.

        End If

    Next iCounter

    ' No duplicate found, adding the item.
    lstFruits.AddItem txtInput.Value

End Sub
```

A few statements may appear new to you in the preceding program code. First, note the use of the ListCount property in the For loop. The ListCount property contains the number of items in a list or combo box. This number starts at 1, but the lowest number in a list box starts with 0. This is why I subtract 1 from the ListCount property in the For loop statement.

To compare what's in the text box to each item in the list box, I can use the list box's ItemData property, which takes an index (in this case the looping variable) as a parameter and passes back the item's value.

Last but not least is the presence of the Exit Sub statement. This statement is very common with Visual Basic programmers when needing to exit a procedure prematurely. In my case, I want to exit the procedure prematurely (of course, after letting the user know) if a duplicate item is found.

If I choose to use a combo box when accepting input from a user, an additional text box control is not needed because the combo box already contains a text box. In reality a combo box is really two controls: a list box and text box. To accept new input from a user with a combo box, your combo box's LimitToList property must be set to No (the default). When retrieving user input from the combo box, work with its Value or Text properties (which is similar to working with a text box).

Removing Items

Removing items from a list or combo box is quite easy. Specifically, you use the RemoveItem method, which takes a single parameter called Index as a value. Generally speaking, items are removed based on a user's selection. Before removing items, however, it is always a good idea to ensure that a user has selected an item first. To do so, simply check the list or combo box's ListIndex property, as the next program demonstrates. Output is seen in Figure 4.4.

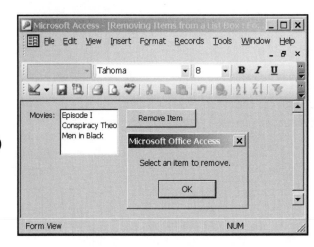

FIGURE 4.4

Checking that an item has been selected before using the RemoveItem method.

```
Option Compare Database
Option Explicit
```

```
Private Sub Form_Load()

    ' Add preliminary items to the list box.
    lstMovies.AddItem "Episode I"
    lstMovies.AddItem "Matrix"
    lstMovies.AddItem "Conspiracy Theory"
    lstMovies.AddItem "Men in Black"

End Sub
```

```
Private Sub cmdRemoveItem_Click()

    ' Has the user selected an item first?
    If lstMovies.ListIndex = -1 Then

        ' The user has not selected an item.
        MsgBox "Select an item to remove."

    Else

        ' The user selected an item, so remove it.
        lstMovies.RemoveItem lstMovies.ListIndex

    End If

End Sub
```

If no items in a list or combo box have been selected, the ListIndex is set to -1. Otherwise the ListIndex contains the index of the currently selected item (starting with index 0 for the first item). This means you can pass the ListIndex property value to the RemoveItem method. This is an efficient and dynamic means of using property values to pass parameters to methods.

Managing Columns

Adding and managing columns with your list and combo boxes is really quite easy. The important rule to remember is that a column header is considered a row or item (index 0) in a list or combo box. This means the header must be treated as an extra item when deleting items or searching for items.

To add and manage columns, you work with the following properties either in design time or through VBA code in runtime:

- ColumnCount: Specifies the number of columns to display
- ColumnHeads: Determines if the list or combo box has a column header
- ColumnWidths: Specifies the width of each column separated by semicolons in inches or centimeters

Remembering that a column header is treated like another item, a column header is added using the list or combo box's AddItem method. Figure 4.5 depicts the visual appearance of columns and column headers.

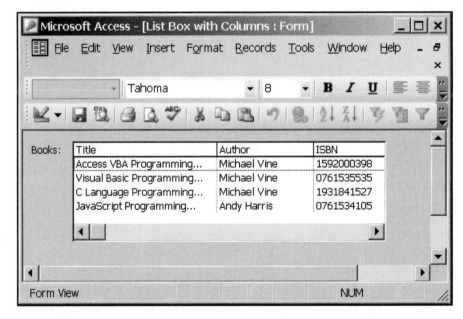

FIGURE 4.5

Adding columns and column headers to a list box.

```
Option Compare Database
Option Explicit
```

```
Private Sub Form_Load()

    lstBooks.ColumnCount = 3
    lstBooks.ColumnHeads = True
    lstBooks.ColumnWidths = "1.5in;1in;1in"

    lstBooks.AddItem "Title;Author;ISBN"
    lstBooks.AddItem "Access VBA Programming...;" & _
        "Michael Vine;1592000398"
    lstBooks.AddItem "Visual Basic Programming...;" & _
        "Michael Vine;0761535535"
    lstBooks.AddItem "C Language Programming...;" & _
        "Michael Vine;1931841527"
    lstBooks.AddItem "JavaScript Programming...;" & _
        "Andy Harris;0761534105"

End Sub
```

When the `ColumnHeads` property is set to `True`, the first `AddItem` method encountered by VBA is used to populate the column headers. Note that when working with columns, you have to remember to separate each column or column data with semicolons.

 Do not confuse the `ColumnHeads` **property with the singular version,** `ColumnHead`. **They are different properties belonging to completely different controls.**

Random Numbers

One of my favorite beginning programming concepts is random numbers. Random numbers allow you to build a wide variety of applications ranging from encryption to games. In this section, I show you how to build and use random numbers in your programs using two VBA functions called `Randomize` and `Rnd`.

The `Randomize` function initializes VBA's internal random number generator. It is only necessary to call this function (no argument required) once during the lifetime of your program. Most often, the `Randomize` function is executed during startup routines such as a form `Load` event. Without the `Randomize` function, the `Rnd` function generates random numbers in a consistent pattern, which of course is not really random at all.

The Rnd function takes a number as an argument and returns a Single data type. When used in conjunction with the Randomize function, the Rnd function can generate random numbers. To create a range of Integer-based random numbers, use the following VBA statements:

```
Dim x as Integer

x = Int((10 * Rnd) + 1)
```

The Int function takes a number as argument and converts it to an integer value (whole number). Remember that the Rnd function returns a Single number type, so the Int function is used to convert a decimal number into a whole number. Adding 1 to the result of (10 * Rnd) creates a random number between 1 and 10. Removing the addition of 1 causes the random number range to be 0 through 9.

One way of utilizing random numbers is through a simulated dice roll. Figure 4.6 reveals the design-time form I used to simulate this. Note that there are eight images, six of which have their Visible property set to False. This way only two dice are visible to the user during runtime.

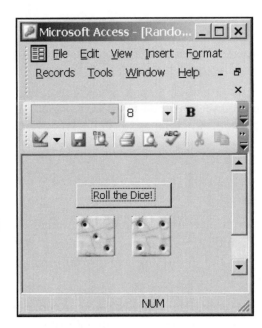

FIGURE 4.6

Using random numbers and image-swapping techniques to emulate rolling of the dice.

```
Option Compare Database
Option Explicit
```

```
Private Sub Form_Load()
    Randomize
End Sub
```

```
Private Sub cmdRoll_Click()

    Dim iRandomNumber As Integer

    ' Generate random number (die) for die 1.
    iRandomNumber = Int((6 * Rnd) + 1)

    Select Case iRandomNumber

        Case 1
            imgDie1.Picture = Image1.Picture
        Case 2
            imgDie1.Picture = Image2.Picture
        Case 3
            imgDie1.Picture = Image3.Picture
        Case 4
            imgDie1.Picture = Image4.Picture
        Case 5
            imgDie1.Picture = Image5.Picture
        Case 6
            imgDie1.Picture = Image6.Picture

    End Select

    ' Generate random number (die) for die 2.
    iRandomNumber = Int((6 * Rnd) + 1)

    Select Case iRandomNumber

        Case 1
            imgDie2.Picture = Image1.Picture
        Case 2
            imgDie2.Picture = Image2.Picture
```

```
    Case 3
        imgDie2.Picture = Image3.Picture
    Case 4
        imgDie2.Picture = Image4.Picture
    Case 5
        imgDie2.Picture = Image5.Picture
    Case 6
        imgDie2.Picture = Image6.Picture

    End Select

End Sub
```

To simulate the dice roll, I use the Click event of a command button to create a random number ranging from 1 to 6 for each die. After that, I perform a bit of image swapping based on a Select Case structure. Image swapping in this case is performed by assigning one Picture property to another. Remember, to work with programs that use images on the accompanying CD-ROM, you will need to change the path of the image's Picture property to a path on you local computer.

CHAPTER PROGRAM: MATH QUIZ

The Math Quiz program in Figure 4.7 is a fun way of learning how to incorporate chapter-based concepts such as loops, random numbers, and list boxes into your VBA applications.

The program prompts a user for the number of math questions she would like to answer. Then, Math Quiz prompts the user with a predetermined number of addition questions using random numbers between 1 and 100. A list box with columns stores each question, the user's response, and the result.

Controls and properties to build the Math Quiz program are described in Table 4.2.

All of the code required to build Math Quiz is seen next.

```
Option Compare Database
Option Explicit
```

```
Private Sub Form_Load()
    Randomize
End Sub
```

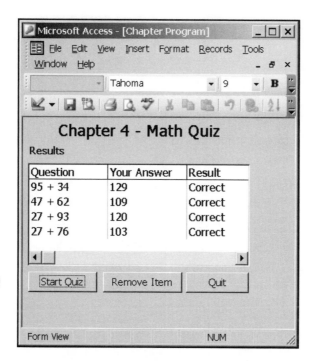

FIGURE 4.7

Using chapter-based concepts to build the Math Quiz program.

TABLE 4.2 CONTROLS AND PROPERTIES OF THE MATH QUIZ PROGRAM

Control	Property	Property Value
Form	Name	Chapter Program
	Caption	Chapter Program
	Record Selectors	No
	Navigation Buttons	No
	Dividing Lines	No
Label	Name	lblTitle
	Caption	Chapter 4—Math Quiz
Label	Name	lblResults
	Caption	Results

(continues)

	TABLE 4.2 CONTROLS AND PROPERTIES OF THE MATH QUIZ PROGRAM (CONTINUED)	
Control	**Property**	**Property Value**
List Box	Name	lstResults
	Row Source Type	Value List
	Column Count	3
	Column Heads	Yes
Command Button	Name	cmdStart
	Caption	Start Quiz
Command Button	Name	cmdRemoveItem
	Caption	Remove Item
Command Button	Name	cmdQuit
	Caption	Quit

```
Private Sub cmdRemoveItem_Click()

    ' Determine if an item has been selected first
    If lstResults.ListIndex = -1 Then
        MsgBox "Select an item to remove."
    Else
        lstResults.RemoveItem lstResults.ListIndex + 1
    End If

End Sub
```

```
Private Sub cmdStart_Click()

    Dim sResponse As String
    Dim sUserAnswer As String
    Dim iCounter As Integer
    Dim iOperand1 As Integer
    Dim iOperand2 As Integer
```

```
' Determine how many math questions to ask.
sResponse = InputBox("How many math questions would you like?")


If sResponse <> "" Then

    ' Add header to each column in the list box if one
    ' hasn't already been added.
    If lstResults.ListCount = 0 Then
        lstResults.AddItem "Question;Your Answer;Result"
    End If


    ' Ask predetermined number of math questions.
    For iCounter = 1 To Val(sResponse)

        ' Generate random numbers between 0 and 100.
        iOperand1 = Int(100 * Rnd)
        iOperand2 = Int(100 * Rnd)

        ' Generate question.
        sUserAnswer = InputBox("What is " & iOperand1 & _
            " + " & iOperand2)

        ' Determine if user's answer was correct and add an
        ' appropriate item to the multi-column list box.
        If Val(sUserAnswer) = iOperand1 + iOperand2 Then
            lstResults.AddItem iOperand1 & " + " & _
                iOperand2 & ";" & sUserAnswer & ";Correct"
        Else
            lstResults.AddItem iOperand1 & " + " & _
                iOperand2 & ";" & sUserAnswer & ";Incorrect"
        End If

    Next iCounter

End If

End Sub
```

CHAPTER SUMMARY

- VBA supports the Do While, Do Until, Loop While, Loop Until, and For loop structures.
- Looping structures use conditions to determine the number of iterations the loop will execute.
- An infinite, or endless, loop is caused when the loop's condition is never met.
- Generally a loop's exiting condition is determined by a counter that is either incremented or decremented.
- The For loop uses a range of numbers to determine how many times the loop iterates.
- Loops are often used to populate list and combo boxes with static data or table information from a database.
- To use the AddItem method of a list or combo box, the RowSourceType property value must be set to Value List.
- The ListIndex property of a list and combo box can be used to determine which item a user has selected.
- If no items are selected in a list or comb box, the ListIndex property is set to -1.
- Columns can be added to list and combo boxes by setting the ColumnCount, ColumnHeads, and ColumnWidths properties.
- Columns are managed through runtime with VBA or through design time by separating individual columns with semicolons.
- VBA uses the Randomize and Rnd functions to generate random numbers.
- The Randomize function initializes VBA's internal random-number generator.
- The Rnd function takes a number as an argument and returns a Single data type.

PROGRAMMING CHALLENGES

1. Place a single command button on a form. Write code in the Click event of the command button to display a message box five times using a Do While loop. Remember to use a counting variable in the loop's condition, which increments each time the loop iterates.

2. Modify Challenge 1 to use a For loop that iterates 20 times with a Step value of 3.

3. Add a combo box and command button to a form. In the form's Load event, add three items to the combo box using the AddItem method. In the Click event of the command button, add input from the combo box's Value property (input from the user). Remember to check for duplicate items.

4. Enhance the Math Quiz program to randomize not only numbers but the type of math problem. More specifically, use an additional variable to hold a random number between 1 and 4 where each number represents addition, subtraction, multiplication, or division.

FUNCTIONS CONTINUED

So far you have learned to use some built-in VBA functions such as InputBox and MsgBox, which provide interactive dialog boxes to the user. What you might not know is that VBA provides many more intrinsic functions for you to use in your programming efforts. Learning how to leverage the power of these built-in functions is all-important in VBA programming and is certainly the key to saving you from unproductive programming time.

To facilitate your learning of VBA functions, this chapter introduces a number of commonly used functions for managing strings, dates, times and for converting data.

STRING-BASED FUNCTIONS

Someone famous once asked, "What's in a name?" Someone less famous (yours truly) once asked, "What's in a string?" So what is in a string? Well, lots. *Strings* are key building blocks in any high-level programming language. More specifically, they are data structures that contain one or more characters. Note that it is also possible for strings to be Null (undefined).

Groupings of characters and numbers comprise strings. These groupings of characters can mean different things depending on their use. Many languages, including VBA, provide popular means for parsing, searching, and managing the individual pieces (characters and numbers) that make up strings.

In this section I show you how to parse, search, and manage strings using some very popular built-in VBA functions, which are described in Table 5.1.

TABLE 5.1 COMMON STRING-BASED FUNCTIONS	
Function Name	**Description**
UCase	Converts a string to uppercase
LCase	Converts a string to lowercase
Len	Returns the number of characters in a string
StrCom	Compares two strings and determines if they are equal to, less than, or greater than each other
Right	Determines the specified number of characters from the right side of a string
Left	Determines the specified number of characters from the left side of a string
Mid	Determines the specified number of characters in a string
InStr	Finds the first occurrence of a string within another
Format	Formats a string based on specified instructions

UCase

The UCase function is an easy function to use. It takes a string as a parameter and returns the string in uppercase letters.

```
Private Sub cmdConvert_Click()

    txtOutput.Value = UCase(txtInput.Value)

End Sub
```

The UCase function can take a string literal ("This is a string literal"), string variable (Dim sFirstName As String), or string type property (txtFirstName.Value) and provide output like that in Figure 5.1.

LCase

The inverse of UCase, the LCase function takes a string parameter and outputs the string in lowercase. Sample code is demonstrated next, with output seen in Figure 5.2.

Figure 5.1

Converting a
string to
uppercase using
the UCase
function.

```
Private Sub cmdConvert_Click()

    txtOutput.Value = LCase(txtInput.Value)

End Sub
```

Figure 5.2

Converting a
string to
lowercase using
the LCase
function.

Len

The Len function is a useful tool for determining the length of a string. It takes a string as input and returns a number of Long data type. The Len function's return value indicates the number of characters present in the string parameter. To demonstrate, the next event procedure determines the number of characters in a person's name. Output can be seen in Figure 5.3.

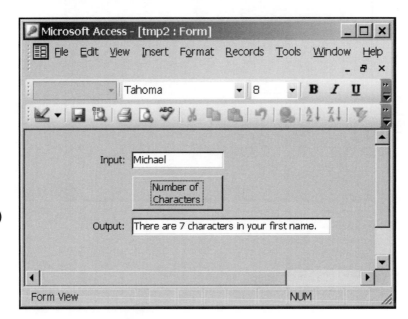

FIGURE 5.3

Using the Len function to determine the number of characters in a string.

```
Private Sub cmdNumberOfCharacters_Click()

    Dim iNumberOfCharacters As Integer

    iNumberOfCharacters = Len(txtFirstName.Value)

    txtOutput.Value = "There are " & iNumberOfCharacters & _
        " characters in your first name."

End Sub
```

StrComp

The StrComp function is useful when comparing the sequence of characters in two strings. The Option Compare statement is used to determine whether binary or textual comparison is done. If a binary comparison is done, characters are treated with case sensitivity. Textual comparisons are not case sensitive.

The StrComp function takes two string parameters and returns one of four numbers, as explained in Table 5.2.

TABLE 5.2 OUTPUT VALUES FOR THE STRCOMP FUNCTION

Return Value	Description
-1	String 1 is less than string 2
0	Both strings are equal
1	String 1 is greater than string 2
Null	One of the strings is Null (undefined)

The next Click event procedure uses the StrComp function to determine the equality of two strings. Figure 5.4 examines sample output from the event procedure.

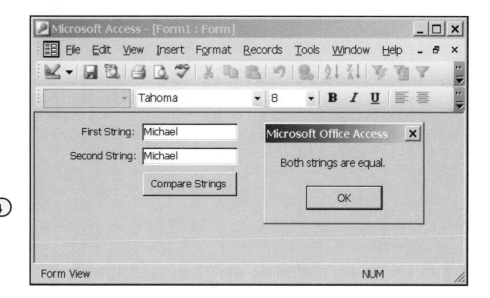

FIGURE 5.4

Using the StrComp to compare two strings for equality.

```
Private Sub cmdCompareStrings_Click()

   Dim iResult As Integer

   iResult = StrComp(txtFirstString.Value, txtSecondString.Value)

   Select Case iResult

      Case -1
         MsgBox "The first string is less than the second."

      Case 0
         MsgBox "Both strings are equal."

      Case 1
         MsgBox "The first string is greater than the second."

      Case Else
         MsgBox "One or more strings are Null."

   End Select


End Sub
```

Right

The Right function takes two parameters and returns a string containing the number of characters from the right side of a string. The first parameter is the evaluated string. The second parameter is a number that indicates how many characters to return from the right side of the string. Sample output is shown in Figure 5.5.

```
Private Sub cmdExtract_Click()
   txtOutput.Value = Right(txtInput.Value, 3)
End Sub
```

FIGURE 5.5

Extracting three characters from the right side of a string.

Left

Working in the opposite direction of the Right function, the Left function extracts a predetermined number of characters from the left side of a string. Like the Right function, the Left function takes two parameters. The first parameter is the evaluated string. The second parameter is a number that indicates how many characters to return from the left side of the string. Sample output is seen in Figure 5.6.

FIGURE 5.6

Extracting three characters from the left side of a string.

```
Private Sub cmdExtract_Click()
    txtOutput.Value = Left(txtInput.Value, 3)
End Sub
```

Mid

The Mid function returns a string containing a predetermined number of characters. It takes three parameters, the first two of which are required. The first parameter is the evaluated string. The next parameter is the starting position from which characters should be taken. The last parameter, which is optional, is the number of characters to be returned. If the last parameter is omitted, all characters from the starting position to the end of the string are returned.

```
Dim sString As String
Dim sMiddleWord As String

sString = "Access VBA Programming"

sMiddleWord = Mid(sString, 8, 3) ' Returns "VBA"
```

InStr

The InStr function can take up to four parameters and returns a number specifying the starting position of a string's first occurrence within another string. The required parameters are two strings, where the first string is being searched and the second parameter is sought after. The optional parameters determine the starting position of the search and the type of string comparison made.

In the next code example, I use both the Mid and InStr functions to extract a person's last name from a string expression. Output is seen in Figure 5.7.

```
Private Sub cmdClickMe_Click()

    Dim sLastName As String
    Dim startPosition

    ' Search the input string for a space character.
    startPosition = InStr(txtInput.Value, " ")

    ' Extract the last name from the string starting
    ' after the space character.
```

```
sLastName = Mid(txtInput.Value, startPosition + 1)

MsgBox "Thanks Mr. " & sLastName

End Sub
```

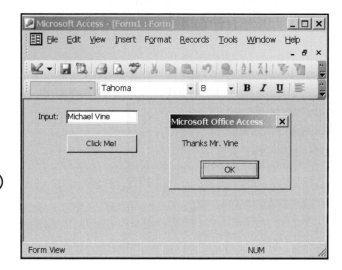

FIGURE 5.7

Using Mid and InStr functions to extract one string from another.

DATE AND TIME FUNCTIONS

Access VBA contains numerous date and time functions such as Date, Time, and Now for accessing your system's date and time. Specifically, I show you how to use the following VBA date/time functions:

- Date
- Day
- WeekDay
- Month
- Year
- Time
- Second
- Minute
- Hour
- Now

With these functions, you can create date/time stamps, stopwatches, clocks, or custom timer functions.

Date

The Date function requires no parameter when executed and returns a Variant data type containing your system's current date. This is that code:

```
MsgBox Date
```

Figure 5.8 demonstrates sample output from the Date function.

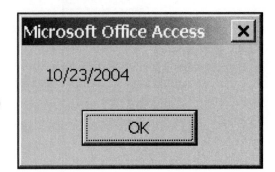

FIGURE 5.8

Displaying the current system's date with the Date function.

Day

The Day function takes a required date argument, such as the output from the Date function, and returns a whole number between 1 and 31, which represents a day within the current month. This is that code:

```
Day(Date) ' Returns a number between 1 and 31.
```

WeekDay

The WeekDay function takes two parameters and returns a whole number containing the current day of the week. The first parameter is the date (Date function output), which is required. The second, optional parameter determines the first day of the week. This is that code:

```
WeekDay(Date) ' Returns a number between 1 and 7.
```

TRICK The default first day of the week is Sunday.

Month

The Month function takes a single parameter, which signifies the current date and returns a whole number representing the current month in the year. This is that code:

```
Month(Date) ' Returns a number between 1 and 12.
```

Year

Much like the preceding date-based functions, the Year function takes a date parameter and returns a whole number representing the current year. Figure 5.9 shows Year at work. Here is that code:

```
Year(Date)
```

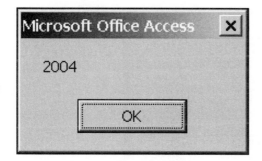

FIGURE 5.9

Displaying the current year with the Year function.

Time

The Time function is another easy-to-use function; it requires no parameters as input and returns a Variant data type with your system's current time. Figure 5.10 shows a sample return value for the Time function. That code is shown here:

```
MsgBox Time
```

When used with other functions and events, the Time function can be quite useful in building many applications. For example, I can use a form's Timer event and TimerInterval property to display the current time updated automatically every second:

```
Private Sub cmdStop_Click()

    ' Stop the Timer event.
    Me.TimerInterval = 0

End Sub
```

```
Private Sub Form_Load()

    Me.TimerInterval = 1000 ' 1000 milliseconds = 1 second

End Sub

Private Sub Form_Timer()

    ' Update the time every 1 second.
    lblTime.Caption = Time

End Sub
```

Note that setting the form's `TimerInterval` property to 0 stops the `Timer` event from executing.

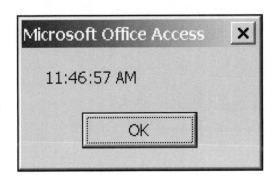

FIGURE 5.10

Displaying the current system time with the `Time` function.

Second

The `Second` function requires a time parameter (the output from the `Time` function) and returns a whole number from 0 to 59 indicating the current second in the current minute. That code looks like this:

```
Second(Time) ' Returns a number from 0 to 59.
```

Minute

Much like the `Second` function, the `Minute` function requires a time parameter (the output from the `Time` function) and returns a whole number from 0 to 59, which indicates the current minute in the current hour. That code looks like this:

```
Minute(Time) ' Returns a number from 0 to 59.
```

Hour

The Hour function takes a required time parameter and returns a whole number between 0 and 23, which represents the current hour according to your system's time. Here is that code:

```
Hour(Time) ' Returns a number from 0 to 23.
```

Now

The Now function incorporates results from both Date and Time functions. It takes no parameters and returns a Variant data type indicating the system's current date and time, respectively.

```
MsgBox Now
```

Sample output from the Now function can be seen in Figure 5.11.

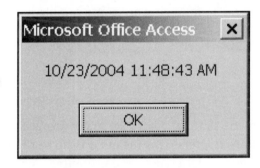

FIGURE 5.11

Displaying the current system date and time with the Now function.

CONVERSION FUNCTIONS

Conversion functions are very powerful; they allow programmers to convert data from one type to another. Access VBA supports many types of conversion functions. Many common uses for data conversion involve converting strings to numbers and numbers to strings. To explore the application of data conversion, I discuss the conversion functions found in Table 5.3.

TABLE 5.3 COMMON VBA CONVERSION FUNCTIONS

Function	Description
Val	Converts recognized numeric characters in a string as numbers
Str	Converts a recognized number to a string equivalent
Chr	Converts a character code to its corresponding character
Asc	Converts a character to its corresponding character code

Val

The Val function takes a string as input and coverts recognizable numeric characters to a number data type. More specifically, the Val function stops reading the string when it encounters a nonnumeric character. The following are some sample return values:

- `Val("123") ' Returns 123`
- `Val("a123") ' Returns 0`
- `Val("123a") ' Returns 123`

Str

The Str function takes a number as argument and converts it to a string representation with a leading space for its sign (positive or negative). An error occurs in the Str function if a non-numeric value is passed as a parameter. The following are some sample return values:

- `Str(123) ' Returns " 123"`
- `Str(-123) ' Returns "-123"`

Chr

You may remember from earlier chapters that data can take many forms. Specifically, numbers can represent both numbers and characters. This means it is up to the programmer to determine how data is stored—variables and data types—and presented—formatting and conversion functions.

Many programming languages, including VBA, support the concept of character codes. *Character codes* are numbers that represent a single character. For example, the character A is represented by the character code 65, and the character a (lowercase letter A) is represented by the character code 97. Appendix A, "Common Character Codes," contains a table of VBA's most common character codes.

To convert a character code to its corresponding character, VBA programmers use the Chr function. The Chr function takes a single character code as a parameter and returns the corresponding character.

Figure 5.12 demonstrates a simple program (given here) that can convert a character code to its corresponding character.

```
Private Sub cmdConvert_Click()

    txtOutput.Value = Chr(txtInput.Value)

End Sub
```

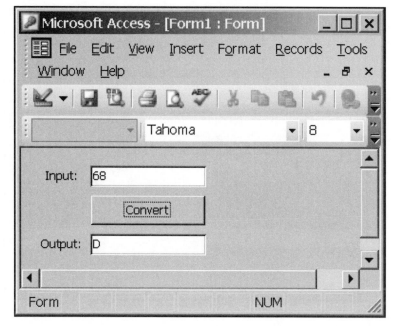

FIGURE 5.12

Converting
character codes
to characters with
the Chr function.

Note that character codes also represent numeric characters and nonprintable characters such as space, tab, and linefeed.

Asc

The Asc function works as the inverse of the Chr function. It takes a single character as input and converts it to its corresponding character code. Sample output from the Asc function can be seen in Figure 5.13.

```
Private Sub cmdConvert_Click()

    txtOutput.Value = Asc(txtInput.Value)

End Sub
```

FORMATTING

It is often necessary to format data to a specific need. For example, you may want to display a date in long format, or a number with a thousandths separator, or numbers as a currency or percentage. Each of these scenarios and many more can be accomplished with a single VBA function called Format.

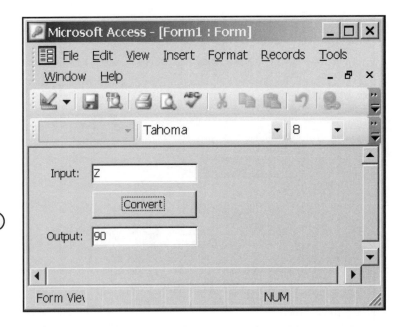

FIGURE 5.13

Using the Asc
function to
convert a
character to its
corresponding
character code.

The Format function takes up to four parameters:

Format(*expression*, *format*, *firstDayOfWeek*, *firstWeekOfYear*)

Table 5.4 describes each of the Format function's parameters in detail.

TABLE 5.4 FORMAT FUNCTION PARAMETERS

Parameter	Description
expression	An expression to format. Required.
format	A valid user-defined or named expression format. Optional.
firstDayOfWeek	A VBA constant that specifies the first day of the week. Optional.
firstWeekOfYear	A VBA constant that specifies the first week of the year. Optional.

In the next three sections, I show you how to use the Format function to format strings, numbers, dates, and times.

Formatting Strings

You have five characters with which to build user-defined strings using the Format function. Each format character seen in Table 5.5 must be enclosed in quotes when passed as a format expression argument in the Format function.

TABLE 5.5 STRING FORMATS

Format Character	Description
@	Displays a character or space as a placeholder
&	Displays a character or nothing as a placeholder
<	Formats all characters in lowercase
>	Formats all characters in uppercase
!	Placeholders are filled left to right

Note that placeholders are displayed from right to left unless an exclamation mark character is present in the format expression. Consult Microsoft Visual Basic Reference for more information on the Format function and format expressions.

In the next code segment, I use the Format function to change a string literal to all upper case:

```
' Returns "HI THERE"
Format("hi there", ">")
```

```
' Returns "access vba programming"
Format("Access VBA Programming", "<")
```

Formatting Numbers

Numbers can be displayed with user-defined formatting expressions. The Format function supports a multitude of formatting characters, which are used in the format argument of the Format function, for numbers. Table 5.6 reveals these number formats.

TABLE 5.6 NUMBER FORMATS

Format Character	Description
0	Displays a digit or 0 as a placeholder
#	Displays a digit or nothing as a placeholder
.	A placeholder that determines how many digits are displayed to the left and right of the decimal
%	Places the percentage character at the location where it appears in the format expression; multiplies the number by 100
,	Separates thousandths from hundredths using the comma character
E- E+ e- e+	Specifies scientific formatting
- + $ ( )	Specifies a literal character
\\	Displays a single backslash

The next three statements demonstrate how the Format function can be used to format numbers as money, format with decimal precision, and format as a percentage:

- s = Format(12345.6, "$##,##00.00") ' Returns $12,345.60
- s = Format("12345.6", "00.0") ' Returns 12345.6
- s = Format("10", "0.0%") ' Returns 1000.0%

Formatting Date and Time

One of the most common reasons to format data is to display dates and times. The Format function supports many named (VBA-defined) and user-defined formatting expressions for display customization.

Table 5.7 describes many date and time formatting options.

In Figure 5.14 sample outputs are shown in a list box from formatting dates and time with the Format function, as follows.

```
Private Sub Form_Load()

    lstFormatDateTime.AddItem Format(Date, "d/m/yy")
    lstFormatDateTime.AddItem Format(Date, "dd/mm/yyyy")
    lstFormatDateTime.AddItem Format(Date, "dddd")
```

TABLE 5.7 DATE AND TIME FORMATS

Format Character	Description
:	Separates time in hours, minutes, and seconds
/	Separates dates in day, month, and year
d	Day displayed as a number without a leading zero
dd	Day displayed as a number with a leading zero
ddd	Day displayed as an abbreviation
dddd	Day displayed with the full name
ddddd	Complete date displayed in short format (m/d/yy)
dddddd	Complete date displayed in long format (mmm dd, yyyy)
w	Day of the week displayed as a number (1 starts on Sunday)
ww	Week of the year displayed as a number
m	Month displayed as a number without a leading zero
mm	Month displayed as a number with a leading zero
mmm	Month displayed as an abbreviation
mmmm	Month displayed with full name
q	Quarters in year displayed as a number
y	Day of the year displayed as a number
yy	Year displayed in two-digit format
yyyy	Year displayed in four-digit format
h	Hour displayed without leading zeros
Hh	Hour displayed with leading zeros
N	Minute displayed without leading zeros
Nn	Minute displayed with leading zeros
S	Second displayed without leading zeros
Ss	Second displayed with leading zeros
ttttt	Time displayed with hour, minute, and second
AM/PM	Displays uppercase AM or PM using 12-hour clock
am/pm	Displays lowercase am or pm using 12-hour clock
A/P	Displays an uppercase A or P using 12-hour clock
a/p	Displays a lowercase a or p using 12-hour clock
p	Displays the date as ddddd and time as ttttt

```
lstFormatDateTime.AddItem Format(Time, "h:m:s")
lstFormatDateTime.AddItem Format(Time, "hh:mm:ss AM/PM")
lstFormatDateTime.AddItem Format(Now, "c")

End Sub
```

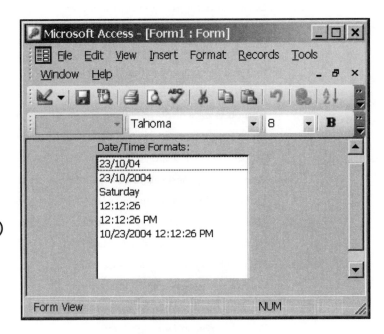

FIGURE 5.14

Using the Format function and user-defined expressions to format date and time.

CHAPTER PROGRAM: SECRET MESSAGE

Secret Message uses built-in VBA functions to build a fun encryption program. Moreover, the Secret Message program uses string-based functions such as Len and Mid and conversion functions Asc and Chr to encrypt and decrypt messages. Figures 5.15 and 5.16 depict sample input and output from the Secret Message program.

Controls and properties to build the Secret Message program are described in Table 5.8.

All of the code required to build the Secret Message program is shown next.

```
Option Compare Database
Option Explicit
```

FIGURE 5.15

Using chapter-based concepts to build the Secret Message program.

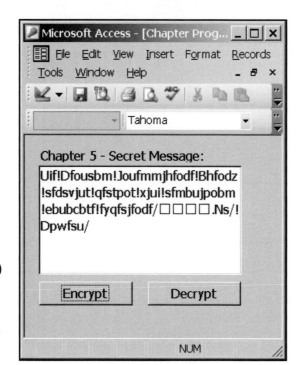

FIGURE 5.16

Using chapter-based concepts to encrypt a message with the Secret Message program.

Control	Property	Property Value
Form	Name	Chapter Program
	Caption	Chapter Program
	Record Selectors	No
	Navigation Buttons	No
	Dividing Lines	No
Label	Name	lblTitle
	Caption	Chapter 5—Secret Message:
	Font Size	10
Text Box	Name	txtMessage
	Enter Key Behavior	New Line in Field
Command Button	Name	cmdEncrypt
	Caption	Encrypt
Command Button	Name	cmdDecrypt
		Decrypt

TABLE 5.8 CONTROLS AND PROPERTIES OF THE SECRET MESSAGE PROGRAM

```vba
Private Sub cmdDecrypt_Click()

    Dim sDecryptedMessage As String
    Dim sDecryptedCharacter As String
    Dim iCounter As Integer

    If txtMessage.Value <> "" Then

        ' Iterate through each encrypted character in the message.
        For iCounter = 1 To Len(txtMessage.Value)

            ' Convert one encrypted character at a time to its
            ' equivalent character code.
            sDecryptedCharacter = Asc(Mid(txtMessage.Value, iCounter, 1))
```

```
                ' Convert the character code (shifted by -1) back
                ' to a character.
                sDecryptedCharacter = Chr(sDecryptedCharacter - 1)

                ' Add the decrypted character to the new decrypted message.
                sDecryptedMessage = sDecryptedMessage + sDecryptedCharacter

        Next iCounter

            ' Display the decrypted message.
            txtMessage.Value = sDecryptedMessage

        End If

End Sub
```

```
Private Sub cmdEncrypt_Click()

    Dim sEncryptedMessage As String
    Dim sEncryptedCharacter As String
    Dim iCounter As Integer

    If txtMessage.Value <> "" Then

        ' Iterate through each character in the message.
        For iCounter = 1 To Len(txtMessage.Value)

            ' Convert one character at a time to its equivalent
            ' character code.
            sEncryptedCharacter = Asc(Mid(txtMessage.Value, iCounter, 1))

            ' Convert the character code (shifted by 1) back
            ' to a character.
            sEncryptedCharacter = Chr(sEncryptedCharacter + 1)

            ' Add the encrypted character to the new encrypted message.
            sEncryptedMessage = sEncryptedMessage + sEncryptedCharacter
```

```
    Next iCounter

    ' Display the encrypted message.
    txtMessage.Value = sEncryptedMessage

  End If

End Sub
```

Chapter Summary

- String case can be managed with UCase and LCase functions.
- Strings can be extracted from other strings using functions such as Left, Right, and Mid.
- Strings can be searched and compared with VBA functions InStr and StrComp, respectively.
- VBA supports a multitude of functions such as Date, Time, and Now for displaying dates and times
- Forms have a Timer event, which can be triggered automatically and regularly using the form's TimerInterval property.
- Data is represented by both numbers and characters using character codes. VBA uses the Chr and Asc functions to convert between character codes and characters.
- Data such as strings, numbers, and date/time can easily be formatted using VBA's Format function.

PROGRAMMING CHALLENGES

1. Using the `Right` function, code the `Click` event of a command button to output the last seven characters in the string `Access VBA Programming`.

2. Using a form's `Timer` event and `TimerInterval` property, build a stopwatch with one label control and two command buttons. Use the `Format` function, `Time` function, and format expression `Ss` to display seconds only.

3. Create a word search game that allows a user to view a string of characters for a predetermined amount of time (say 5 to 10 seconds). Build a timer to accomplish this). After time is up, hide the string of characters and prompt the user to enter one or more words he saw in the string. For example, the string of characters `keoixakaccessqcinmsboxeamlz` contains the words `access` and `box`. Use the `InStr` function to determine whether the user's guess is contained in the word search string.

4. Build a form with one text box and one command button. Allow the user to enter multiple lines into the text box. In the `Click` event of the command button, use a `For` loop and the `Len` function to iterate through each character in the text box. Every time a space character is found, increment a procedure-level variable by 1. After the loop has completed, output the number of spaces found in a message box.

CODE REUSE AND
DATA STRUCTURES

I n this chapter I show you how to increase your programming productivity by building your own procedures for reuse throughout a program. I also show you how to build collections of related information using data structures such as arrays and user-defined types.

CODE REUSE

Remember that Visual Basic and VBA are *event-driven* programming languages. This means VBA programmers could easily duplicate work when writing code in two or more event procedures. For example, consider a bookstore program that contains three separate places (forms or windows) a user could search for a book by entering a book title and clicking a command button. As a VBA programmer, you could easily write the same code in each command button's Click event. This approach is demonstrated in the next three event procedures.

```
Private Sub cmdSearchFromMainWindow_Click(BookTitle As String)

    ' Common code to search for a book based on book title.

End Sub
```

```
Private Sub cmdSearchFromHelpWindow_Click(BookTitle As String)
```

```
' Common code to search for a book based on book title.

End Sub
```

```
Private Sub cmdSearchFromBookWindow_Click(BookTitle As String)

    ' Common code to search for a book based on book title.

End Sub
```

The program statements required to search for a book could be many lines long and needlessly duplicated in each event procedure. To solve this problem, you could build your own user-defined procedure called SearchForBook, which implements all the required code only once to search for a book. Then each event procedure need only call SearchForBook and pass in a book title as a parameter.

To remove duplicate code, I must first build the SearchForBook user-defined procedure.

```
Public Sub SearchForBook(sBookTitle As String)

    ' Search for a book based on book title.

End Sub
```

Instead of duplicating the Search statements in each Click event, I simply call the SearchForBook subprocedure, passing it a book title.

```
Private Sub cmdSearchFromMainWindow_Click()

    SearchForBook(txtBookTitle.Value)

End Sub
```

```
Private Sub cmdSearchFromHelpWindow_Click()

    SearchForBook(txtBookTitle.Value)

End Sub
```

```
Private Sub cmdSearchFromBookWindow_Click()

    SearchForBook(txtBookTitle.Value)

End Sub
```

This new approach eliminates duplicate code and logic by creating what's known as code-reuse. Specifically, *code reuse* is the process by which programmers pull out commonly used statements and put them into unique procedures or functions, which can be referenced from anywhere in the application.

Code reuse makes your life as a programmer much easier and more enjoyable. It is an easy concept to grasp and is really more applied than theoretical. In the world of VBA, code reusability is implemented as subprocedures and function procedures. Programmers create user-defined procedures for problems that need frequently used solutions.

Introduction to User-Defined Procedures

In previous chapters, you learned how to use built-in VBA functions (also known as *procedures*) such as `MsgBox` and `InputBox`. You may have wondered how those functions were implemented. In this section, you learn how to build your own functions using user-defined procedures.

Access VBA supports three types of procedures: subprocedures, function procedures, and property procedures. I specifically discuss subprocedures and function procedures while saving property procedures for Chapter 10, "Object Oriented Programming with Access VBA," when I discuss object-oriented programming, also known as OOP!

 The main difference between subprocedures and function procedures is that subprocedures do not return values. Many other programming languages, such as C or Java, simply refer to a procedure that returns no value as a *void function*.

Though different in implementation and use, both subprocedures and function procedures share some characteristics, such as beginning and ending statements, executable statements, and incoming arguments. The main difference between the two revolves around a return value. Specifically, subprocedures do not return a value, whereas function procedures do.

User-defined procedures are added to your Visual Basic code modules manually or with a little help from the Add Procedure dialog box. To access the Add Procedure dialog box, open your VBE (Visual Basic Environment) and make sure the Code window portion has the focus. Select Insert, Procedure from the menu.

The Procedure menu item appears unavailable (disabled) if the code window in the VBE does not have the focus.

The Add Procedure dialog box in Figure 6.1 allows you to name your procedure and select a procedure type and scope.

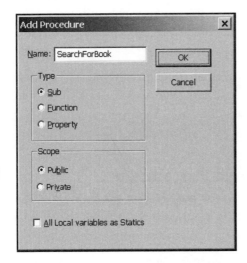

FIGURE 6.1

Adding a procedure with the Add Procedure dialog box.

If you select All Local Variables as Statics, your procedure-level variables maintain their values through your program's execution.

After creating your procedure, the Add Procedure dialog box tells VBA to create a procedure shell with Public Sub and End Sub statements, as shown in Figure 6.2.

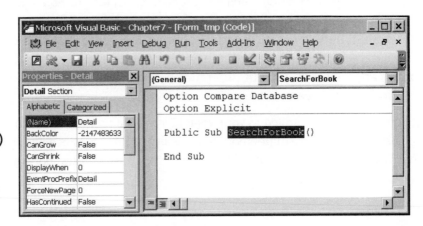

FIGURE 6.2

An empty procedure created with the Add Procedure dialog box.

Subprocedures

Subprocedures must have a Sub statement and corresponding End Sub statement. They can contain executable Visual Basic statements such as declaration and assignment statements. Subprocedures can take arguments such as variables, constants, and expressions. If no arguments are provided, the beginning Sub statement must contain an empty set of parentheses:

```
Public Sub DisplayCurrentTime()

    MsgBox "The time is " & Time

End Sub
```

The next procedure implements adding two numbers, which are passed in as arguments.

```
Public Sub AddTwoNumbers(iNumber1 As Integer, iNumber2 As Integer)

    MsgBox "The result of " & iNumber1 & " and " & iNumber2 & _
           " is " & iNumber1 + iNumber2

End Sub
```

When executed by itself, the AddTwoNumbers procedure requires no parentheses to surround its parameter list:

```
AddTwoNumbers 4, 6
```

When used in an assignment statement, however, the comma-separated parameter list must be enclosed in parentheses:

```
lblOutput.Caption = AddTwoNumbers(4, 6)
```

Note again that subprocedures only execute statements and do not return a value to the calling procedure. If a return value is required, consider using a function procedure (discussed next).

Function Procedures

Function procedures are very much like subprocedures in that they consist of Visual Basic statements and take arguments. Unlike subprocedures, function procedures begin with a Function statement and end with an End Function statement. Function procedures return values to the calling procedure by assigning a value to the function name:

```
Public Function MultiplyTwoNumbers(dNumber1 As Double, dNumber2 As Double)
```

```
    MultiplyTwoNumbers = dNumber1 * dNumber2

End Function
```

The `MultiplyTwoNumbers` function procedure takes two arguments and assigns the result of their multiplication to the function name, thereby returning the result to the calling function.

```
lblResult.Caption = MultiplyTwoNumbers(6, 9)
```

To be more dynamic, I could pass `Value` properties of two text boxes directly in as arguments.

```
lblResult.Caption = MultiplyTwoNumbers(Val(txtNumber1.Value), _
Val(txtNumber2.Value))
```

To ensure that the `MultiplyTwoNumbers` function receives numbers (doubles) as arguments, I use the `Val` function inside the parameter list to convert strings to numbers.

Arguments and Parameters

The words *arguments* and *parameters* are often used in the same context. They differ in purpose and definition. *Arguments* are constants, variables or expressions that are passed to a procedure whereas *parameters* are variables that hold the arguments and can be used in the procedure that it was passed to. Confusing, I know, but know there is technically a difference between the two words.

Many programming languages, including VBA, allow arguments to be passed either by value or by reference. When arguments are passed by value, VBA makes a copy of the original variable's contents and passes the copy to the procedure. This means the procedure can't modify the original contents of the argument, only the copy.

To pass arguments by value, you need to preface the parameter name with the `ByVal` keyword as shown in the `Increment` procedure.

```
Private Sub cmdProcess_Click()

    Dim iNumber As Integer

    iNumber = 1

    Increment iNumber

    MsgBox "The value of iNumber is " & iNumber

End Sub
```

```
Public Sub Increment(ByVal x As Integer)

    x = x + 5

End Sub
```

Looking at Figure 6.3, you can see that it is not required to give the argument the same name as the variable passed in.

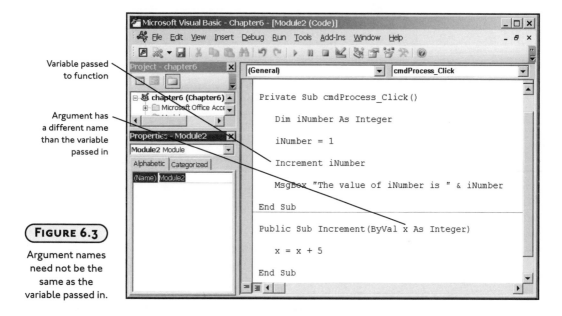

Variable passed to function

Argument has a different name than the variable passed in

FIGURE 6.3

Argument names need not be the same as the variable passed in.

TRAP

When not used in assignment statements, argument lists can't be enclosed in parentheses. Here is an example:

```
Increment iNumber
```

Keep in mind that Visual Basic does not always produce a runtime error when parentheses are used and yet not required. Instead, Visual Basic may simply pass the argument incorrectly, producing unexpected results.

On the other hand, arguments passed by reference send the procedure a reference to the argument's memory location. In a nutshell, a memory address is sent to the procedure when arguments are passed by reference. This means the procedure is able to modify the original data. Passing arguments by reference is the default argument behavior in VBA.

Moreover, passing arguments by reference is the most efficient means of passing arguments to procedures because only a reference (memory address) to the argument is passed, not the data itself.

To pass arguments by reference, simply preface the argument name using the ByRef keyword or use no preface keyword at all.

```
Private Sub cmdProcess_Click()

    Dim iNumber As Integer

    iNumber = 1

    Increment iNumber

    MsgBox "The value of iNumber is " & iNumber

End Sub
```

```
Public Sub Increment(ByRef x As Integer)

    x = x + 5

End Sub
```

TRICK Arguments are passed by reference automatically. It is not necessary to preface the argument name with the ByRef keyword.

Passing the iNumber variable by reference allows the Increment procedure to modify the argument's value directly.

STANDARD MODULES

Access VBA supports two types of modules: class and standard. Class modules are directly related to an object, such as a form or report. Form class modules contain event procedures for the associated controls and objects. Standard modules, however, have no association with an object. They store a collection of variables and user-defined procedures, which can be shared among your Access programs.

You can add a standard module from the Visual Basic environment by selecting Insert, Module from the menu.

To see how you could utilize a standard module, I've revised the Secret Message program from Chapter 5, "Functions Continued." Specifically, I added one standard module and two public functions called Encrypt and Decrypt. Using public functions allows me to reuse the code in these functions from anywhere in my application.

To move the Encrypt and Decrypt functionality from event procedures to functions, I first create the function shells using the Add Procedure dialog box. Next, I add a string parameter to both functions. This argument is passed into each function when called. Moreover, the parameter called sMessage replaces the hard-coded text-box value from the previous version of Secret Message. All occurrences of the text-box name are replaced with the parameter name. This is truly code reuse, as I can now call these functions and pass my message from anywhere in my Access application. Last but not least, I assign the function's output to the function's name.

The new standard module code from the enhanced Secret Message program is shown next.

```
Option Compare Database
Option Explicit


Public Function Decrypt(sMessage As String)

    Dim sDecryptedMessage As String
    Dim sDecryptedCharacter As String
    Dim iCounter As Integer

    For iCounter = 1 To Len(sMessage)

        sDecryptedCharacter = Asc(Mid(sMessage, iCounter, 1))
        sDecryptedCharacter = Chr(sDecryptedCharacter - 1)
        sDecryptedMessage = sDecryptedMessage + sDecryptedCharacter

    Next iCounter

    ' Assign decrypted message to function name.
    Decrypt = sDecryptedMessage


End Function
```

```
Public Function Encrypt(sMessage As String)

    Dim sEncryptedMessage As String
    Dim sEncryptedCharacter As String
    Dim iCounter As Integer

    For iCounter = 1 To Len(sMessage)

        sEncryptedCharacter = Asc(Mid(sMessage, iCounter, 1))
        sEncryptedCharacter = Chr(sEncryptedCharacter + 1)
        sEncryptedMessage = sEncryptedMessage + sEncryptedCharacter

    Next iCounter

    ' Assign encrypted message to function name.
    Encrypt = sEncryptedMessage

End Function
```

With my `Encrypt` and `Decrypt` functions implemented in a standard module, I simply need to call them and pass the `Value` property from the text box. After the function call is executed, the function's return value is assigned back to the text box's `Value` property.

```
Option Compare Database
Option Explicit
```

```
Private Sub cmdDecrypt_Click()

    ' Call the Decrypt function passing the encrypted
    ' message as an argument. Assign function's result
    ' to the text box's Value property.
    If txtMessage.Value <> "" Then
        txtMessage.Value = Decrypt(txtMessage.Value)
    End If

End Sub
```

```
Private Sub cmdEncrypt_Click()

    ' Call the Encrypt function passing the plain text
    ' message as an argument. Assign function's result
    ' to the text box's Value property.
    If txtMessage.Value <> "" Then
        txtMessage.Value = Encrypt(txtMessage.Value)
    End If

End Sub
```

You should understand that the changes made to the Secret Message program are transparent to the user. In other words, the use of user-defined functions and standard modules does not change the way the user interacts with the program, nor does it change the program's functionality. The important concept is that the changes were made to provide a more modular program, which implements code reuse through user-defined procedures and modules.

ARRAYS

Arrays are one of the first data structures learned by beginning programmers. Not only common as a teaching tool, arrays are frequently used by professional programmers to store like data types as one variable. In a nutshell, *arrays* can be thought of as a single variable that contains many elements. Moreover, VBA arrays share many common characteristics:

- Elements in an array share the same variable name.
- Elements in an array share the same data type.
- Elements in an array are accessed with an index number.

As noted, elements in an array share the same variable name and data type. Individual members in an array are called *elements* and are accessed via an index. Just like any other variable, arrays occupy memory space. To explain further, an array is a grouping of contiguous memory segments, as demonstrated in Figure 6.4.

Notice the five-element array in Figure 6.4 starts with index 0. This is an important concept to remember, so it's worth repeating in italics: *Unless otherwise stated, elements in an array begin with index number zero.* With that said, there are five array elements in Figure 6.1, starting with index 0 and ending with index 4.

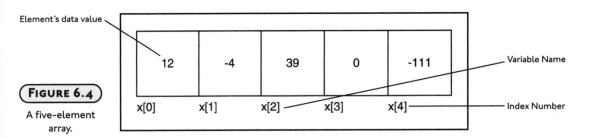

Element's data value

| 12 | -4 | 39 | 0 | -111 |

x[0]   x[1]   x[2]   x[3]   x[4]

Variable Name

Index Number

TRAP

A common programming error is not accounting for the zero-based index in arrays. This programming error is often called the *off-by-one error*. Errors like this are generally not caught during compile time, but rather at runtime when a user or your program attempts to access an element number in an array that does not exist. For example, if you have a five-element array and your program tries to access the fifth element with index number 5, a runtime program error ensues. This is because the last index in a five-element array is index 4!

Single-Dimension Arrays

Using the keywords Dim, Static, Public, and Private, arrays are created just like any other variable.

TRICK

Unless Option Base 1 is specified, or *dimensioned*, with an explicit range, arrays by default begin with a zero base index.

- Dim myIntegerArray(5) As Integer ' Creates six Integer elements
- Dim myVariantArray(10) ' Creates eleven Variant elements
- Dim myStringArray(1 to 7) As String ' Creates 7 String elements

In the preceding declarations, the number of elements in an array is determined during array declaration using either a number or a range of numbers surrounded by parentheses.

A nice feature of VBA is its ability to initialize variables for use. Specifically, VBA initializes number-based array elements to 0 and string-based array elements to "" (indicating an empty string).

Individual elements in an array are accessed via an index:

```
lblArrayValue.Caption = myStringArray(3)
```

The next Click event procedure initializes a String array using a For loop and adds the array contents to a list box.

```
Private Sub cmdPopulateListBox_Click()

    ' Declare a seven element String array.
    Dim myStringArray(1 To 7) As String
    Dim x As Integer

    ' Initialize array elements.
    For x = 1 To 7

        myStringArray(x) = "The value of myStringArray is " & x

    Next x

    ' Add array contents to a list box.
    For x = 1 To 7

        lstMyListBox.AddItem myStringArray(x)

    Next x

End Sub
```

VBA provides two array-based functions called LBound and UBound for determining an array's upper and lower bounds. The LBound function takes an array name and returns the array's lower bound. Conversely, the UBound function takes an array name and returns the array's upper bound. These functions are demonstrated in this Click event procedure.

```
Private Sub cmdPopulateListBox_Click()

    ' Declare an eleven element Integer array.
    Dim myIntegerArray(10) As Integer
    Dim x As Integer

    ' Initialize array elements using LBound and UBound functions
    ' to determine lower and upper bounds.
    For x = LBound(myIntegerArray) To UBound(myIntegerArray)
```

```
    myIntegerArray(x) = x

  Next x


  ' Add array contents to a list box.
  For x = LBound(myIntegerArray) To UBound(myIntegerArray)

    lstMyListBox.AddItem myIntegerArray(x)

  Next x


End Sub
```

Two-Dimensional Arrays

Two-dimensional arrays are most often thought of in terms of a table or matrix. For example, a two-dimensional array containing four rows and five columns creates 20 elements, as seen in Figure 6.5.

```
Dim x(3,4) As Integer ' Two dimensional array with 20 elements.
```

	Column 0	Column 1	Column 2	Column 3	Column 4
Row 0	x(0,0)	x(0,1)	x(0,2)	x(0,3)	x(0,4)
Row 1	x(1,0)	x(1,1)	x(1,2)	x(1,3)	x(1,4)
Row 2	x(2,0)	x(2,1)	x(2,2)	x(2,3)	x(2,4)
Row 3	x(3,0)	x(3,1)	x(3,2)	x(3,3)	x(3,4)

Column index →

Row index →

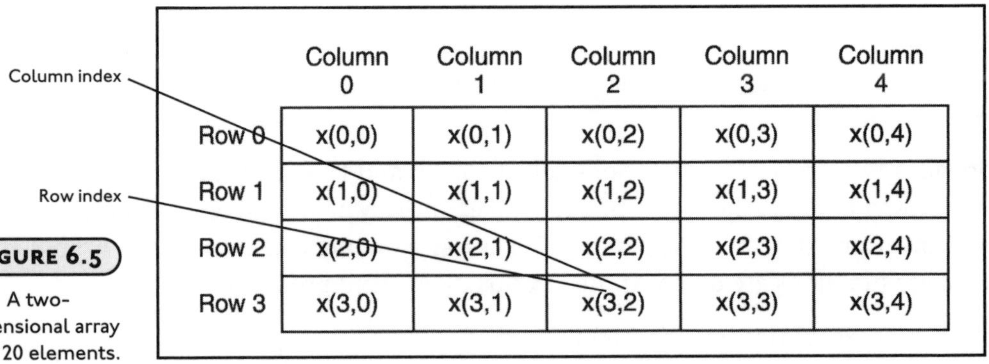

FIGURE 6.5

A two-dimensional array with 20 elements.

The first index (also known as a *subscript*) in a two-dimensional array represents the row in a table. The second index represents the table's column. Together, both subscripts specify a single element within an array.

A nested looping structure is required to iterate through all elements in a two-dimensional array.

```
Private Sub cmdInitializeArray_Click()
```

```
' Create a 20 element two dimensional array.
Dim x(3, 4) As Integer
Dim iRow As Integer
Dim iColumn As Integer

' Loop through one row at a time.
For iRow = 0 To 3

    ' Loop through each column in the row.
    For iColumn = 0 To 4

        ' Populate each element with the result of
        ' multiplying the row and column.
        x(iRow, iColumn) = iRow * iColumn

    Next iColumn

Next iRow

End Sub
```

As shown in the previous Click event, the outer For loop iterates through one column at a time. Each time the outer loop is executed, a nested For loop is executed five times. The inner loop represents each column (in this case five columns) in a row. After each column in a row has been referenced, the outer loop executes again, which moves the array position to the next row and the inner loop to the next set of columns.

Dynamic Arrays

Arrays are useful when you know how many elements you need. What if you don't know how many array elements your program requires? One way to circumvent this problem is by creating a huge array that most definitely holds any number of elements you throw at it. I don't recommend this, however. When arrays are *declared* (created), VBA reserves enough memory to hold data for each element. If you're guessing on the number of elements required, you're most certainly wasting memory! A more professional way of solving this dilemma is with dynamic arrays.

If you've worked in other programming languages such as C, you might be cringing about the thought of dynamic arrays implemented with linked lists. You will be relieved to learn that VBA makes building and working with dynamic arrays very easy.

When your program logic uses dynamic arrays, it can size and resize your array while the application is running. To create a dynamic array, simply eliminate any references to subscripts or indexes in the array declaration.

```
Option Compare Database
Option Explicit


Dim iDynamicArray() As Integer ' Dynamic array.
```

Leaving the parentheses empty tells VBA your array is dynamic. I will be able to use my dynamic array in all subsequent form-level procedures by dimensioning the dynamic array in the general declaration area. To set the number of elements in a dynamic array, use the ReDim keyword.

```
Private Sub cmdDynamicArray_Click()

    Dim sUserResponse As String

    sUserResponse = InputBox("Enter number of elements:")

    ' Set number of array elements dynamically.
    ReDim iDynamicArray(sUserResponse)

    MsgBox "Number of elements in iDynamicArray is " _
        & UBound(iDynamicArray) + 1

End Sub
```

Using the ReDim keyword, I can set my array size after the program is running. The only problem with this approach is that each time the ReDim statement is executed, all previous element data is lost. To correct this, use the Preserve keyword in the ReDim statement, as follows.

```
Private Sub cmdIncreaseDynamicArray_Click()

    Dim sUserResponse As String

    sUserResponse = InputBox("Increase number of elements by:")

    ' Set number of array elements dynamically, while
    ' preserving existing elements.
```

```
ReDim Preserve iDynamicArray(UBound(iDynamicArray) _
    + sUserResponse)

MsgBox "Number of elements in iDynamicArray is now " _
    & UBound(iDynamicArray) + 1

End Sub
```

To preserve current elements while increasing a dynamic array, you must tell VBA to add elements to the array's existing upper bound. This can be accomplished using the UBound function, as demonstrated in the previous Click event procedure cmdIncreaseDynamicArray.

 TRAP The Preserve keyword allows to you to change a dynamic array's upper bound only. You cannot change a dynamic array's lower bound with the Preserve keyword.

Passing Arrays as Arguments

Passing an array to a function or subprocedure is not as difficult in VBA as one might think. You must follow a couple of rules, however, to ensure a valid argument pass.

To pass all elements in an array to a procedure, simply pass the array name with no parentheses. Next, you must define the parameter name with an empty set of parentheses, as the next two procedures demonstrate.

```
Private Sub cmdPassEntireArray_Click()

    Dim myArray(5) As Integer

    HowMany myArray

End Sub
```

```
Private Sub HowMany(x() As Integer)

    MsgBox "There are " & UBound(x) & " elements in this array."

End Sub
```

To pass a single element in an array, it is not necessary to define the parameter name as an array. Rather, simply pass one array element as a normal variable argument:

```
Private Sub cmdPassArrayElement_Click()

    Dim myArray(5) As Integer

    CheckItOut myArray(3)

End Sub
```

```
Private Sub CheckItOut(x As Integer)

    MsgBox "The parameter's value is " & x & "."

End Sub
```

Passing arrays and elements of arrays as arguments is that easy!

User-Defined Types

In other programming languages such as C, user-defined types are commonly referred to as *structures*. *User-defined types* are collections of one or more related elements, which can be of different data types. User-defined types must be declared at the module level (also known as the *general declarations area*) in a standard module. Programmers can leverage user-defined types to group like variables as one, much as a record in a database does.

Type and End Type Statements

User-defined types are created with the Type and End Type statements at the module level. More specifically, user-defined types must be declared outside of any procedure in a standard module. To demonstrate, I created a user-defined type called EmployeeData.

```
Type EmployeeData

    EmployeeLastName As String
    EmployeeFirstName As String
    EmployeeID As Integer
    EmployeeSalary As Currency
    EmployeeHireDate As Date
```

```
End Type
' …is the same as
Public Type EmployeeData

    Dim EmployeeLastName As String
    Dim EmployeeFirstName As String
    Dim EmployeeID As Integer
    Dim EmployeeSalary As Currency
    Dim EmployeeHireDate As Date

End Type
```

 TRICK   It is not necessary to use the Dim keyword when declaring variables (members) inside a user-defined type.

Note that declaring a user-defined type does not instantiate a variable, nor does it reserve any space in memory. The declaration of a user-defined type simply provides VBA with a blueprint when variables of your user-defined type are created.

By default, user-defined types are public, though they can be declared using the keyword Private, which makes them available only to the current module from where they are created.

```
' Available only in the current module.
Private Type BookData

    Title As String
    ISBN As String
    Author As String
    Publisher As String
    PublishDate As Date
    Price As Currency

End Type
```

Declaring Variables of User-Defined Type

As mentioned, declaring a user-defined type does not create a variable, but rather defines a template for VBA programmers to use later. To create variables of your user-defined types, define a user-defined type in a standard module.

```
Option Compare Database
Option Explicit


' Define user defined type in a standard module.
Type BookData

    Title As String
    ISBN As String
    Author As String
    Publisher As String
    PublishDate As Date
    Price As Currency


End Type
```

Then you can create variables of your user-defined type at a module level.

```
' Declare 5 element array of BookData Type
Dim myFavoriteBook As BookData
```

Because user-defined types are public by default, you can create type variables in other module, such as form class modules:

```
Private Sub cmdEnterBookData_Click()


' Declare one variable of BookData Type
    Dim myCookingBook As BookData


End Sub
```

Managing Elements

Once a variable has been declared as a user-defined type, you can use it much like any other variable. To access elements within type variables, simply use the dot notation to assign and retrieve data, as the next program demonstrates.

```
Private Sub cmdEnterBookData_Click()

    Dim myBook As BookData ' Declare one variable of BookData Type

    myBook.Title = txtTitle.Value
    myBook.ISBN = txtISBN.Value
```

```
    myBook.Author = txtAuthor.Value
    myBook.Publisher = txtPublisher.Value
    myBook.PublishDate = txtPublishDate.Value
    myBook.Price = txtPrice.Value

    MsgBox myBook.Title & " has been entered."

End Sub
```

Note that a public user-defined type must have already been created in a standard module.

Remember that user-defined types can be thought of as rows in a database table: Both table rows and user-defined types maintain a grouping of like elements of one or more data types.

So far, you have only seen how to create a single variable of user-defined type (analogous to a single row in a database). To create multiple variables of the same user-defined type (much like multiple rows in a database), simply create an array of user-defined type, as shown in the next program.

```
Option Compare Database
Option Explicit

Dim myBooks() As BookData ' Declare dynamic array of BookData Type
Dim currentIndex As Integer
```

```
Private Sub cmdAddNewBook_Click()

    ' Add one array element to the dynamic array.
    ReDim Preserve myBooks(UBound(myBooks) + 1)

    ' Clear text boxes
    txtTitle.Value = ""
    txtISBN.Value = ""
    txtAuthor.Value = ""
    txtPublisher.Value = ""
    txtPublishDate.Value = ""
    txtPrice.Value = ""

End Sub
```

```vba
Private Sub cmdEnterBookData_Click()

    myBooks(UBound(myBooks)).Title = txtTitle.Value
    myBooks(UBound(myBooks)).ISBN = txtISBN.Value
    myBooks(UBound(myBooks)).Author = txtAuthor.Value
    myBooks(UBound(myBooks)).Publisher = txtPublisher.Value
    myBooks(UBound(myBooks)).PublishDate = txtPublishDate.Value
    myBooks(UBound(myBooks)).Price = txtPrice.Value

    MsgBox myBooks(UBound(myBooks)).Title & " has been entered."

End Sub
```

```vba
Private Sub cmdNext_Click()

If currentIndex <= UBound(myBooks) Then

    If currentIndex < UBound(myBooks) Then
      ' Increment index.
      currentIndex = currentIndex + 1
    End If

    txtTitle.Value = myBooks(currentIndex).Title
    txtAuthor.Value = myBooks(currentIndex).Author
    txtISBN.Value = myBooks(currentIndex).ISBN
    txtPublisher.Value = myBooks(currentIndex).Publisher
    txtPublishDate.Value = myBooks(currentIndex).PublishDate
    txtPrice.Value = myBooks(currentIndex).Price

End If

End Sub
```

```vba
Private Sub cmdPrevious_Click()

If currentIndex >= 1 Then
```

```
If currentIndex > 1 Then
   ' Decrement index.
   currentIndex = currentIndex - 1
End If


txtTitle.Value = myBooks(currentIndex).Title
txtAuthor.Value = myBooks(currentIndex).Author
txtISBN.Value = myBooks(currentIndex).ISBN
txtPublisher.Value = myBooks(currentIndex).Publisher
txtPublishDate.Value = myBooks(currentIndex).PublishDate
txtPrice.Value = myBooks(currentIndex).Price


End If


End Sub
```

```
Private Sub Form_Load()

   ' Add one array element to the dynamic array.
   ReDim myBooks(1)

   currentIndex = 1

End Sub
```

The Integer variable—called currentIndex in the previous Form_Load event procedure—was declared in the general declarations section. It therefore can be used throughout the form's class module. I use this variable to maintain the current index of the array as I navigate through the elements in the array. Also note the use of dynamic array techniques to add elements of BookData type to my array variable in the cmdAddNewBook_Click event procedure.

CHAPTER PROGRAM: DICE

The chapter program Dice in Figure 6.6 is an easy-to-build, fun game. Mimicking basic poker rules, the player rolls the dice by pressing a command button and hopes for either three of a kind (worth 10 points) or, better yet, four of a kind (worth 25 points).

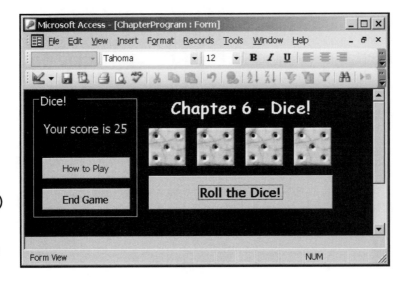

FIGURE 6.6

Using chapter-based concepts to build the Dice program.

The Dice program implements code reuse by leveraging chapter-based concepts such as arrays, user-defined procedures, and standard code modules. In addition to chapter-based concepts, the Dice program uses random number techniques to simulate a roll. (This is discussed in Chapter 4, "Looping Structures.")

Controls and properties that build the Dice program are described in Table 6.1.

TABLE 6.1 CONTROLS AND PROPERTIES OF THE DICE PROGRAM

Control	Property	Property Value
Form	Name	Chapter Program
	Caption	Chapter Program
	Record Selectors	No
	Navigation Buttons	No
	Dividing Lines	No
Frame	Name	fraGameBoard
Command Button	Name	cmdHowToPlay
	Caption	How to Play
Command Button	Name	cmdQuit
	Caption	End Game

	TABLE 6.1 CONTROLS AND PROPERTIES OF	
	THE DICE PROGRAM (CONTINUED)	

Control	Property	Property Value
Command Button	Name	cmdRoll
	Caption	Roll the Dice!
Label	Name	lblTitle
	Caption	Chapter 6—Dice!
Image	Name	imgSlot1
	Picture	blank.jpg
	Size Mode	Stretch
Image	Name	imgSlot2
	Picture	blank.jpg
	Size Mode	Stretch
Image	Name	imgSlot3
	Picture	blank.jpg
	Size Mode	Stretch
Image	Name	imgSlot4
	Picture	blank.jpg
	Size Mode	Stretch
Image	Name	imgDice1
	Picture	die1.jpg
	Size Mode	Stretch
Image	Name	imgDice2
	Picture	die2.jpg
	Size Mode	Stretch
Image	Name	imgDice3
	Picture	die3.jpg
	Size Mode	Stretch
Image	Name	imgDice4
	Picture	die4.jpg
	Size Mode	Stretch

(continues)

	TABLE 6.1 CONTROLS AND PROPERTIES OF THE DICE PROGRAM (CONTINUED)	

Control	Property	Property Value
Image	Name	imgDice5
	Picture	die5.jpg
	Size Mode	Stretch
Image	Name	imgDice6
	Picture	die6.jpg
	Size Mode	Stretch

All of the code required to implement the form class module in the Dice program is seen next.

```vba
Option Compare Database
Option Explicit
```

```vba
Private Sub cmdQuit_Click()
    DoCmd.Quit
End Sub
```

```vba
Private Sub cmdRoll_Click()

    ' Roll the Dice!
    RollTheDice

    ' Check the player's hand.
    DetermineCurrentHand iCurrentHand

End Sub
```

```vba
Private Sub cmdHowToPlay_Click()
```

```
MsgBox "Dice! Version 1.0" & Chr(13) & _
  "Developed by Michael Vine." & Chr(13) & Chr(13) & _
  "Roll the dice and win points with four of a kind (25 points), " _
  & Chr(13) & _
  "and three of a kind (10 points).", , "Chapter 6—Dice!"

End Sub
```

```
Private Sub Form_Load()
    Randomize
    lblScore.Caption = "Your score is " & iScore
End Sub
```

The algorithms to roll the dice and check the players hand is implemented in a standard code module, which is shown next.

```
Option Compare Database
Option Explicit

' Public variables available to all procedures in
' all modules
Public iScore As Integer
Public iCurrentHand(3) As Integer
```

```
Public Sub DetermineCurrentHand(a() As Integer)

    ' Look for valid hands worth points.
    ' Valid hands with points are:
    '      3 of a kind—10 points
    '      4 of a kind—25 points

    Dim iCounter As Integer

    ' Holds possibilities of a win
    Dim iNumbers(1 To 6) As Integer

    ' Count the number of occurrences for each die
    For iCounter = 0 To 3
```

```
    Select Case a(iCounter)
        Case 1
            iNumbers(1) = iNumbers(1) + 1
        Case 2
            iNumbers(2) = iNumbers(2) + 1
        Case 3
            iNumbers(3) = iNumbers(3) + 1
        Case 4
            iNumbers(4) = iNumbers(4) + 1
        Case 5
            iNumbers(5) = iNumbers(5) + 1
        Case 6
            iNumbers(6) = iNumbers(6) + 1
    End Select
Next iCounter


' Determine if player has four of a kind
If iNumbers(1) = 4 Or iNumbers(2) = 4 Or iNumbers(3) = 4 Or _
    iNumbers(4) = 4 Or iNumbers(5) = 4 Or iNumbers(6) = 4 Then

    MsgBox "Four of a kind! 25 points!"
    iScore = iScore + 25
    Forms("ChapterProgram").lblScore.Caption = _
        "Your score is " & iScore
    Exit Sub

End If


' Player did not have a four of a kind, see if they
' have three of a kind.
If (iNumbers(1) = 3 Or iNumbers(2) = 3 Or iNumbers(3) = 3 Or _
    iNumbers(4) = 4 Or iNumbers(5) = 3 Or iNumbers(6) = 3) Then

    MsgBox "Three of a kind! 10 points!"
    iScore = iScore + 10
    Forms("ChapterProgram").lblScore.Caption = _
        "Your score is " & iScore
    Exit Sub
```

```
        End If

End Sub
```

```
Public Sub RollTheDice()

    Dim iCounter As Integer

    ' Reset current hand
    For iCounter = 0 To 3
        iCurrentHand(iCounter) = Int((6 * Rnd) + 1)
    Next iCounter

    ' Assign a die to the first slot
    Select Case iCurrentHand(0)
        Case 1
            Forms("ChapterProgram").imgSlot1.Picture =
Forms("ChapterProgram").imgDice1.Picture
        Case 2
            Forms("ChapterProgram").imgSlot1.Picture =
Forms("ChapterProgram").imgDice2.Picture
        Case 3
            Forms("ChapterProgram").imgSlot1.Picture =
Forms("ChapterProgram").imgDice3.Picture
        Case 4
            Forms("ChapterProgram").imgSlot1.Picture =
Forms("ChapterProgram").imgDice4.Picture
        Case 5
            Forms("ChapterProgram").imgSlot1.Picture =
Forms("ChapterProgram").imgDice5.Picture
        Case 6
            Forms("ChapterProgram").imgSlot1.Picture =
Forms("ChapterProgram").imgDice6.Picture
    End Select

    ' Assign a die to the second slot
    Select Case iCurrentHand(1)
```

```
      Case 1
         Forms("ChapterProgram").imgSlot2.Picture =
Forms("ChapterProgram").imgDice1.Picture
      Case 2
         Forms("ChapterProgram").imgSlot2.Picture =
Forms("ChapterProgram").imgDice2.Picture
      Case 3
         Forms("ChapterProgram").imgSlot2.Picture =
Forms("ChapterProgram").imgDice3.Picture
      Case 4
         Forms("ChapterProgram").imgSlot2.Picture =
Forms("ChapterProgram").imgDice4.Picture
      Case 5
         Forms("ChapterProgram").imgSlot2.Picture =
Forms("ChapterProgram").imgDice5.Picture
      Case 6
         Forms("ChapterProgram").imgSlot2.Picture =
Forms("ChapterProgram").imgDice6.Picture
   End Select

   ' Assign a die to the third slot
   Select Case iCurrentHand(2)
      Case 1
         Forms("ChapterProgram").imgSlot3.Picture =
Forms("ChapterProgram").imgDice1.Picture
      Case 2
         Forms("ChapterProgram").imgSlot3.Picture =
Forms("ChapterProgram").imgDice2.Picture
      Case 3
         Forms("ChapterProgram").imgSlot3.Picture =
Forms("ChapterProgram").imgDice3.Picture
      Case 4
         Forms("ChapterProgram").imgSlot3.Picture =
Forms("ChapterProgram").imgDice4.Picture
      Case 5
         Forms("ChapterProgram").imgSlot3.Picture =
Forms("ChapterProgram").imgDice5.Picture
      Case 6
```

```
        Forms("ChapterProgram").imgSlot3.Picture =
Forms("ChapterProgram").imgDice6.Picture
   End Select


   ' Assign a die to the fourth slot
   Select Case iCurrentHand(3)
      Case 1
         Forms("ChapterProgram").imgSlot4.Picture =
Forms("ChapterProgram").imgDice1.Picture
      Case 2
         Forms("ChapterProgram").imgSlot4.Picture =
Forms("ChapterProgram").imgDice2.Picture
      Case 3
         Forms("ChapterProgram").imgSlot4.Picture =
Forms("ChapterProgram").imgDice3.Picture
      Case 4
         Forms("ChapterProgram").imgSlot4.Picture =
Forms("ChapterProgram").imgDice4.Picture
      Case 5
         Forms("ChapterProgram").imgSlot4.Picture =
Forms("ChapterProgram").imgDice5.Picture
      Case 6
         Forms("ChapterProgram").imgSlot4.Picture =
Forms("ChapterProgram").imgDice6.Picture
   End Select

End Sub
```

CHAPTER SUMMARY

- Code reuse is implemented as user-defined subprocedures and function procedures.
- Function procedures return a value; subprocedures do not.
- Both subprocedures and function procedures can take one or more arguments.
- Arguments are the data passed into procedures. Parameters are the variables inside the procedure, which represent the argument data.
- Arguments can be passed by value and by reference.

- Arguments passed by value contain a copy of the original data. This prevents the procedure from modifying the original data.
- Arguments passed by reference contain a reference to the variable's memory address. The procedure can modify the original data.
- Arguments are passed by reference automatically.
- Standard modules are used to group commonly referenced user-defined procedures together.
- Arrays are used to store groupings of like data types as one variable.
- An array is a grouping of contiguous memory segments.
- Variables in an array are called elements.
- Each variable in an array shares the same name.
- Elements in an array are accessed via an index.
- VBA arrays are zero based by default.
- Arrays are created just like other variables using the keywords `Dim`, `Static`, `Public`, and `Private`.
- Two-dimensional arrays are often thought of in terms of a table or matrix.
- Two looping structures (one of which is nested) are required to iterate through each element in a two-dimensional array.
- Dynamic arrays can be created and managed using the `ReDim` and `Preserve` keywords.
- Arrays can be passed as arguments to procedures.
- User-defined types are commonly referred to as structures.
- User-defined types are groupings of like information, which can be of different data types.
- User-defined types are created using the `Type` and `End Type` statements.
- User-defined types must be declared in a standard module in the general declarations area (outside of any procedure).
- Variables of user-defined type are analogous to rows in a database.

PROGRAMMING CHALLENGES

1. Build a form with two text boxes that receive numbers as input and one command button that displays a message box containing the larger of the two numbers. To accomplish this, write code in the Click event of the command to call a user-defined function named FindLargestNumber. Pass it two arguments (text box values) and display the result in a message box. Write code in the FindLargestNumber function to determine the larger number and return the result to the calling procedure (command button Click event in this case).

2. Create a one-dimensional string-based array with five elements. Assign five different names to the array. Use a For loop to iterate through each of the array elements, displaying the names in a message box.

3. Declare a user-defined type called HomeData with elements StreetAddress, City, State, SquareFootage, LotSize, and SalePrice in a standard module. Create a form with six text boxes to add values to each variable type element. In the general declarations area of the form, create a single variable of HomeType to store the user-entered value. Add two command buttons to the form, one called cmdAddHome and the other cmdDisplayHomeData. In cmdAddHome Click event, store the data entered by the user into your user-defined type variable. In cmdDisplayHomeData Click event, display each element's value in a message box.

4. Update the chapter program Dice to check for two pairs.

Debugging, Input Validation, File Processing, and Error Handling

This chapter teaches you techniques for preventing runtime errors through input validation and error handling. You also see how to debug your VBA code using common VBE debugging windows. In addition, I show you how VBA manages file input and output (*file I/O*).

DEBUGGING

Sooner or later, all programmers seek the holy grail of debugging. The holy grail of debugging is different for each programming language. VBA programmers are very lucky the VBE provides a multitude of debugging facilities not found in many other programming environments.

As a programming instructor and lecturer, I've often encouraged my Visual Basic students to use the VBE debugging facilities not only to debug programs, but to see how the program flows, how variables are populated, and how and when statements are executed. In other, less friendly languages, programmers must take for granted the order in which their statements are executed. In VBA, you can actually step through your application one statement at a time. You can even go back in time to reexecute statements, something I show you a little later on.

In this section, I show you how to leverage each of the following VBE debugging facilities:

- Break statements
- Immediate window
- Locals window
- Watch window

IN THE REAL WORLD

Debugging can be one of the most challenging processes in software development, and unfortunately it's sometimes very costly. In a nutshell, *debugging* is the process by which programmers identify, find, and correct software errors.

There are three common types of bugs in software. *Syntax errors* are the most common form of software bugs. They are caused by misspellings in the program code and are most commonly recognized by the language's compiler. Syntax errors are generally easy to fix.

The next type of bug is called a runtime error. *Runtime errors* occur once the program is running and an illegal operation occurs. These errors generally occur because the programmer has not thought ahead of time to capture them (for example, File Not Found, Disk Not Ready, or Division by Zero). Runtime errors are most often easy to find and sometimes easy to fix.

The last common type of bug, and the most difficult to identify and fix, is known as the logic error. *Logic errors* are not easily identified, as they don't necessarily generate an error message. Logic errors are the result of wrong logic implemented in the program code.

Stepping Through Code

By now you should be fairly comfortable with the design-time and runtime environments. Moreover, you may have discovered the break mode environment. As a refresher, the following bulleted list reviews each type of Access VBA environment.

- **Design time** is the mode by which you add controls to containers (such as forms) and write code to respond to events.
- The **runtime** environment allows you to see your program running the same way a user would. During runtime you can see all your Visual Basic code, but you cannot modify it.
- **Break mode** allows you to pause execution of your Visual Basic program (during runtime) to view, edit, and debug your program code.

The VBE allows you to step through your program code one line at a time. Known as *stepping* or *stepping into*, this process allows you to graphically see what line of code is currently executing as well as values of current variables in scope. Using function keys or menu items, you can navigate through program code with ease. For example, once in break mode, you can press the F8 key to skip to the next line.

During break mode, it is also possible to step over a procedure without having to graphically execute the procedure's statements one at a time. Known as *procedure stepping* or *stepping over*, this process can be accomplished during break mode by pressing Shift + F8 simultaneously.

There are times when you may wish to skip ahead in program code to a predetermined procedure or statement. The VBE provides this functionality through the use of breakpoints.

Breakpoints

Breakpoints can be inserted into your Visual Basic procedures during design time or break mode, as seen in Figure 7.1.

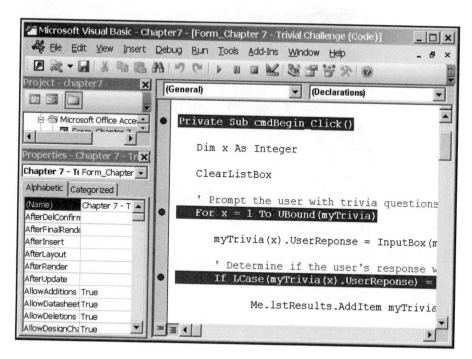

FIGURE 7.1

Inserting
breakpoints
on program
statements.

To create a breakpoint, simply click in the left margin of the Code window where you wish program execution to pause. When your program's execution reaches the statement where a breakpoint has been placed, program execution pauses. To continue execution to the next breakpoint, simply press F5. To continue program execution one statement at a time, with or without a breakpoint, press the F8 key.

TRICK Breakpoints cannot be placed on empty lines in the code window or on variable declarations.

There are occasions when you want to go back in time and reexecute a particular program statement without having to halt the entire program and rerun it. Believe it or not, the VBE provides a facility for traveling back in time while in break mode. To do so, simply click the yellow arrow in the left margin of the Code window (seen in Figure 7.2) and drag it to a previous program statement.

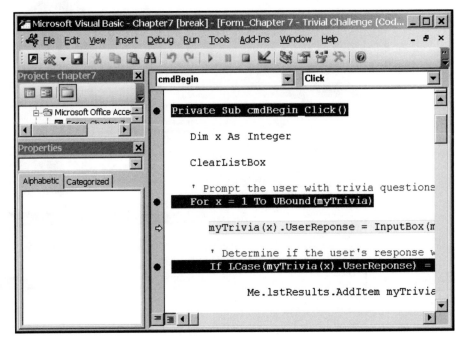

FIGURE 7.2

Going back in time to reexecute program statements while in break mode.

The yellow arrow in Figure 7.2 is the current line of execution. Using your mouse, you can move the arrow to other valid lines of execution.

Immediate Window

During testing or debugging, it is not always desirable to change the values of variables and properties by modifying program code. A safer way of testing program code is through the use of the Immediate window. The Immediate window can be used during design time or break mode. Most popular in break mode, the Immediate window can be accessed by pressing CTRL + G or through the View menu.

The Immediate window allows you to verify and change the values of properties or variables, as shown in Figure 7.3.

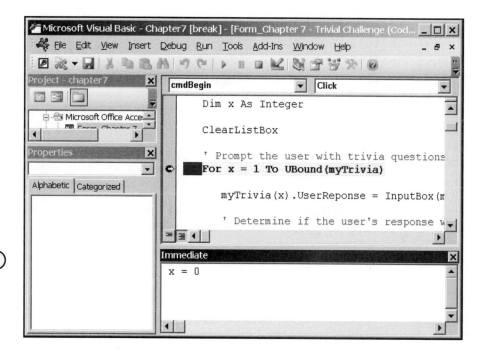

FIGURE 7.3

Changing a variable's value through the Immediate window.

Interestingly, you can type statements that do not directly correspond with your current program execution. For example, in Figure 7.4 I entered the following expression into the Immediate window.

```
Print 25 + 25
```

After I press the Enter key, the Immediate window produces the result of my expression (in this case, 50). The keyword `Print` tells the Immediate window to print the expression's result to the Immediate window's screen.

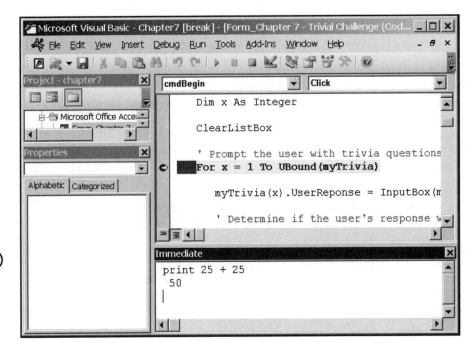

FIGURE 7.4

Using the Print keyword to display results in the Immediate window.

You can reexecute a statement in the Immediate window by moving the cursor to the statement's line and pressing Enter.

Locals Window

The Locals window, a friendly companion to any VBA programmer, provides valuable information about variables and control properties in current scope. Accessed from the View menu group, the Locals window (seen in Figure 7.5) not only supplies information on variables and properties, but also allows for the changing of control property values.

To change a property or variable's value using the Locals window, simply click the item in the Value column and type a new variable or property value.

Watch Window

In addition to breakpoints, the Watch window can aid you in troubleshooting or debugging program code. Accessed from the View menu item, the Watch window can track values of expressions and break when expressions are true or have been changed. In a nutshell, the Watch window keeps track of Watch expressions, as seen in Figure 7.6.

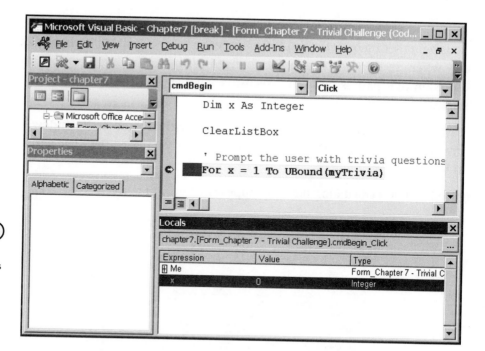

FIGURE 7.5

The Locals window provides information on variables and control properties in current scope.

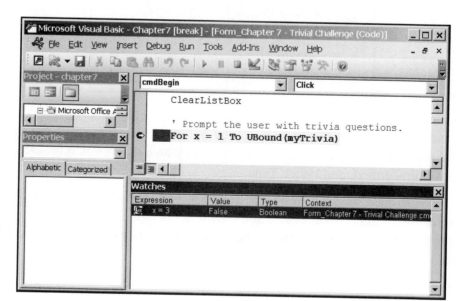

FIGURE 7.6

Tracking Watch expressions through the Watch window.

A basic Watch expression allows you to graphically track the value of an expression throughout the life of a program. Moreover, you can create a Watch expression that pauses program execution when an expression has been changed or is `true`.

For example, let's say you know a bug occurs in your program because the value of a variable is being set incorrectly. You know the value of the variable is changing, but you do not know where in the code it is being changed. Using a Watch expression, you can create an expression that pauses program execution whenever the value of the variable in question changes.

Though Watch expressions can be created from within the Watch window, it is much easier to create them by right-clicking a variable or property name in the Code window and choosing Add Watch.

Figure 7.7 shows the dialog box that appears when you add a watch.

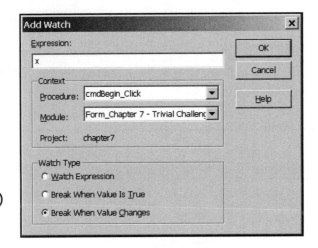

The Add Watch dialog box provides many options for creating Watch expressions. Essentially, creating a Watch expression with the Add Watch dialog box is broken into three parts: Expression, Context, and Watch Type.

An *expression* is a variable, property, function call, calculation, or combination of valid expressions. By default, the expression's value is the name of the variable or property you're trying to watch. The *context* is the scope of the variable or property being watched. There are three values displayed:

- **Procedure.** Defines the procedure where the expression is evaluated.
- **Module.** Defines the module where the variable or property resides.
- **Project.** Displays the name of the current project.

The Watch Type determines how Visual Basic responds to the expression:

- **Watch expression.** Displays the Watch expression and expression value in the Watch window.
- **Break When Value Is True.** Visual Basic breaks program execution when the value of the Watch expression is `true`.
- **Break When Value Changes.** Visual Basic breaks program execution when the value of the expression changes.

INPUT VALIDATION

Input validation is a great place to begin learning about error handling and bug fixing. This is because a good portion of program errors come from unexpected user input or responses.

For example, what do you think would happen if a user entered a letter or character as an operand into a math quiz game? A better question is, "How do I prevent a user from entering a letter into a text box intended for numbers?" What about a game that prompts a user for a level; would testing that the input is a number be enough? Probably not, as most games have only a few levels, so you would also need to test for a range of numbers. In a nutshell, the art of input validation depends on a talented programmer with enough foresight to prevent errors before they happen.

In Microsoft Access, developers can create input validation for forms, tables, and queries with an input mask. In this section, I show you how to build input validation using VBA.

IsNumeric

Sometimes preventing input errors can be as easy as determining whether a user has entered a number or a string. There are times when you may wish the user to enter his or her name, or maybe you are looking for a number such as age. Either way, Visual Basic provides the `IsNumeric` function for testing such scenarios.

The `IsNumeric` function takes a variable or expression as a parameter and returns a `Boolean` value of `True` if the variable or expression is a number, `False` if it is not.

```
Private Sub cmdCheckForNumber_Click()

    If IsNumeric(txtNumbersOnly.Value) = False Then

        MsgBox "Enter numbers only please."
```

```
   Else

      MsgBox "Thank you for entering numbers."

   End If

End Sub
```

In the preceding example, you can see that by testing the Value of the text box with the IsNumeric function, I want the user to enter a number. If the IsNumeric function returns the Boolean value of False, I know that the user has entered something other than a number.

Conversely, you could use the IsNumeric function to check for a string value. Simply change the conditional expression in the If statement.

```
Private Sub cmdCheckForNumber_Click()

   If IsNumeric(txtStringDataOnly.Value) = True Then

      MsgBox "Enter string data only please."

   Else

      MsgBox "Thank you for entering non-numeric data."

   End If

End Sub
```

 Remember that Access 2003 VBA returns a Null value for an empty text box.

When testing for numeric or nonnumeric data, it is also common to test for an empty text box using the IsNull function, as the next procedure demonstrates.

```
Private Sub cmdCheckForNumber_Click()

   If IsNull(txtStringDataOnly.Value) Then
```

```
    MsgBox "Please enter a string value into the text box."
    Exit Sub

End If

If IsNumeric(txtStringDataOnly.Value) = True Then

    MsgBox "Enter string data only please."

Else

    MsgBox "Thank you for entering non-numeric data."

End If

End Sub
```

The IsNull function takes an expression as a parameter (in my example the Value property of a text box), and returns a Boolean value (True or False) depending whether or not the expression is Null.

Checking a Range of Values

You may find at times that testing a value for a particular data type (such as number or string) is not enough to prevent input errors. Sometimes it is necessary to check for a range of values. For example, you may wish to prompt a user to enter a number from 1 to 100. Maybe you want a person to pick a letter from *a* to *z*.

Testing for a range of values involves a little more thought from the programmer. Specifically, your first thought should be to know the range(s) needing to be tested and if the ranges are numeric or character based. Testing ranges of values with numbers or strings uses the same programming constructs consisting of compound conditions.

Let's take the 1 to 100 example I mentioned earlier. As seen here, I continue to use the IsNumeric function as part of the overall testing for a range of numbers (1 to 100):

```
Private Sub cmdCheckRange_Click()

    If IsNumeric(txtInput.Value) = True Then
```

```
      If Val(txtInput.Value) >= 1 And _
         Val(txtInput.Value) <= 100 Then

         MsgBox "You entered a number between 1 and 100."

      Else

         MsgBox "Your number is out of range."

      End If

   Else

      MsgBox "Please enter a number from 1 to 100."

   End If

End Sub
```

Testing for a range of letters (characters) is not much different, if you remember that all characters (letters or numbers) can be represented with ANSI (American National Standards Institute) values. For example, say I want a user to enter a letter in the range of a through m (including both upper- and lowercase letters within the range). I can still use the IsNumeric function to help me out, but I need to perform some additional tests.

```
Private Sub cmdCheckRange_Click()

   If IsNumeric(txtInput.Value) = False Then

      If Asc(UCase(txtInput.Value)) >= 65 And _
         Asc(UCase(txtInput.Value)) <= 77 Then

         MsgBox "You entered a letter between a and m."

      Else

         MsgBox "Your letter is out of range."

      End If
```

```
   Else

       MsgBox "Please enter a letter between a and m."

   End If

End Sub
```

In the preceding code, I'm looking for the `IsNumeric` function to return a `False` value, which means the input was not a number. Next I use the `Asc` function, which converts a character to its corresponding ANSI value.

Using compound conditions, I specifically look for an ANSI range between `65` and `77`, the numbers that represent the capital letters A and M. You may also notice that I used the function `UCase` in association with the `Asc` function. The `UCase` function converts lowercase letters to uppercase letters. If I didn't convert the characters to uppercase, I would have needed to check for the lowercase letters as well (ANSI numbers `97` to `109`).

ERROR HANDLING

Whenever your program interacts with the outside world, you should provide some form of error handling to counteract unexpected inputs or outputs. One way of providing error handling is to write your own error-handling routines.

Error-handling routines are the traffic control for your program. Such routines can handle any kind of programming or human-generated errors you can think of. They should not only identify the error, but try to fix it—or at least give the program or interacting human a chance to do so.

To begin error handling in a procedure, use the `On Error GoTo` statement to signify that you are going to use an error-handling routine:

```
On Error GoTo ErrorHandler
```

This statement can go anywhere in your procedure, but should be placed toward the top, generally right after any procedure-level variable declarations.

`ErrorHandler` is the name I've chosen for my error-handling routine. Error-handling routines can be given any name: `ErrorBin`, `ErrorBucket`, or whatever you like.

The keyword GoTo is a carryover from of an old programming practice made popular in various languages such as BASIC and COBOL. A GoTo was regularly used for designing and building modularized programs. To break programs into manageable pieces, programmers would create modules and link them together using the keyword GoTo.

After years of programming with GoTo, programmers began to realize that this created messy "spaghetti-like" code, which at times became nearly impossible to debug. Fortunately, event-driven and object-oriented programming techniques have virtually eliminated the use of GoTo.

Once an error handler has been declared, errors generated in the procedure are directed to the error-handling routine, as seen in this example.

```
Public Function Verify_Input() As Boolean

On Error GoTo ErrorHandler

    'get Input from user

    Exit Function

ErrorHandler:

    MsgBox ("An error has occurred.")
    Resume

End Function
```

It is necessary to execute the Exit Function or Exit Sub statements before program execution enters the error-handling routine. Without these statements, a procedure that executes without errors executes the error handler as well. That's an important note, so let me repeat it again in italics: *Without an* Exit *statement, a procedure that executes without errors executes the error-handling routine as well.*

Error-handling begins by typing the name of the error handler followed by a colon. Within the error handler, you write code to respond to the error. In the previous example, I simply use a message box to report that an error has occurred.

The Resume keyword takes program execution back to the statement where the error occurred. Note that there are three possible ways for returning program control to the procedure:

- Resume. By itself, the keyword Resume returns program control to where the error occurred.
- Resume Next. The Resume Next statement returns program control to the statement after the statement where the error occurred.
- Resume Label. The Resume Label statement returns program control to a predetermined line number, as seen in the following code.

```
Public Function Verify_Input() As Boolean

    On Error GoTo ErrorHandler

    'get Input from user

    BeginHere:

    Exit Function

ErrorHandler:

    MsgBox ("An error has occurred.")
    Resume BeginHere:

End Function
```

Generally speaking, message boxes are good ways to let a user know an error has occurred. However, knowing that an error has occurred is not enough; the user also needs to know what caused the error and what options there are for resolving the error.

In the next section you learn how to identify specific and custom errors using the Err object.

The Err Object

When a user encounters an error in your program, he should be provided with a clear, precise description of the problem and resolution. The Err object provides VBA programmers with an accessible means of finding or triggering Microsoft Windows-specific errors.

Essentially the Err (short for error) object maintains information about errors that occur in the current procedure. This information is stored in the form of properties. The most common of the Err's properties follow:

- Description contains a description of the current error.
- Number contains the error number of the current error (0 to 65,535).
- Source contains the name of the object that generated the error.

Table 7.1 contains just a few of VBA's more common trappable error numbers and descriptions. For a complete list of error numbers and descriptions, consult Appendix C, "Trappable Errors," of this book.

TABLE 7.1 COMMON ERROR NUMBERS AND DESCRIPTIONS

Error Number	Error Description
11	Division by 0
53	File Not Found
61	Disk Full
71	Disk Not Ready
76	Path Not Found

In the next program example, I use an error handler to check for division by 0.

```
Private Sub cmdDivide_Click()

   On Error GoTo ErrorBin

   MsgBox "Result is " & Val(txtOperand1.Value) _
   / Val(txtOperand2.Value)

   Exit Sub

ErrorBin:

   MsgBox "Error Number " & Err.Number & ", " & Err.Description
```

```
    Resume Next

End Sub
```

There may be times when an error occurs in your program that is similar to that of a given `Err` description, but does not trigger the specific `Err` number. The ability to trigger errors can be achieved through the `Err` object's `Raise` method.

The `Raise` method allows you to trigger a specific error condition, thus displaying a dialog box to the user. The `Raise` method takes a number as a parameter. For example, the following statement triggers a Disk Not Ready dialog box:

```
Err.Raise 71
```

Besides providing descriptive error messages, error handling prevents many unwanted problems for your users. In other words, error handling may prevent your program from crashing. Users expect an error for division by 0, but they don't expect division by 0 to crash their applications.

The Debug Object

The `Debug` object is quite common with many VBA and Visual Basic programmers for troubleshooting problems by sending output to the Immediate window. The `Debug` object has two methods: `Print` and `Assert`. The `Print` method prints the value of its parameter and sends it to the Immediate window.

The `Assert` method conditionally breaks program execution when the method is reached. More specifically, the `Assert` method takes an expression as a parameter, which evaluates to a `Boolean` value. If the expression evaluates to `False`, the program's execution is paused. Otherwise, program execution continues. The next procedure demonstrates the use of the `Assert` method.

```
Private Sub cmdDivide_Click()

    Dim passedTest As Boolean

    On Error GoTo ErrorBin

    If Val(txtOperand2.Value) = 0 Then
        passedTest = False
    Else
        passedTest = True
```

```
    End If

    ' Conditionally pause program execution.
    Debug.Assert passedTest

    MsgBox "Result is " & Val(txtOperand1.Value) _
      / Val(txtOperand2.Value)

    Exit Sub

ErrorBin:

    MsgBox "Error Number " & Err.Number & ", " & Err.Description

    Resume Next

End Sub
```

FILE PROCESSING

You're probably aware that Access is a database. What is a *database*? Loosely, it's a collection of data. Do you know that you, too, can build your own database? You can—and you can do it with file I/O (input/output) and a little help from this chapter.

Within VBA there are many techniques for building and managing file I/O routines. File I/O is the approach taken by programmers to manage data stored in files. Data files that you create can be viewed and edited through Microsoft text editors such as Notepad.

Most data files that you work with are built upon a common foundation, much like a database. The data files you learn about in this chapter share the following relationships and building blocks:

- **Data File**. A collection of data that stores records and fields
- **Record**. A row of related data that contains one or more fields, separated by a space, tab, or comma
- **Field**. An attribute in a record, which is the smallest component in a data file

An example data file is shown in Figure 7.8. The trivia.dat data file is used in the chapter-based program. It has five records, with each record containing three fields separated by commas. This is called a *comma-delimited file*.

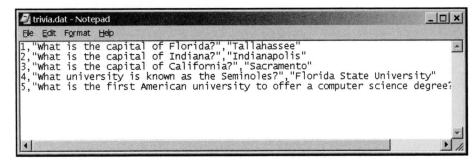

FIGURE 7.8

A sample
data file.

In the sections to come, I show you how to build and manage your own data files using sequential file access.

About Sequential File Access

Data files created with sequential file access have records stored in a file, one after another, in sequential order. When you access data files with sequential file access, records must be read in the same order in which they were written to the file. In other words, if you wish to access the 20th record in a data file, you must first read records 1 to 19.

Sequential file access is useful and appropriate for small data files. If you find that your sequential file access program is starting to run slowly, you may wish to change file access to an RDBMS such as Microsoft Access.

Opening a Sequential Data File

The first step in creating or accessing a data file is to open it. Microsoft provides an easy-to-use facility for opening a data file through the Open function.

```
Open "Filename" For {Input | Output | Append} As #Filenumber [Len = Record Length]
```

The Open function takes three parameters. Filename describes the name of the file you wish to open or create. Input|Output|Append is a list from which you pick one to use. #Filenumber is a number from 1 to 511 that is used for referencing the file. Len is an optional parameter that can control the number of characters buffered. The sequential access modes are shown in Table 7.2.

I use the Open method to create a new file for output called quiz.dat.

```
Open "quiz.dat" For Output As #1
```

TABLE 7.2 SEQUENTIAL ACCESS MODES	
Mode	**Description**
Input	Reads records from a data file
Output	Writes records to a data file
Append	Writes or appends records to the end of a data file

TRICK

The Filename attribute can contain paths in addition to filenames. For example, if you want to create employee records in a file named employee.dat on a floppy diskette, you could use the following syntax.

```
Open "a:\employee.dat" For Output As #1
```

The result of the Open function varies depending on the initial action chosen. If the Input parameter is chosen, the Open function searches for the file and creates a buffer in memory. If the file is not found, VBA generates an error.

TRICK

A *buffer* is an area where data is temporarily stored.

If the file specified is not found, a new file is created using the Filename parameter as the filename. Note that the Output mode always overwrites an existing file. Once a data file has been successfully opened, you can then read from it, write to it, and close it.

Reading Sequential Data from a File

If you want to read records from a data file, you must use the Input parameter with the Open function.

```
Open "quiz.dat" For Input As #1
```

Once the file is opened for input, use the Input function to retrieve fields from the file.

```
Input #Filenumber, Fields
```

The Input function takes two parameters: #Filenumber and a list of fields. For example, if you want to read the first record in a data file called quiz.dat (assuming quiz.dat contains three fields for each record), you could use the following program statements.

```
Dim liQuestionNumber as Integer
Dim lsQuestion as String
Dim lsAnswer as String

Open "quiz.dat" For Input As #1

Input #1, liQuestionNumber, lsQuestion, lsAnswer
```

Notice that I pass three variables as the field list to the Input function. These variables hold the contents of the first record found.

By now, you may be thinking, "So far, so good, but how do I read all records in a data file?" The answer involves something new and something old. First, you have to use a loop to search through the data file. Second, your loop's condition should use the EOF function.

The EOF (end of file) function tests for the end of the data file. It takes a file number as a parameter, returning a True Boolean value if the end of the file is found or False if the end of file has not been reached.

To test for the end of file, the EOF function looks for an EOF marker placed at the end of a file by the Close function. I discuss closing data files later in the chapter.

```
Dim liQuestionNumber as Integer
Dim lsQuestion as String
Dim lsAnswer as String

Open "quiz.dat" For Input As #1

Do Until EOF(1)
   Input #1, liQuestionNumber, lsQuestion, lsAnswer
   List1.AddItem "Question number:  " & _
     liQuestionNumber & lsQuestion
Loop
```

The preceding loop iterates until the EOF function returns a True value. Inside the loop, each record is read one at a time. After a record is read, the print method of a picture box control is used to output two of the fields (liQuestionNumber and lsQuestion) for display.

Writing Sequential Data to a File

In order to write data to a sequential file, you want to use either the Output mode, which creates a new file for writing, or the Append mode, which writes records to the end of a data file. Note that these are two separate lines of code.

```
Open "quiz1.dat" For Output As #1
Open "quiz.dat" For Append As #1
```

After opening a file for writing, you can use the Write function to write records.

```
Write #Filenumber, Fields
```

The Write function takes two parameters: #Filenumber and a list of fields. #Filenumber denotes the file number used in the Open function and the Fields parameter is a list of strings, numbers, variables, and properties that you want to use as fields.

For example, if I want to create a data file and write quiz records to it, I could use the following syntax.

```
Open "quiz.dat" For Output As #1
Write #1, 1, "Is Visual Basic an Event Driven language?", "Yes"
```

I could also use variable names for my fields list.

```
Write #1, liQuestionNumber, lsQuestion, lsAnswer
```

Either way, VBA outputs numbers as numbers and strings as strings surrounded with quote marks.

Closing Data Files

As you may have guessed, closing a data file is an important part of file processing. Specifically, closing a data file performs the following operations:

- Writes the EOF marker
- When using the Output or Append mode, writes records to the physical file in the sequential order in which they were created
- Releases the file number and buffer for memory conservation

To close a data file, simply use the Close function after all file processing has completed.

```
Close #FileNumber
```

The Close function takes the file number as its only parameter. For example, to close the file quiz.dat after writing one record, I could use the Close function:

```
Open "quiz.dat" For Output As #1

Write #1, 1, "Is Visual Basic an Event Driven language?", "Yes"

Close 1
```

If the `Close` function is used without any parameters, it closes all open sequential data files.

Error Trapping for File Access

Error trapping is almost always a must when dealing with file I/O. Why? Have you ever tried to access your floppy diskette from Windows Explorer, only to get an error message because there is no floppy diskette in the drive? What if the diskette is in the drive, but the file is not found, or better yet—the file is there but it's corrupt?

There are all types of potential errors when dealing with data files and file I/O. Your best bet is to plan ahead and create error-trapping or error-handling routines. In fact, it is safe to promote error trapping in any procedure that opens, writes, reads, appends, or closes files.

An adequate facility for capturing file I/O errors is to use VBA's `Err` object. The `Err` object contains preexisting codes for various known errors such as File Not Found, Disk Not Ready, and many more that can be used to your advantage.

Here's an error-handling routine for a quiz game that uses the `Err` object to check for specific errors when the game attempts to open a file in the form `Load` event:

```
Private Sub Form_Load()

    On Error GoTo ErrorHandler:
```

Like any other error-handling routine, I start my procedure off by declaring an error-handling label with an `On Error GoTo` statement. You can actually put unique labels throughout your code as I've done here with the `BeginHere:` label.

```
    BeginHere:
```

Labels can serve useful purposes so long as you keep their existence minimal and easy to follow. As you see later in the code, I choose the `BeginHere:` label as a good starting point in this procedure.

```
    Open "quiz.dat" For Input As #1

    Exit Sub
```

After opening the sequential data file, the procedure is exited, providing no errors have occurred.

```
ErrorHandler:
  Dim liResponse As Integer
```

If an error does occur in opening the file, my guess is that it is one of the following error conditions (error codes). You can see in the following code that I'm using the Select Case structure to check for specific Err object codes. If an error code is found, the user is prompted with an opportunity to fix the problem. If the user decides to retry the operation, the program resumes control to the BeginHere: label.

```
Select Case Err.Number

    Case 53

        'File not found
        liResponse = MsgBox("File not found!", _
            vbRetryCancel, "Error!")

        If liResponse = 4 Then 'retry
            Resume BeginHere:
        Else
            cmdQuit_Click
        End If

    Case 71

        'Disk not ready
        liResponse = MsgBox("Disk not ready!", _
            vbRetryCancel, "Error!")

        If liResponse = 4 Then 'retry
            Resume BeginHere:
        Else
            cmdQuit_Click
        End If

    Case 76

        liResponse = MsgBox("Path not found!", _
            vbRetryCancel, "Error!")

        If liResponse = 4 Then 'retry
```

```
        Resume BeginHere:
    Else
        cmdQuit_Click
    End If

  Case Else

    MsgBox "Error in program!", , "Error"
    cmdQuit_Click

  End Select

End Sub
```

CHAPTER PROGRAM: TRIVIAL CHALLENGE

The Trivial Challenge program, shown in Figure 7.9, is a fun game that uses chapter-based techniques and concepts such as data files, sequential file access, and error handling.

Program code for the game is broken into two separate code modules. The standard module contains a public user-defined type, which stores and manages quiz components such as question numbers, question, answer, and user's response. Most of the program code is in the form class module where the game's logic is managed.

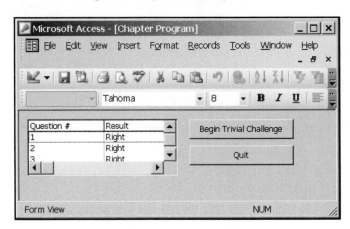

FIGURE 7.9

Using chapter-based concepts to build the Trivial Challenge program.

Controls and properties that build the Trivial Challenge program are described in Table 7.3.

TABLE 7.3 CONTROLS AND PROPERTIES OF THE TRIVIAL CHALLENGE PROGRAM		
Control	**Property**	**Property Value**
Form	Name	Chapter 7—Trivial Challenge
	Caption	Chapter Program
	Record Selectors	No
	Navigation Buttons	No
	Dividing Lines	No
List Box	Name	lstResults
	Row Source Type	Value List
	Column Count	2
	Column Heads	Yes
Command Button	Name	cmdBegin
	Caption	Begin Trivial Challenge
Command Button	Name	cmdQuit
	Caption	Quit

Module-level code defines a public user-defined type.

```
Option Compare Database
Option Explicit
```

```
Public Type Trivia

    QuestionNumber As Integer
    Question As String
    Answer As String
    UserReponse As String

End Type
```

Shown next is the form class module code for building the remainder of the Trivial Challenge program.

```
Option Compare Database
Option Explicit

' Declare dynamic array of Trivia type.
Dim myTrivia() As Trivia
```

```
Private Sub cmdBegin_Click()

   Dim x As Integer

   ClearListBox ' Call a user-defined procedure

   ' Prompt the user with trivia questions.
   For x = 1 To UBound(myTrivia)

      myTrivia(x).UserReponse = InputBox(myTrivia(x).Question)

      ' Determine if the user's response was right, wrong or empty.
      If LCase(myTrivia(x).UserReponse) = LCase(myTrivia(x).Answer) Then

            Me.lstResults.AddItem myTrivia(x).QuestionNumber _
               & ";" & "Right"

      Else

         If myTrivia(x).UserReponse = "" Then
            ' User did not respond (pressed Cancel on input box).
            Me.lstResults.AddItem myTrivia(x).QuestionNumber _
               & ";" & "No Response"
         Else
            Me.lstResults.AddItem myTrivia(x).QuestionNumber _
               & ";" & "Wrong"
         End If

      End If
```

```
    Next x

End Sub
```

```
 Private Sub cmdQuit_Click()
     DoCmd.Quit
 End Sub
```

```
 Private Sub Form_Load()

    ' Create initial element in dynamic array.
    ReDim myTrivia(1)

    ' Add header to each column in the list box if one
    ' hasn't already been added.
    If lstResults.ListCount = 0 Then
        Me.lstResults.AddItem "Question #;Result"
    End If

    ' Load trivia questions into memory.
    LoadTrivia

 End Sub
```

```
 Public Sub ClearListBox()

  Dim x As Integer

  ' Clear list box
  For x = 1 To (lstResults.ListCount - 1)
      Me.lstResults.RemoveItem lstResults.ListCount - 1
  Next x

 End Sub
```

```vb
Public Sub LoadTrivia()

  On Error GoTo ErrorHandler

  ' Open file for sequential input using
  ' the application's current path.
  Open Application.CurrentProject.Path & "\" & "trivia.dat" For Input As #1

  ' Read all records until end of file is reached.
  ' Store each question and answer in a user defined type.
  Do While EOF(1) = False

      ' Read trivia data into variables.
      Input #1, myTrivia(UBound(myTrivia)).QuestionNumber, _
        myTrivia(UBound(myTrivia)).Question, _
        myTrivia(UBound(myTrivia)).Answer

      ' Print debug data to the immediate window.
      'Debug.Print myTrivia(UBound(myTrivia)).QuestionNumber, _
        'myTrivia(UBound(myTrivia)).Question, myTrivia(UBound(myTrivia)).Answer

      If EOF(1) = False Then

          ' Increment dynamic array for each next trivia question.
          ReDim Preserve myTrivia(UBound(myTrivia) + 1)

      End If

  Loop

  ' Close the sequential file.
  Close #1

  Exit Sub
```

```
ErrorHandler:

    MsgBox "Error number " & Err.Number & Chr(13) & _
            Err.Description

End Sub
```

```
Private Sub lstResults_Click()

   ' Display the selected question back to the user.
   If lstResults.ListIndex = -1 Then
      Exit Sub
   End If

   MsgBox myTrivia(lstResults.ListIndex + 1).Question

End Sub
```

CHAPTER SUMMARY

- Debugging is the process by which programmers identify, find, and correct software errors.
- Software bugs are generally grouped into one of three categories: syntax errors, runtime errors, and logic errors.
- The Visual Basic Environment includes many debugging features such as breakpoints, the Immediate window, the Locals window, and the Watch window.
- Breakpoints are used to pause program execution.
- The Immediate window can be used to ascertain variable and property values.
- Variable and property values can be altered in the Immediate window.
- Variable and property values within scope can be viewed and managed in the Locals window.
- Watch expressions can be created and managed in the Watch window.
- Input validation generally involves checking for numeric or nonnumeric data entered by the user.
- Programmers can use input validation to check for a range of numbers or characters.
- The IsNull function takes an expression as a parameter and returns a Boolean value (True or False) depending whether or not the expression is Null.

- VBA programmers often use the Err and Debug objects to aid in debugging and error handling.
- The Err object contains properties for discerning the current error number and error description.
- The Debug object contains methods commonly used in conjunction with the Immediate window for pausing program execution and displaying program output.
- VBA error-handling routines are initiated using the On Error GoTo statement.
- There are three possible ways to return program control to the procedure using the keywords Resume, Resume Next, and Resume Label.
- Data files contain records and fields.
- In VBA, file processing can be achieved with sequential file access using the Open, Write, Input, and Close methods.
- Error handling should always be incorporated into file-processing routines.

PROGRAMMING CHALLENGES

1. Build a form with one text box and one command button. The text box should receive the user's name. In the Click event of the command button, write code to validate that the user has entered nonnumeric data and display the outcome in a message box. Test your program by entering numeric data into the text box.

2. Build a form with one text box and one command button. The text box should receive a number between 1 and 10. In the Click event of the command button, write code to validate that the data entered is a number and that it is in the range of 1 to 10. Use a message box to display the outcome.

3. Create a data file called friends.dat. Insert a few records into the friends.dat file. The record layout should have three fields (phone number, first name, and last name), which should look similar to this:

```
"111-222-3333", "Michael", "Massey"
```

4. Create a form that allows a user to view all records in the friends.dat file. Populate a list box on the form with the phone numbers and names of friends. Remember to use error handling when opening the friends.dat file.

5. Create a form that allows a user to enter more friends into the friends.dat file. Retrieve information from the user with text boxes on the form. Remember to use the Append option when opening the friends.dat file and use error handling accordingly.

MICROSOFT JET SQL

I n this chapter I show you how to use the Microsoft Jet SQL for querying and managing databases without the help of Access wizards. I specifically show you two subsets of the Jet SQL language, called DML and DDL.

If you're new to database languages such as SQL, consider this chapter a prerequisite for Chapter 9, "Database Programming with ADO." Even if you've worked with SQL before, you may find this chapter a refreshing account of Microsoft Jet SQL syntax and common functionality.

INTRODUCTION TO JET SQL

Most databases, including Microsoft Access, incorporate one or more data languages for querying information and managing databases. The most common of these data languages is SQL (Structured Query Language), which contains a number of commands for querying and manipulating databases. SQL commands are typically grouped into one of two categories known as *data manipulation language (DML)* commands and *data definition language (DDL)* commands.

Microsoft Jet SQL follows a standard convention known as ANSI SQL, which is used by many database vendors, including Microsoft, Oracle, and IBM. Each manufacturer, however, incorporates its own proprietary language-based functions and syntax with Microsoft Jet SQL. Access is no exception with key differences in reserved words and data types.

To demonstrate Jet SQL, I use Access Queries in SQL View with Microsoft's sample Northwind database. Shown in Figure 8.1 is Microsoft's Northwind database.

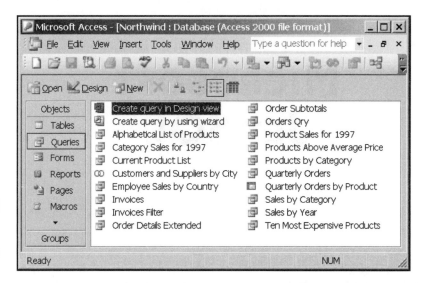

FIGURE 8.1

Looking at the Queries window of the Northwind database.

After opening the Queries window in the Northwind database, you can see that the Access developers at Microsoft have created many queries.

Building queries in Microsoft Access is much like the experience of building tables and forms in Access. Essentially, Microsoft provides wizards and graphical interfaces for building everything, including queries. In this chapter, I show you how to go beyond Access wizards to build your own queries using SQL!

To access the SQL window in Access, select a query and then press the Design button as I've done with the Northwind Current Product List query in Figure 8.2.

Once the query is open in Design mode, select View, SQL View from the menu, which I've done for the Northwind Current Product List query in Figure 8.3.

 TRICK You can also access the SQL View menu item when creating a new query, but the SQL View menu item is only available when a query is in Design mode.

SQL is not considered to be full-fledged programming language like VBA, C, or Java. In this author's mind, a real programming language must, at minimum, contain facilities for creating variables, as well as structures for conditional logic branches and iteration through loops. Regardless, SQL is a powerful language for asking the database questions (also known as *querying*).

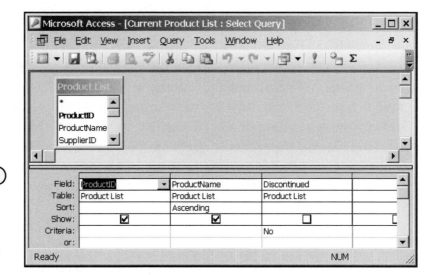

FIGURE 8.2

Viewing the Northwind Current Product List query in Design mode.

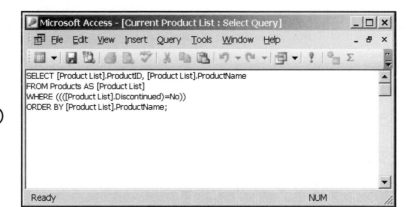

FIGURE 8.3

Viewing the Northwind Current Product List query in SQL View.

IN THE REAL WORLD

Pronounced *sequel*, SQL was originally developed by IBM researchers in the 1970s. It has become the de facto database manipulation language for many database vendors. For database users, mastering SQL has become a sought-after skill set in the information technology world. Most persons who master the SQL language have no trouble finding well-paid positions.

To provide readability in the sections to come, I use a preferred syntax nomenclature for SQL:

- All SQL commands and reserved language keywords are in uppercase. For example, SELECT, FROM, WHERE, and AND are all Jet SQL commands and reserved keywords.

- Even though Microsoft Access is not a case-sensitive application, table and column names used in SQL statements use the same case as defined in the database. For example, a column defined as EmployeeId is spelled EmployeeId in the SQL query.

- Table and column names that contain spaces must be enclosed in brackets. For example, the column name Customer Number must be contained in SQL as [Customer Number]. Failure to do so causes errors or undesired results when executing your queries.

- A query can be written on a single line. For readability, I break SQL statements into logical blocks on multiple lines. For example, look at this SQL statement:

```
SELECT [Order Details].OrderID, Sum(CCur([UnitPrice]*[Quantity]*(1-[Discount])/
100)*100) AS Subtotal FROM [Order Details] GROUP BY [Order Details].OrderID;
```

It should look like this:

```
SELECT      [Order Details].OrderID,
SUM         (CCur([UnitPrice]*[Quantity]*(1-[Discount])/100)*100)
AS          Subtotal
FROM        [Order Details]
GROUP BY    [Order Details].OrderID;
```

DATA MANIPULATION LANGUAGE

SQL contains many natural-language commands for querying, computing, sorting, grouping, joining, inserting, updating, and deleting data in a relational database. These querying and manipulation commands fall under the Data Manipulation Language subset also known as DML.

Simple SELECT Statements

To retrieve information from a relational database, SQL provides the simple SELECT statement. A simple SELECT statement takes the following form.

```
SELECT    ColumnName, ColumnName
FROM      TableName;
```

The SELECT clause identifies one or more column names in a database table(s). After identifying the columns in the SELECT clause, you must tell the database which table(s) the columns live in using the FROM clause. It is customary in SQL to append a semicolon (;) after the SQL statement to indicate the statement's ending point.

To retrieve all rows in a database table, the wildcard character (*) can be used like this.

```
SELECT    *
FROM      Employees;
```

You can execute SQL queries in Access in one of a couple of ways. You can simply save your query, return to the Queries window, and double-click your newly saved query. Or, leaving your SQL View window open, select View, Datasheet View from the menu.

Another way to execute your SQL queries is to select Query, Run item from the menu, or click the red exclamation mark (!) on the Toolbar. Either way, the results from the preceding query running against the Northwind database are shown in Figure 8.4.

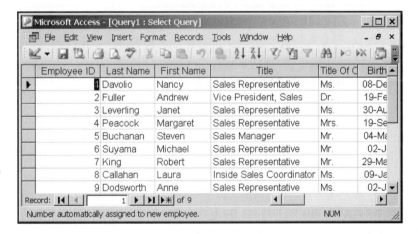

FIGURE 8.4

Viewing the results of a simple query.

The Datasheet window shown in Figure 8.4 displays the result set returned from the SQL query.

TRICK A *result set* is a common phrase used to describe the result or records returned by a SQL query.

Sometimes it is not necessary to retrieve all columns in a query. To streamline your query, supply specific column names separated by commas in the SELECT clause.

```
SELECT    LastName, FirstName, Title
FROM      Employees;
```

In the preceding query I ask the database to retrieve only the last names, first names, and titles of each employee record. Output is shown in Figure 8.5.

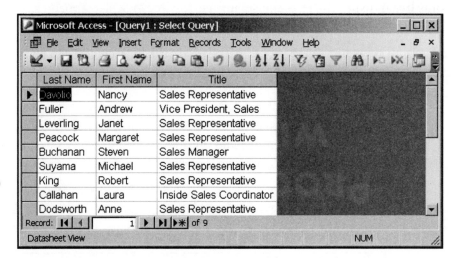

 TRAP Microsoft Access allows users to create table and column names with spaces. Use brackets ([ ]) to surround table and column names with spaces in SQL queries. Failure to do so can cause errors when running your queries.

You can change the order in which the result set displays columns by changing the column order in your SQL queries.

```
SELECT    Title, FirstName, LastName
FROM      Employees;
```

Changing the order of column names in a SQL query does not alter the data returned in a result set, but rather its column display order.

Conditions

SQL queries allow basic conditional logic for refining the result set returned by the query. Conditions in SQL are built using the WHERE clause.

```
SELECT    Title, FirstName, LastName
FROM      Employees
WHERE     Title = 'Sales Representative';
```

In the preceding query I use a condition in the WHERE clause to eliminate rows returned by the query where the employee's title equals Sales Representative. Output from this query is seen in Figure 8.6.

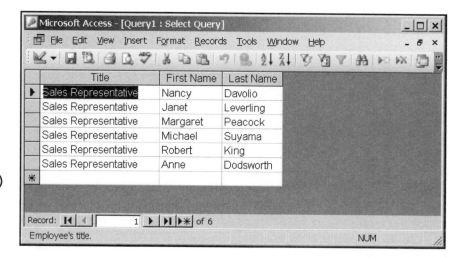

FIGURE 8.6

Using conditions in the WHERE clause to refine the result set.

Note that textual data such as 'Sales Representative' in the WHERE clause's expression must always be enclosed by single quotes.

SQL conditions work much like the conditions you've already learned about in Access VBA in that the WHERE clause's condition evaluates to either true or false. You can use the operators seen in Table 8.1 in SQL expressions.

TABLE 8.1 CONDITIONAL OPERATORS USED IN SQL EXPRESSIONS

Operator	Description
=	Equals
<>	Not equal
>	Greater than
<	Less than
>=	Greater than or equal to
<=	Less than or equal to

To demonstrate conditional operators, the next query returns the rows in the Products table where the value for units in stock is less than or equal to 5. Output is seen in Figure 8.7.

```
SELECT    *
FROM      Products
WHERE     UnitsInStock <= 5;
```

![Microsoft Access Query1 Select Query window showing Products result set with Product ID, Product Name, and Supplier columns]

Microsoft Access - [Query1 : Select Query]

File Edit View Insert Format Records Tools Window Help

Product ID	Product Name	Supplier
5	Chef Anton's Gumbo Mix	New Orleans Cajun Delights
17	Alice Mutton	Pavlova, Ltd.
21	Sir Rodney's Scones	Specialty Biscuits, Ltd.
29	Thüringer Rostbratwurst	Plutzer Lebensmittelgroßmärkte AG
31	Gorgonzola Telino	Formaggi Fortini s.r.l.
45	Røgede sild	Lyngbysild
53	Perth Pasties	G'day, Mate
66	Louisiana Hot Spiced Okra	New Orleans Cajun Delights
74	Longlife Tofu	Tokyo Traders

Record: |◄| ◄| 1 |►|►||►*| of 9

Number automatically assigned to new product.   NUM

FIGURE 8.7

Refining the products result set with conditional operators.

TRAP

> Note that single quotes are not used to surround numeric data when searching numeric data types.

SQL queries also can contain compound conditions using the keywords AND, OR, and NOT. The next two SQL queries demonstrate the use of compound conditions in the WHERE clause.

```
SELECT    *
FROM      Products
WHERE     UnitsInStock < 5 AND UnitPrice > 10;

SELECT     *
FROM       Products
WHERE NOT  (UnitsInStock = 0);
```

Before moving on to the next section on SQL, I'd like to share with you a paradigm shift. Believe it or not, most SQL programmers are the translators for their companies' information needs. To better understand this, think of SQL programmers as the intermediaries between business people and the unwieldy database. The business person comes in to your office and says, "I'm concerned about low inventories. Could you tell me what products we have in stock with unit quantities less than or equal to 5?" As the SQL programmer, you smile and say, "Sure, give me a minute." After digesting what your colleague is asking, you translate the inquiry into a question the database understands—in other words, a SQL query such as the following.

```
SELECT    *
FROM      Products
WHERE     UnitsInStock <= 5;
```

Within seconds, your query executes and you print out the results for your amazed and thankful colleague. You're the superstar, the genius, the miracle worker. But most of all, you're the translator.

Computed Fields

Computed fields do not exist in the database as columns. Instead, computed fields are generated using calculations on columns that do exist in the database. Simple calculations such as addition, subtraction, multiplication, and division can be used to create computed fields.

When creating computed fields in SQL, the AS clause assigns a name to the computed field. The next SQL statement uses a computed field to calculate subtotals based on two columns (Unit Price and Quantity) in the Order Details table. Output is seen in Figure 8.8.

```
SELECT    OrderID, (UnitPrice * Quantity) AS SubTotals
FROM      [Order Details];
```

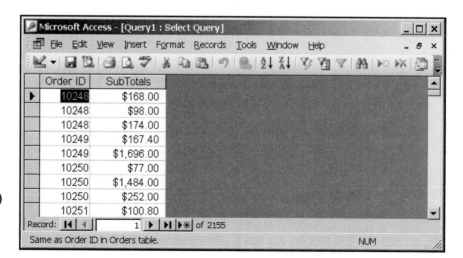

FIGURE 8.8

Using SQL to build computed fields.

Note the presence of the SubTotals column name in Figure 8.8. The SubTotals field does not exist in the Order Details table. Rather, the SubTotals field is created in the SQL statement using the AS clause to assign a name to an expression. Though parentheses are not required, I use them in my computed field's expression to provide readability and order of operations, if necessary.

Built-In Functions

Just as VBA incorporates many intrinsic functions such as Val, Str, UCase, and Len, SQL provides many built-in functions for determining information on your result sets. You learn about these SQL *aggregate functions* in this section:

- AVG
- COUNT
- FIRST, LAST
- MIN, MAX
- SUM
- DISTINCT

The AVG function takes an expression such as a column name for a parameter and returns the mean value in a column or other expression.

```
SELECT          AVG(UnitPrice)
FROM            Products;
```

The preceding SQL statement returns a single value, which is the mean value of the UnitPrice column in the Products table. Output is seen in Figure 8.9.

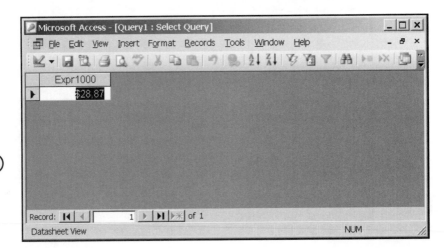

FIGURE 8.9

Using the AVG function to calculate the mean value of a column.

Notice in Figure 8.9 that the column heading gives no clue as to the meaning of the SQL statement's return value. To correct this, simply use the AS clause.

```
SELECT    AVG(UnitPrice) AS [Average Unit Price]
FROM      Products;
```

The COUNT function is a very useful function for determining how many records are returned by a query. For example, the following SQL query uses the COUNT function to determine how many customer records are in the Customers table.

```
SELECT    COUNT(*) AS [Number of Customers]
FROM      Customers;
```

Figure 8.10 reveals the output from the COUNT function in the preceding SQL statement. Note that it's possible to supply a column name in the COUNT function, but the wildcard character (*) performs a faster calculation on the number of records found in a table.

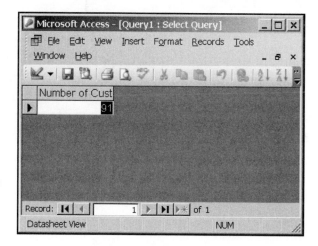

FIGURE 8.10

Displaying the result of a COUNT function.

The FIRST and LAST functions return the first and last records in a result set, respectively. Because records are not necessarily stored in alphanumeric order, the FIRST and LAST functions may produce seemingly unexpected results. The results, however, are accurate. These functions report the first and last expressions in a result set as stored in a database and returned by the SQL query.

```
SELECT    FIRST(LastName) AS [First Employee Last Name],
          LAST(LastName) AS [Last Employee Last Name]
FROM      Employees;
```

The preceding SQL statement uses the FIRST and LAST functions to retrieve the first and last names (specifically the last name) of employee records in the Employees table. Output is seen in Figure 8.11.

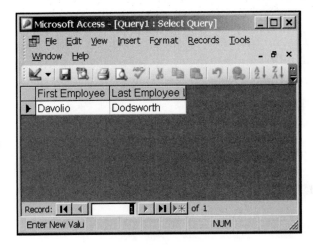

FIGURE 8.11

Using the FIRST and LAST functions to retrieve the first and last values of a result set.

To determine the minimum and maximum values of an expression in SQL, use the MIN and MAX functions, respectively. Like other SQL functions, the MIN and MAX functions take an expression and return a value. The next SQL statement uses these two functions to determine the minimum and maximum unit prices found in the Products table. Output is seen in Figure 8.12.

```
SELECT    MIN(UnitPrice) AS [Minimum Unit Price],
          MAX(UnitPrice) AS [Maximum Unit Price]
FROM      Products;
```

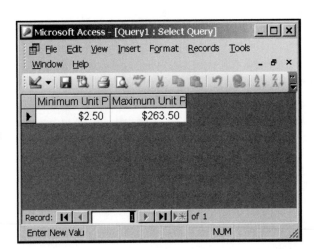

FIGURE 8.12

Retrieving the minimum and maximum values from an expression using the MIN and MAX functions.

The SUM function takes an expression as argument and returns the sum of values. The SUM function is used in the next SQL statement, which takes a computed field as an argument to derive the sum of subtotals in the Order Details table.

```
SELECT    SUM(UnitPrice * Quantity) AS [Sum of Sub Totals]
FROM      [Order Details];
```

Output from the SQL statement using the SUM function is in Figure 8.13.

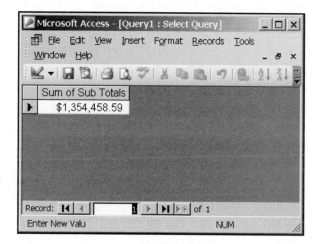

FIGURE 8.13

Displaying the
output of the SUM
function.

The last built-in function for this section is DISTINCT, which returns a distinct set of values for an expression. To demonstrate, if I want to find a unique list of countries for the suppliers in the Northwind database, I need to sift through every record in the Suppliers table and count each distinct country name. Or, I could use the DISTINCT function to return a distinct value for each country in the Country column.

```
SELECT    DISTINCT(Country)
FROM      Suppliers;
```

Sorting

You may recall from the discussions surrounding the FIRST and LAST functions that data stored in a database is not stored in any relevant order, including alphanumeric. Most often, data is stored in the order in which it was entered, but not always. If you need to retrieve data in a sorted manner, learn how to work with the ORDER BY clause.

The ORDER BY clause is used at the end of a SQL statement to sort a result set (records returned by a SQL query) in alphanumeric order. Sort order for the ORDER BY clause can either be ascending (A to Z, 0 to 9) or descending (Z to A, 9 to 0). Use the keyword ASC for ascending or DESC for descending.

Note that neither the ASC nor DESC keywords are required with the ORDER BY clause, and that the default sort order is ascending.

To properly use the ORDER BY clause, simply follow the clause with a *sort key*, which is a fancy way of saying a column name to sort on. The optional keywords ASC and DESC follow the sort key.

To exhibit SQL sorting techniques, study the next two SQL statements and their outputs, shown in Figures 8.14 and 8.15.

```
SELECT      *
FROM        Products
ORDER BY    ProductName ASC;
```

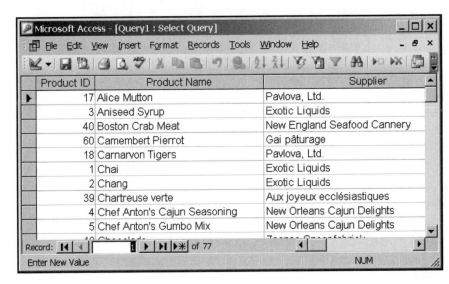

FIGURE 8.14

Using the ORDER BY clause and the ASC keyword to sort product records by product name in ascending order.

```
SELECT      *
FROM        Products
ORDER BY    ProductName DESC;
```

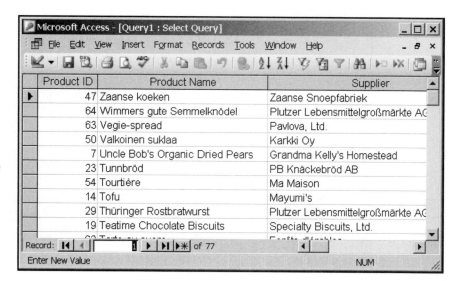

FIGURE 8.15

Using the ORDER
BY clause and the
DESC keyword to
sort product
records by
product name in
descending order.

Grouping

Grouping in SQL provides developers with an opportunity to group like data together. Without the use of grouping, built-in functions such as SUM and AVG calculate every value in a column. To put like data into logical groups of information, SQL provides the GROUP BY clause.

In the next SQL statement, I use the GROUP BY clause to group a computed field by product ID in the Products table.

```
SELECT      ProductID, SUM(UnitPrice * Quantity) AS [Sub Total by Product]
FROM        [Order Details]
GROUP BY    ProductID;
```

Notice the output from the preceding SQL statement in Figure 8.16. Even though I specified ProductID as the desired column, the output column and the data it contains show as a product name. This occurs because the Products table uses a SQL lookup to retrieve the product name by product ID.

There are times when you need conditions on your groups. In these events, you cannot use the WHERE clause. Instead, SQL provides the HAVING clause for condition building when working with groups. To demonstrate, I modify the previous SQL statement to use a HAVING clause, which asks the database to retrieve only groups that have a subtotal byproduct greater than 15,000.00.

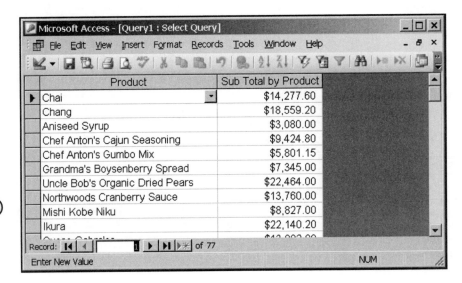

FIGURE 8.16

Using the GROUP
BY clause to
group like data
together.

```
SELECT       ProductID, SUM(UnitPrice * Quantity) AS [Sub Total by Product]
FROM         [Order Details]
GROUP BY     ProductID
HAVING SUM   (UnitPrice * Quantity) > 15000.00;
```

Joins

Joins are used when you need to retrieve data from more than one table. Specifically, a SQL join uses keys to combine records from two tables where a primary key from one table is matched up with a foreign key from another table. The result is a combination of result sets from both tables where a match is found. If a match is not found, information from either table is discarded in the final result set.

SQL joins are created by selecting columns from more than one table in the SELECT clause, including both table names in the FROM clause, and matching like columns from both tables in the WHERE clause. The following example join's output is in Figure 8.17.

```
SELECT   FirstName, LastName, OrderDate, ShipName
FROM     Employees, Orders
WHERE    Employees.EmployeeID = Orders.EmployeeID;
```

In Figure 8.17, I've retrieved columns from both the Employees and Orders table where the EmployeeID values from both tables match. Because the join keys from both tables (EmployeeID)

First Name	Last Name	Order Date	Ship Name
Nancy	Davolio	17-Jul-1996	Ernst Handel
Nancy	Davolio	01-Aug-1996	Wartian Herkku
Nancy	Davolio	07-Aug-1996	Magazzini Alimentari Riuniti
Nancy	Davolio	20-Aug-1996	QUICK-Stop
Nancy	Davolio	28-Aug-1996	Tradição Hipermercados
Nancy	Davolio	29-Aug-1996	Tortuga Restaurante
Nancy	Davolio	12-Sep-1996	Tortuga Restaurante
Nancy	Davolio	16-Sep-1996	Romero y tomillo
Nancy	Davolio	20-Sep-1996	Du monde entier
Nancy	Davolio	25-Sep-1996	Rattlesnake Canyon Grocery

FIGURE 8.17

Joining the
Employees and
Orders table with
the WHERE clause.

are spelled the same, I must explicitly tell SQL what table name I'm referring to by using dot notation, as seen again here.

```
WHERE Employees.EmployeeID = Orders.EmployeeID;
```

TRAP If the expression in the WHERE clause is incorrect, a Cartesian join results. A *Cartesian result* is when the query returns every possible number of combinations from each table involved.

The preceding join is typically called a *natural join*, where a row from one table matches a row from another table using a common column and matching column value. There are times, however, when you want rows from one table that do not match rows in the other table. SQL solves this dilemma with an *outer join*.

There are two types of outer joins: left outer joins and right outer joins. A *left outer join* includes all records from the left (first) of the two tables even if there are no matching rows from right (second) table. The *right outer join* includes all rows from the right (second) table even if there are no matching rows from the left (first) table.

To demonstrate, let's say I want to find out who my suppliers are and what products they offer. I could start off by using a natural join as seen next, with output in Figure 8.18.

```
SELECT    Products.ProductName, Suppliers.CompanyName
FROM      Products, Suppliers
WHERE     Products.SupplierID = Suppliers.SupplierID
```

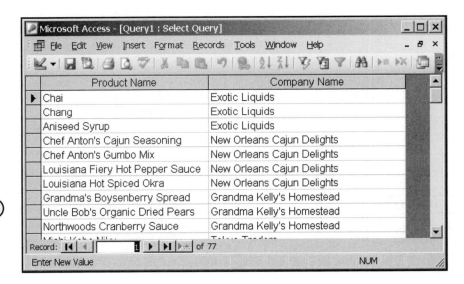

FIGURE 8.18

Using a natural join to find suppliers and their products.

There's only one problem with this join—it's possible I have suppliers who have no products as of yet. The natural join in this case does not show me the suppliers who have no products. I can, however, view not only suppliers with products but suppliers with no products by using a right outer join. You can see this in the following code and in Figure 8.19.

```
SELECT    Products.ProductName, Suppliers.CompanyName
FROM      Products RIGHT JOIN Suppliers
ON        Products.SupplierID = Suppliers.SupplierID
```

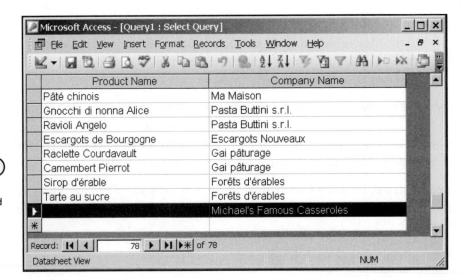

FIGURE 8.19

Using a right outer join to find suppliers and their products even though suppliers have no products.

Looking at Figure 8.19, you can see there's an extra supplier in my query output (Michael's Famous Casseroles) that has no product, which the natural join missed. Note that I added this extra supplier to my copy of the Northwind database.

To use outer joins, you need to leverage the RIGHT JOIN or LEFT JOIN keywords in the FROM clause and replace the WHERE keyword with ON.

```
FROM    Products RIGHT JOIN Suppliers
ON      Products.SupplierID = Suppliers.SupplierID
```

INSERT INTO Statement

You can use SQL to insert rows into a table with the INSERT INTO statement. The INSERT INTO statement inserts new records into a table using the VALUES clause.

```
INSERT INTO    Books
VALUES         ('1234abc456edf', 'Beginning SQL', 'Vine',
               'Michael', 'Technology Press');
```

Though not required, matching column names can be used in the INSERT INTO statement to clarify the fields with which you're working.

```
INSERT INTO    Books (ISBN, Title, LastName, FirstName, Publisher)
VALUES         ('1234abc456edf', 'Beginning SQL', 'Vine',
               'Michael', 'Technology Press');
```

Using matching column names is necessary, not just helpful, when you only need to insert data for a limited number of columns in a table. A case in point is when working with the AutoNumber field type, which Access automatically creates for you when inserting a record.

The concept of working with an AutoNumber and an INSERT INTO statement is shown in the following SQL statement and Figure 8.20.

```
INSERT INTO    Shippers (CompanyName, Phone)
VALUES         ('Slow Boat Express', '123-456-9999');
```

FIGURE 8.20

Inserting new records into a table with INSERT INTO statement.

Microsoft Office Access

You are about to append 1 row(s).

Once you click Yes, you can't use the Undo command to reverse the changes.
Are you sure you want to append the selected rows?

[Yes]   [No]

UPDATE Statement

You can use the UPDATE statement to change field values in one or more tables. The UPDATE statement works in conjunction with the SET keyword:

```
UPDATE    Products
SET       UnitsInStock = UnitsInStock + 5;
```

You supply the table name to the UPDATE statement and use the SET keyword to update any number of fields that belong to the table in the UPDATE statement. In my example, I'm updating every record's UnitsInStock field by adding the number 5. Notice that I said every record. Because I didn't use a WHERE clause, the UPDATE statement updates every row in the table.

In the next UPDATE statement, I use a WHERE clause to put a condition on the number of rows that receive updates.

```
UPDATE    Products
SET       UnitsInStock = UnitsInStock + 5
WHERE     SupplierID = 1;
```

It is possible for SQL programmers to forget to place conditions on their UPDATE statements. Because there is no undo or rollback feature in Access, pay attention to the dialog box, which you see in Figure 8.20, that appears before you commit changes.

DELETE Statement

The DELETE statement removes one or more rows from a table. It's possible to delete all rows from a table using the DELETE statement and a wildcard.

```
DELETE    *
FROM      Products;
```

More often than not, conditions are placed on DELETE statements using the WHERE clause.

```
DELETE    *
FROM      Products
WHERE     UnitsInStock = 0;
```

Once again, pay close attention to Access's informational dialog boxes when performing any inserts, updates, or deletes on tables.

The DELETE statement can perform cascade deletes on tables with one-to-many relationships if the Cascade Delete Related Records option is chosen in the Edit Relationships window, as seen in Figure 8.21.

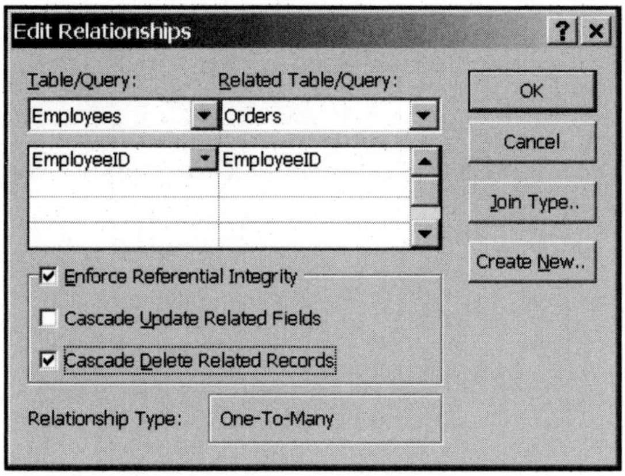

FIGURE 8.21

Selecting cascade deletes on one-to-many table relationships.

With the Cascade Delete Related Records option chosen for the Employees and Orders tables, any employee records deleted also initiate a corresponding deletion in the Orders table where a matching EmployeeID was found.

DATA DEFINITION LANGUAGE

Data definition language, also known as DDL, contains commands that define a database's attributes. Most commonly, DDL creates, alters, and drops tables, indexes, constraints, views, users, and permissions.

In this section you investigate a few of the more common uses for DDL in beginning database programming:

- Creating tables
- Altering tables
- DROP statements

Creating Tables

Creating tables in DDL involves using the CREATE TABLE statement. With the CREATE TABLE statement, you can define and create a table, its columns, column data types, and any constraints that might be needed on one or more columns. In its simplest form, the CREATE TABLE syntax and format is shown here.

```
CREATE TABLE   TableName
               ( FieldName FieldType,
               FieldName FieldType,
               FieldName FieldType);
```

The TableName attribute defines the table to be created. Each FieldName attribute defines the column to be created. Each FieldName has a corresponding FieldType attribute, which defines the column's data type.

The next CREATE TABLE statement creates a new table called Books that contains seven columns.

```
CREATE TABLE    Books
                (ISBN Text,
                Title Text,
                AuthorLastName Text,
                AuthorFirstName Text,
                Publisher Text,
                Price Currency,
                PublishDate Date);
```

The CREATE TABLE statement allows you to specify if one or more columns should not allow NULL values. By default, columns created in the CREATE TABLE statement allow NULL entries. To specify a not NULL column, use the Not Null keywords.

```
CREATE TABLE    Books
                (ISBN Text Not Null,
                Title Text,
                AuthorLastName Text,
                AuthorFirstName Text,
                Publisher Text,
                Price Currency,
                PublishDate Date);
```

Using the Not Null keywords sets the column's Required attribute to Yes.

Altering Tables

You can use the ALTER TABLE statement to alter tables that have already been created. Three common uses of the ALTER TABLE statement are to add column(s) to an existing table, to change the field type attributes of one or more columns, or to remove a column from a table.

The next ALTER TABLE statement adds a Salary column to the Employees table with the help of the ADD COLUMN keywords.

```
ALTER TABLE    Employees
ADD COLUMN     Salary Currency;
```

Adding the Salary column with the ALTER TABLE statement appends the new column to the end of the Employees table.

To change a column's data type, use the ALTER COLUMN keywords in conjunction with the ALTER TABLE statement.

```
ALTER TABLE      Employees
ALTER COLUMN     Extension Number;
```

In the preceding ALTER TABLE statement, I changed the data type of the Extension column from a Text data type to a Number data type.

To remove a column from a table in Access, use the DROP COLUMN keywords in conjunction with the ALTER TABLE statement:

```
ALTER TABLE      Employees

DROP COLUMN      Salary;
```

TRAP Access does not always warn you of your impending database alterations. In the case of dropping (removing) a column, Access simply performs the operation without mention.

DROP Statement

The DROP statement can be used to remove many entities from a database such as tables, indexes, procedures, and views. In this section you see how the DROP statement is used to drop a table from a database.

Removing a table from a database with the DROP statement is really quite easy. Simply supply the entity type to be dropped, along with the entity name.

```
DROP TABLE Books;
```

In the preceding example, the dropped entity typed is a TABLE and the entity name is Books. Once again, beware: Access does not always warn you when it modifies the database. In the DROP TABLE example, Access simply executes the command without any confirmation.

CHAPTER SUMMARY

- Most relational databases include a version of SQL for retrieving data and manipulating database entities.
- Data definition language (DDL) is a set of SQL commands used to define attributes, such as tables and columns, of a relational database.

- Data manipulation language (DML) is a set of commands for querying, computing, sorting, grouping, joining, inserting, updating, and deleting data in a relational database.
- SQL statements are freeform, meaning one SQL statement can be written on one or more lines. For readability, SQL programmers break SQL statements into one or more logical groups on multiple lines.
- Information is retrieved from a relational database using SELECT statements.
- Simple and compound conditions can be used in SQL statements using the WHERE clause.
- Computed fields do not exist as columns in a table; instead they are derived data using calculations in SQL statements.
- Computed fields are given display names using the AS clause.
- SQL contains many aggregate, or built-in, functions such as COUNT, DISTINCT, MIN, MAX, and SUM.
- Database records returned by a SQL statement are not sorted by default. To sort SQL query results, use the ORDER BY clause.
- SQL query results can be grouped using the GROUP BY clause.
- Natural joins are created by matching key fields in two or more tables in the WHERE clause.
- Incorrect joins can produce an unwanted Cartesian product.
- A left outer join includes all records from the left (first) of the two tables even if there are no matching rows from the right (second) table.
- A right outer join includes all rows from the right (second) table even if there are no matching rows from the left (first) table.
- Records can be manually inserted into a table using the INSERT INTO statement.
- The UPDATE statement can be used to update fields in a database table.
- Records in a table can be removed using the DELETE statement.
- Tables can be manually created using the CREATE TABLE statement.
- In its simplest form, the CREATE TABLE statement defines the table's name, its columns, and its column types.
- The ALTER TABLE statement can be used to add columns to an existing table, update a column's data type, and remove a column from a table.
- The DROP statement is used for removing tables, indexes, views, and procedures from a database.

PROGRAMMING CHALLENGES

USE THE MICROSOFT NORTHWIND DATABASE AND A SQL VIEW WINDOW FOR ALL THE FOLLOWING CHALLENGES.

1. Write and test a SQL query that retrieves all columns from the Categories table.

2. Write and test a SQL query that retrieves only the contact name and contact title from the Customers table.

3. Write and test a SQL query that uses a computed field to calculate the total cost of each record in the Order Details table.

4. Write and test the SQL query that returns the total number of records in the Employees table.

5. Use the Orders table to write and test the SQL query that returns the sum of freight shipments grouped by customer.

6. Using the INSERT INTO statement, write a SQL query that inserts a new record into the Employees table.

7. Update the unit price by $3.25 in the Products table for all products by the supplier Tokyo Traders.

8. Delete all records in the Products table where the product has been discontinued.

9. Using DDL commands, create a new table called HomesForSale. The HomesForSale table should contain the following fields: StreetAddress, City, State, ZipCode, SalePrice, and ListDate. Ensure that the StreetAddress column does not allow Null values.

10. Using DDL commands, add three new columns to the HomesForSale table: AgentLastName, AgentFirstName, and AgentPhoneNumber.

11. Using DDL commands, remove the HomesForSale table from the database.

DATABASE
PROGRAMMING
WITH ADO

With a basic knowledge of VBA programming, you can leverage the power of Microsoft's ActiveX Data Objects (commonly referred to as ADO) to access and manage data sources such as Microsoft Access. In this chapter I show you the essentials for programming with ADO's application programming interface.

ADO OVERVIEW

For a number of years, Microsoft has implemented and supported quite a few database programming models such as *RDO (Remote Data Objects)*, *DAO (Data Access Objects)*, and most recently *ADO (ActiveX Data Objects)*.

ADO is an object-based programming model that allows programmers in many Microsoft programming languages such as Visual C++, Visual Basic, ASP (Active Server Pages), C#, and of course VBA to access and manage data sources. ADO has become Microsoft's most important and reliable method for data source connectivity, retrieval, and management.

Data sources can be as simple as text files, or they can be more sophisticated relational data sources such as Microsoft Access, Microsoft SQL Server, or even non-Microsoft databases like Oracle's RDBMS. Specifically, ADO allows you to connect to data sources that support *open database connectivity (ODBC)*. ADO also allows you to leverage the power of *structured query language (SQL)* for those data sources that support it.

Each ADO programming endeavor involves working with the ADO API, also called the *ADO object model*. An *API (application programming interface)* is a set of interfaces, or classes, that allow you to access the low-level functionality of programming models such as ADO. The ADO API consists of many objects, collections, events, methods, and properties.

Though most Microsoft programming languages support the ADO object model, there are some slight differences in how ADO is implemented and used within each language. In this chapter, you learn how ADO is implemented and used in Access VBA.

Before getting started, you may wish to familiarize yourself with some key ADO terminology and objects as outlined in Table 9.1.

TABLE 9.1   KEY ADO TERMINOLOGY

Item	Description
Connection	A connection is how you gain access to a data source. In ADO, connections are achieved through the Connection object.
Command	In ADO, commands are defined as a set of instructions such as SQL statements or a stored procedure that typically inserts, deletes, or updates data. ADO commands are embodied in the Command object.
Field	ADO recordsets contain one or more fields. ADO fields are implemented with the Field object, which contain properties for field names, data types, and values.
Parameter	Parameters allow you to use variables to pass information to commands such as SQL statements. ADO uses the Parameter object to build parameterized queries and stored procedures.
Recordset	Rows returned by a command such as a SQL statement are stored in recordsets. ADO's Recordset object allows you to iterate through the returned rows and insert, update, and delete rows in the recordset.

CONNECTING TO A DATABASE

Before you and ADO can work with data in a data source, you must first establish a connection using the Connection object. To declare variables of ADO object type, use the ADODB library name followed by a period and a specific ADO object type such as Connection. An example of declaring an ADO object variable of Connection type is seen here.

```
Dim myConnection As ADODB.Connection
```

If you're using ADO to connect to your current Microsoft Access application, you can use the CurrentProject object's AccessConnection property to set an ADO connection object to your Connection object variable. An example of connecting to a local database is shown next.

```
Private Sub cmdConnectToLocalDB_Click()

    On Error GoTo ConnectionError

    'Declare connection object variable
    Dim localConnection As ADODB.Connection

    'Set current Access connection to Connection object variable
    Set localConnection = CurrentProject.AccessConnection

    MsgBox "Local connection successfully established."

    Exit Sub

ConnectionError:

    MsgBox "There was an error connecting to the database. " & Chr(13) _
            & Err.Number & ", " & Err.Description

End Sub
```

Using the Set statement, I'm able to assign the current Access ADO connection to my Connection object variable, which is called localConnection. Note that whenever you open a connection, it's important to utilize error handling.

Many ADO programming occasions involve connecting to a remote database. Connecting to a remote database through ADO involves working with one or more Connection object properties and its Open method, as demonstrated here.

```
Private Sub cmdConnectToRemoteDB_Click()

    On Error GoTo ConnectionError

    'Declare connection object variable
    Dim remoteConnection As New ADODB.Connection
```

```
    'Assign OLEDB provider to the Provider property
    'Use the Open method to establish a connection to the database
    With remoteConnection
      .Provider = "Microsoft.Jet.OLEDB.4.0"
      .Open "C:\Documents and Settings\mivine\Desktop\home" & _
        "\tmp\current_2003\chp9\programs\chapter9.mdb"
    End With

    MsgBox "Remote connection successfully established."

    'Close the current database connection
    remoteConnection.Close

    Exit Sub

ConnectionError:

    MsgBox "There was an error connecting to the database. " & Chr(13) _
           & Err.Number & ", " & Err.Description

End Sub
```

TRICK   Remote database access using ADO can be one of two types: connecting to Access databases on your local machine or connecting to databases across the network.

Depending on the type of database you're connecting to, you use either ODBC or OLE DB as your connection provider. In the case of Microsoft Access databases, you assign an OLE DB provider name to the Connection object's Provider property. Microsoft's Jet 4.0 OLE DB provider uses the Microsoft Jet database engine to open a database in shared mode.

Once a provider has been set, use the Open method to establish a connection to your Access database. In the preceding example, I pass a connection string to the Connection object's Open method. This connection string tells ADO what my database name is and where it is located.

TRAP   When working with examples in this book, you need to change the string of the Connection object's Open method to reflect your database's name and location.

After working with the ADO object model for some time, you learn there are many programming methods for accomplishing the same task. Some ADO programmers like to use the Connection object's Properties collection to assign name/value pairs of connection attributes. As an example, the next procedure uses this technique for connecting to a remote Access database.

```
Private Sub cmdConnectToRemoteDB_Click()

    On Error GoTo ConnectionError

    'Declare connection object variable
    Dim remoteConnection As New ADODB.Connection

    'Assign OLEDB providers
    'Assign database name / location to Data Source
    'Use the Open method to establish a connection to the database
    With remoteConnection
        .Provider = "Microsoft.Access.OLEDB.10.0"
        .Properties("Data Provider").Value = "Microsoft.Jet.OLEDB.4.0"
        .Properties("Data Source").Value = _
            "C:\Documents and Settings\mivine\Desktop\home" & _
            "\tmp\current_2003\chp9\programs\chapter9.mdb"
        .Open
    End With

    MsgBox "Connection successfully established."

    remoteConnection.Close

    Exit Sub

ConnectionError:

    MsgBox "There was an error connecting to the database. " & Chr(13) _
            & Err.Number & ", " & Err.Description

End Sub
```

A common problem in beginning ADO programming is troubleshooting connection errors. One frequent error is to overlook the path and filename passed to the `Data Source` property or `Open` method. Make sure these values match correctly with the location and name of your database.

Regardless of your connection choice, you should always close your database connections using the `Connection` object's `Close` method. The ADO `Close` method frees application resources, but does not remove the object from memory. To remove objects from memory, set the object to `Nothing`.

In general, connections should be opened once when the application is first loaded (`Load` event, for example) and closed once when the application is closing (`UnLoad` event, for example).

WORKING WITH RECORDSETS

The ADO programming model uses recordsets to work with rows in a database table. Using ADO recordsets, you can add, delete, and update information in database tables.

The `Recordset` object represents all rows in a table or all rows returned by a SQL query. The `Recordset` object, however, can refer to only a single row of data at time. Once a database connection has been established, `Recordset` objects can be opened in one of three ways:

- Using the `Open` method of the `Recordset` object.
- Using the `Execute` method of the `Command` object.
- Using the `Execute` method of the `Connection` object.

The most common way of opening recordsets is through the `Open` method of a `Recordset` object.

`Recordset` object variables are declared like any other variable—using the ADODB library:

```
Dim rsEmployees As New ADODB.Recordset
```

Once a `Recordset` object variable has been declared, you can use its `Open` method to open a recordset and navigate through the result set. The `Open` method takes five arguments:

```
rsEmployees.Open Source, ActiveConnection, CursorType, LockType, Options
```

Before moving further into recordsets, let's investigate the concept of database locks and cursors and how Microsoft ADO uses them in conjunction with result sets and the `Recordset` object.

TRICK A *result set* is the set of rows retrieved by a command or SQL query. In Microsoft ADO, recordsets are embodied in the `Recordset` object, which is used to manage result sets. In an abstract sense, however, the notion of a recordset is synonymous with a result set.

INTRODUCTION TO DATABASE LOCKS

Whether or not your `Recordset` objects can update, add, or delete rows depends on your database lock type. Most RDBMS implement various forms of table and row-level locking. Database locking prevents multiple users (or processes) from updating the same row at the same time. For example, suppose both my friend and I attempt to update the same row of information at the same time. Left to its own devices, this type of simultaneous updating could cause memory problems or data loss. To solve this, very smart RDBMS developers designed sophisticated software-locking techniques using a variety of algorithms.

Even though the locking dilemma has been solved and implemented for us, ADO developers still need to identify a valid locking mechanism such as read only, batch update, optimistic, or pessimistic. These types of locking mechanisms can be specified in the `LockType` property of the `Recordset` object. Table 9.2 describes available recordset lock types.

TABLE 9.2 LOCKTYPE PROPERTY VALUES

Lock Type	Description
`adLockBatchOptimistic`	Used for batch updates.
`adLockOptimistic`	Records are locked only when the `Recordset` object's `Update` method is called. Other users can access and update the same row of data while you have it open.
`adLockPessimistic`	Records are locked as soon as record editing begins. Other users can't access or modify the row of data until you have called the `Recordset`'s `Update` or `CancelUpdate` methods.
`adLockReadOnly`	Records are read only (default lock type).

Generally speaking, most VBA programmers need decide whether their database locks should be read only or not. As a rule of thumb, use the read-only lock type (`adLockReadOnly`) when you simply need to scroll forward through a result set without modifying its contents. If you need to perform any updates on the result set, an optimistic locking solution (`adLockOptimistic`) is sufficient.

Introduction to Cursors

Since Recordset objects represent a single row of data, VBA programmers need a way to iterate through a list of rows. The ability to maneuver through a result set is implemented through database cursors.

In database terms, a *cursor* is a structure that names and manages a storage area in memory. Programmers use cursors to point to a row of data in a result set one row at a time. The concepts of a cursor and a result set are depicted in Figure 9.1.

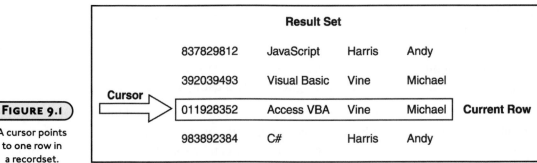

FIGURE 9.1

A cursor points to one row in a recordset.

Using a combination of other structures such as loops and objects, programmers navigate through a recordset with the cursor pointing to the current row. You can think of programming with cursors as similar to file processing (discussed in Chapter 7, "Debugging, Input Validation, File Processing, and Error Handling") where you open a data file and read one record at a time. When programming with cursors, you establish a cursor and move the cursor's pointer to one row in a recordset at a time.

When working with ADO's Recordset object, you can specify one of four cursor types in the CursorType property. Table 9.3 outlines this.

You should use forward-only (adOpenForwardOnly) cursors when updating rows is not required and reading rows in a result set from start to finish is acceptable. If you require dynamic updates (adOpenDynamic) in your result set, a dynamic cursor type is recommended.

In addition to cursor types, ADO allows programmers to specify a cursor location for the Recordset and Connection objects via the CursorLocation property. Depending on the location of your database and the size of your result set, cursor locations can have a considerable effect on your application's performance.

As outlined in Table 9.4, cursor locations can be either server side or client side.

TABLE 9.3   CURSORTYPE PROPERTY VALUES

Lock Type	Description
adOpenForwardOnly	Provides optimal performance through limited scrolling (forward only).
adOpenKeyset	Provides all types of movement in a Recordset object. Does not contain added or deleted rows.
adOpenDynamic	Provides all types of movement in a Recordset object. Includes added, deleted, and updated rows.
adOpenStatic	Provides all types of movement in a static Recordset object. Changes are not seen by users until the Recordset object is updated.

TABLE 9.4   CURSORLOCATION PROPERTY VALUES

Lock Type	Description
adUseClient	Records in the recordset are stored in local memory.
adUseServer	Builds a set of keys locally for Access databases and on the server for Microsoft SQL Server. The set of keys is used to retrieve and navigate through the result set.

When considering cursor locations, Microsoft recommends server-side cursors when working with Microsoft Access databases and client-side cursors when working with Microsoft SQL Server databases.

Retrieving and Browsing Data

Once you have successfully established a connection to a database with ADO, retrieving and browsing data is quite easy. To retrieve data with ADO, you work with the Recordset object. In addition to cursors and locks, the Recordset object has many features for managing record-based data.

In this section, I use Microsoft's sample database Northwind.mdb to demonstrate retrieving and browsing data with ADO. Figure 9.2 depicts a form I built, which remotely connects to the Northwind database and allows a user to browse through data found in the Categories table.

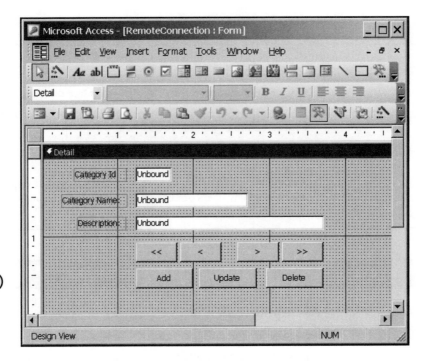

FIGURE 9.2

Using ADO to connect and browse record-based data.

To build the application seen in Figure 9.2, use the controls and properties in Table 9.5. I cover the VBA code for the Add, Update, and Delete command buttons later in the chapter.

TABLE 9.5 CONTROLS AND PROPERTIES OF THE REMOTE CONNECTION PROGRAM

Control	Property	Property Value
Form	Name	Remote Connection
	Caption	Remote Connection
	Record Selectors	No
	Navigation Buttons	No
	Dividing Lines	No
Text Box	Name	txtCategoryId
Label	Name	lblCategoryId
	Caption	Category Id:

(continues)

**TABLE 9.5 CONTROLS AND PROPERTIES OF
THE REMOTE CONNECTION PROGRAM** (CONTINUED)

Control	Property	Property Value
Text Box	Name	txtCategoryName
Label	Name	lblCategoryName
	Caption	Category Name:
Text Box	Name	txtDescription
Label	Name	lblDescription
	Caption	Description:
Command Button	Name	cmdMoveFirst
	Caption	<<
Command Button	Name	cmdMovePrevious
	Caption	<
Command Button	Name	cmdMoveNext
	Caption	>
Command Button	Name	cmdMoveLast
	Caption	>>
Command Button	Name	cmdAdd
	Caption	Add
Command Button	Name	cmdUpdate
	Caption	Update
Command Button	Name	cmdDelete
	Caption	Delete

Next, add the following VBA code to your form class module.

```
Option Compare Database

Dim remoteConnection As New ADODB.Connection
Dim rsCategories As New ADODB.Recordset
```

```vba
Private Sub Form_Load()
    Connect
    SetRecordset
End Sub
```

```vba
Private Sub Form_Unload(Cancel As Integer)
    Disconnect
End Sub
```

```vba
Public Sub Disconnect()

    On Error GoTo ConnectionError

    rsCategories.Close
    remoteConnection.Close

    Exit Sub

ConnectionError:
    MsgBox "There was an error closing the database." & _
        Err.Number & ", " & Err.Description

End Sub
```

```vba
Private Sub Connect()

    On Error GoTo ConnectionError

    With remoteConnection
        .Provider = "Microsoft.Jet.OLEDB.4.0"
        .Open "C:\Documents and Settings\mivine\" & _
            "Desktop\home\tmp\current_2003\" & _
            "Northwind Sample Database\Northwind.mdb"
    End With
```

```
    Exit Sub

ConnectionError:

    MsgBox "There was an error connecting to the database. " & _
        Chr(13) & Err.Number & ", " & Err.Description

End Sub
```

```
Public Sub SetRecordset()

    Dim sql As String

    On Error GoTo DbError

    sql = "select * from Categories"

    rsCategories.CursorType = adOpenKeyset
    rsCategories.LockType = adLockReadOnly

    rsCategories.Open sql remoteConnection, _
        , , adCmdText

    If rsCategories.EOF = False Then
        Me.txtCategoryId = rsCategories!CategoryID
        Me.txtCategoryName = rsCategories.Fields.Item("CategoryName")
        Me.txtDescription = rsCategories.Fields.Item(2)
    End If

    Exit Sub

DbError:

    MsgBox "There was an error retrieving information " & _
        "from the database." _
        & Err.Number & ", " & Err.Description

End Sub
```

I've created two procedures that handle connecting to the Northwind database and disconnecting from it. The Connect subprocedure is called during the form Load event and Disconnect subprocedure is called during the form Unload event, which is triggered when the form is closed or unloaded from memory.

TRAP When applying code from this book in your own applications, remember to change the path of the Northwind.mdb database (or any other database, for that matter) in the Open method of the Connection object.

Notice in the form's Load event that I call another subprocedure: SetRecordset. This procedure sets up my Recordset object by establishing a SQL query, opening the recordset, and applying the first row of data to the text boxes.

Keep in mind that I declared my Recordset object variable (rsCategories) as a form-level variable. This allows me to access it throughout my form class module.

Before going any further, consider the following numbered list, which describes a common process for opening a recordset with ADO:

1. Define a SQL query using a String variable, which tells the Recordset object how it should be opened.

2. Assign cursor and lock type values to corresponding Recordset object properties. Note that you can set these properties on separate lines (as I did) or in the Open method of the Recordset object.

3. Use the Open method and pass in three of five optional parameters. The first parameter (sql) tells the Recordset object how to open the recordset. In addition to SQL statements, you can use a table name surrounded by double quotes ("Categories", for example). The second parameter (remoteConnection) is the name of the active connection variable that points to my copy of the Northwind.mdb database. Note: This connection must have already been successfully opened. The last parameter is in the fifth parameter position. This is the options parameter, which tells the Recordset object how to use its first parameter. If the first parameter is a SQL string, use the constant adCmdText. If the first parameter is a table name ("Categories", for instance), use the constant adCmdTable.

4. After the Recordset object has been successfully opened, I ensure that rows have been returned by using the EOF (end of file) property. If the EOF property is true, no records were returned and no further processing is done.

5. If the `Recordset` object contains one or more rows (`EOF` = `False`), I can access fields in a couple of ways. In my example, I use the `Recordset` object name (`rsCategories`) followed by an exclamation mark (!) and then the field name found in the database table. This is probably the most common way for ADO programmers to access recordset fields. Other ways of accessing fields involve using the `Fields` collection shown here.

```
Me.txtCategoryName = rsCategories.Fields.Item("CategoryName")
Me.txtDescription = rsCategories.Fields.Item(2)
```

The first example passes a column name to the `Item` property of the `Fields` collection. The second example uses what's known as the *ordinal position* of the field returned. Ordinal positions start with 0.

Once data is successfully retrieved from a field, you can assign its value to variables or properties.

In ADO/database terms, the *ordinal position* refers to the relative position of a field or column in a collection such as `Fields`. Believe it or not, using ordinal positions for accessing fields is not uncommon in ADO. Consider an example of accessing the return value of the SQL function `Count`. Since SQL does not return a column name, you must work with ordinal position in the `Fields` collection.

Here is an example of using ordinal positions to retrieve the result of a SQL function.

```
Private Sub cmdCount_Click()

    Dim sql As String
    Dim rsCount As New ADODB.Recordset

    On Error GoTo DbError

    sql = "select count(*) from Categories"

    rsCount.Open sql, remoteConnection, adOpenForwardOnly, _
        adLockReadOnly, adCmdText

    If rsCategories.EOF = False Then
        MsgBox "There are " & rsCount.Fields.Item(0) & _
        " rows in the Categories table."
    End If
```

```
        Exit Sub

    DbError:

        MsgBox "There was an error retrieving information from the
        database." _
        & Err.Number & ", " & Err.Description

    End Sub
```

To browse through rows in a recordset, ADO's Recordset object provides the following four methods:

- MoveFirst. Moves the cursor to the first record in the result set.
- MoveLast. Moves the cursor to the last record in the result set.
- MoveNext. Moves the cursor to the next record in the result set.
- MovePrevious. Moves the cursor to the previous record in the result set.

When working with the MoveNext and MovePrevious methods, it's important to use cursors that allow forward and backward scrolling. Also, you need to check that the cursor's position is not already at the beginning of the recordset before moving to a previous entry or at the end of the recordset before moving to the next entry. Use the Recordset object's AbsolutePosition and RecordCount properties for these conditions.

The AbsolutePosition property contains the ordinal position of the current record in the result set. The AbsolutePosition property contains a whole number beginning at 1. The RecordCount property contains the total number of rows contained in the recordset.

Using these properties and methods, you can build conditions for browsing through ADO records. To demonstrate, I continue my Remote Connection program by adding VBA/ADO code to the following four event procedures.

```
Private Sub cmdMoveFirst_Click()

    On Error GoTo DbError

    'Move to the first record in the result set.
    rsCategories.MoveFirst
    Me.txtCategoryId = rsCategories!CategoryID
    Me.txtCategoryName = rsCategories!CategoryName
    Me.txtDescription = rsCategories!Description
```

```
        Exit Sub

DbError:

        MsgBox "There was an error retrieving information " & _
            "from the database." _
            & Err.Number & ", " & Err.Description

End Sub
```

```
Private Sub cmdMoveLast_Click()

        On Error GoTo DbError

        'Move to the last record in the result set.
        rsCategories.MoveLast
        Me.txtCategoryId = rsCategories!CategoryID
        Me.txtCategoryName = rsCategories!CategoryName
        Me.txtDescription = rsCategories!Description

        Exit Sub

DbError:

        MsgBox "There was an error retrieving information " & _
            "from the database." _
            & Err.Number & ", " & Err.Description

End Sub
```

```
Private Sub cmdMoveNext_Click()

        On Error GoTo DbError
```

```
'Move to the next record in the result set if the cursor is not
'already at the last record.
If rsCategories.AbsolutePosition < _
    rsCategories.RecordCount Then

    rsCategories.MoveNext
    Me.txtCategoryId = rsCategories!CategoryID
    Me.txtCategoryName = rsCategories!CategoryName
    Me.txtDescription = rsCategories!Description

End If

Exit Sub

DbError:

MsgBox "There was an error retrieving information " & _
    "from the database." _
    & Err.Number & ", " & Err.Description

End Sub
```

```
Private Sub cmdMovePrevious_Click()

On Error GoTo DbError

'Move to the previous record in the result set, if the
'current record is not the first record.
If rsCategories.AbsolutePosition > 1 Then

    rsCategories.MovePrevious
    Me.txtCategoryId = rsCategories!CategoryID
    Me.txtCategoryName = rsCategories!CategoryName
    Me.txtDescription = rsCategories!Description

End If
```

```
    Exit Sub

DbError:

    MsgBox "There was an error retrieving information " & _
        "from the database." _
        & Err.Number & ", " & Err.Description

End Sub
```

Updating Records

Updating records using ADO's `Recordset` object is relatively easy. Generally speaking, you perform the following tasks:

1. Declare a new `Recordset` object variable.
2. Define and create a SQL string that identifies the record you want to update.
3. Assign updatable cursor and lock types for updating a record.
4. Open the recordset, which should contain only one record, the record you wish to update.
5. Assign new data to the recordset fields.
6. Update the recordset using the `Recordset` object's `Update` method.
7. Close the recordset using the `Recordset` object's `Close` method.
8. Refresh other recordsets, if applicable, by closing and reopening the recordset or calling the `Recordset` object's `Requery` method.

The tricky part in updating records is ensuring that your SQL queries are well defined. For example, to update a record in the `Categories` table of the `Northwind` database, I want to qualify my recordset using the table's primary key. In this case that's the `CategoryID` field.

```
sql = "select * from Categories where CategoryID = " & _
    Val(Me.txtCategoryId.Value)
```

In the preceding SQL string, I assign the value of the text box containing the category ID. Since I'm using a `String` variable, I can build a dynamic SQL statement using control properties—input from the user. By using a condition in my SQL string and supplying it with the primary key of a record, I'm making sure that only the record with the primary key is contained in the result set.

When concatenating string or text values to a dynamic SQL statement, you must use single quotes inside of double quotes to surround the expression.

```
sql = "select * from Categories where CategoryName = '" & _

    Val(Me.txtCategoryName.Value) & "'"
```

You may be asking yourself, "How do I know what record to update?" The answer to this question is based on the record selected in the graphical interface. So long as your GUI allows a user to select only one record, you are in good shape. To demonstrate, I now add VBA/ADO code to the Update command button's Click event in the Remote Connection program.

```
Private Sub cmdUpdate_Click()

    Dim sql As String
    Dim rsUpdate As New ADODB.Recordset

    On Error GoTo DbError

    'Build dynamic SQL statement based on record
    'selected by the user.
    sql = "select * from Categories where CategoryID = " & _
        Val(Me.txtCategoryId.Value)

    'Assign updatable cursor and lock type properties.
    rsUpdate.CursorType = adOpenDynamic
    rsUpdate.LockType = adLockOptimistic

    'Open the Recordset object.
    rsUpdate.Open sql, remoteConnection, , , adCmdText

    'Don't try to update the record, if the recordset
    'did not find a row.
    If rsUpdate.EOF = False Then

        'Update the record based on input from the user.
        With rsUpdate
            !CategoryName = Me.txtCategoryName
            !Description = Me.txtDescription
```

```
            .Update
            .Close
        End With

    End If

    MsgBox "Record updated.", vbInformation

    'Close the form-level Recordset object and
    'refresh it to include the newly updated row.
    rsCategories.Close
    SetRecordset

    Exit Sub

DbError:

    MsgBox "There was an error updating the database." _
        & Err.Number & ", " & Err.Description

End Sub
```

 The Recordset object's Update method is synonymous with saving.

Adding Records

Adding records with ADO does not necessarily require the use of SQL queries. In most scenarios, you simply need a record added to a table based on user input. In the simplest form, records are added to tables using the following steps:

1. Declare a new Recordset object variable.
2. Assign updatable cursor and lock types for adding a record.
3. Open the Recordset object using its Open method with a table name as the first parameter and the associated adCmdTable constant name for the options parameter.
4. Call the Recordset object's AddNew method.

5. Assign new data to the recordset fields.
6. Save the new row of data using the Recordset object's Update method.
7. Close the recordset using the Recordset object's Close method.
8. Refresh other recordsets, if applicable, by closing and reopening the recordset or calling the Recordset object's Requery method.

Using the preceding steps, the following code implements the Click event procedure of the Add command button from Figure 9.2.

```
Private Sub cmdAdd_Click()

    Dim sql As String
    Dim rsAdd As New ADODB.Recordset

    On Error GoTo DbError

    'Assign updatable cursor and lock type properties.
    rsAdd.CursorType = adOpenDynamic
    rsAdd.LockType = adLockOptimistic

    'Open the Recordset object.
    rsAdd.Open "Categories", remoteConnection, , , adCmdTable

    'Add the record based on input from the user
    '(except for the AutoNumber primary key field).
    With rsAdd
        .AddNew
        !CategoryName = Me.txtCategoryName
        !Description = Me.txtDescription
        .Update
        .Close
    End With

    MsgBox "Record Added.", vbInformation

    'Close the form-level Recordset object and refresh
    'it to include the newly updated row.
```

```
    rsCategories.Close
    SetRecordset

    Exit Sub

DbError:

    MsgBox "There was an error adding the record." _
        & Err.Number & ", " & Err.Description

End Sub
```

Deleting Records

Deleting records using ADO is somewhat similar to updating records in that you need to use SQL queries to identify the record for updating—in this case, deleting. The numbered steps identify a typical ADO algorithm for deleting a record:

1. Declare a new Recordset object variable.
2. Assign updatable cursor and lock types for deleting a record.
3. Construct a dynamic SQL string that uses a condition to retrieve the record selected by the user. The condition should use a field, which is a key (unique) value selected by the user.
4. Open the recordset, which should contain only one record (the record you wish to delete).
5. If the record was found, call the Recordset object's Delete method.
6. Save the record operation using the Recordset object's Update method.
7. Close the recordset using the Recordset object's Close method.
8. Refresh other recordsets, if applicable, by closing and reopening the recordset or calling the Recordset object's Requery method.

Using these steps, I can implement ADO program code in the Click event procedure of the Delete command button shown in Figure 9.2.

```
Private Sub cmdDelete_Click()

    Dim sql As String
    Dim rsDelete As New ADODB.Recordset
```

```
On Error GoTo DbError

'Build dynamic SQL statement based on
'record selected by the user.
sql = "select * from Categories where CategoryID = " & _
    Val(Me.txtCategoryId.Value)"

'Assign updatable cursor and lock type properties.
rsDelete.CursorType = adOpenDynamic
rsDelete.LockType = adLockOptimistic

'Open the Recordset object.
rsDelete.Open sql, remoteConnection, , , adCmdText

'Don't try to delete the record, if the
'recordset did not find a row.
If rsDelete.EOF = False Then

    'Update the record based on input from the user.
    With rsDelete
        .Delete
        .Update
        .Close
    End With

End If

MsgBox "Record deleted.", vbInformation

'Close the form-level Recordset object and refresh
'it to include the newly updated row.
rsCategories.Close
SetRecordset

Exit Sub

DbError:
```

```
MsgBox "There was an error deleting the record." _
    & Err.Number & ", " & Err.Description

End Sub
```

CHAPTER PROGRAM: CHOOSE MY ADVENTURE

Without a doubt, Choose My Adventure is one of my favorites of the programs I've built for any of my *Absolute Beginner* books. Choose My Adventure uses ADO programming techniques to access tables that contain a short story. The story presents questions on various pages and allows the reader to select an outcome. Depending on the selected outcome, the reader gets a different story and ending.

I used two forms to build Choose My Adventure—one to show about details (see Figure 9.3) and the other to house the program's main functionality (see Figure 9.4). Controls and properties of the Choose My Adventure About form is shown next.

FIGURE 9.3

The About form of the Choose My Adventure program.

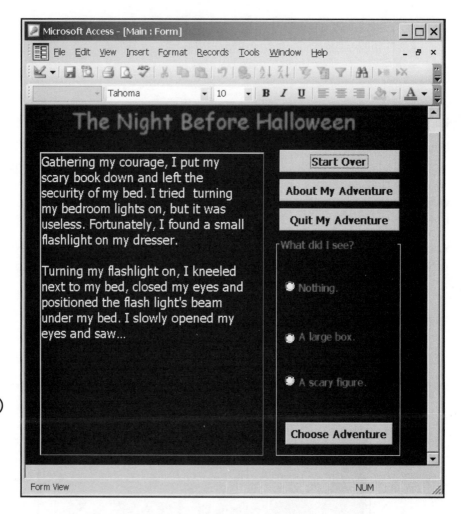

FIGURE 9.4

Using chapter-based concepts to build the Choose My Adventure program.

There is minimal code required for the About form, which uses the DoCmd object's Close method to close the form.

```
Private Sub cmdOK_Click()
    DoCmd.Close acForm, "About"
End Sub
```

The core functionality of the Choose My Adventure program is contained in the Main form with controls and properties described in Table 9.7.

TABLE 9.6 CONTROLS AND PROPERTIES OF THE ABOUT FORM

Control	Property	Property Value
Form	Name	About
	Caption	Chapter 9
	Record Selectors	No
	Navigation Buttons	No
	Dividing Lines	No
Image	Name	imgBanner
	Picture	banner.jpg (located on CD)
	Size Mode	Stretch
Image	Name	imgSkeleton
	Picture	skeleton.jpg (located on CD)
	Size Mode	Stretch
Label	Name	lblAbout
	Caption	A Choose My Adventure book
Command Button	Name	cmdOK
	Caption	OK

TABLE 9.7 CONTROLS AND PROPERTIES OF THE MAIN FORM

Control	Property	Property Value
Form	Name	Main
	Caption	Chapter 9
	Record Selectors	No
	Navigation Buttons	No
	Dividing Lines	No
Image	Name	imgBanner
	Picture	banner.jpg (located on CD)
	Size Mode	Stretch

(continues)

	TABLE 9.7 CONTROLS AND PROPERTIES OF THE MAIN FORM (CONTINUED)	
Control	**Property**	**Property Value**
Text Box	Name	txtPage
	Enter Key Behavior	New Line in Field
Command Button	Name	cmdRead
	Caption	Start Over
Command Button	Name	cmdAbout
	Caption	About My Adventure
Command Button	Name	cmdQuit
	Caption	Quit My Adventure
Command Button	Name	cmdChoose
	Caption	Choose Adventure
Frame	Name	fraQuestionAndOutcomes
Frame Label	Name	lblQuestion
Option Button	Name	optOption1
Option Button Label	Name	lblOption1
Option Button	Name	optOption2
Option Button Label	Name	lblOption2
Option Button	Name	optOption3
Option Button Label	Name	lblOption3

All of the code required to implement the Choose My Adventure Main form follows.

```
Option Compare Database
Option Explicit

'Declare form-level Connection object variable.
Dim localConnection As ADODB.Connection
```

```
Private Sub cmdAbout_Click()
    'Show the About form.
    DoCmd.OpenForm "About"
End Sub
```

```
Private Sub cmdChoose_Click()
    ' Use the assigned option button value to get
    ' the next page in the book.
    GetPage Me.fraQuestionAndOutcomes.Value
End Sub
```

```
Private Sub cmdQuit_Click()
    'Quit the application.
    DoCmd.Quit
End Sub
```

```
Private Sub cmdRead_Click()

    MsgBox "Welcome to The Night Before Halloween, " & _
            " a Choose My Adventure book by Michael Vine.", _
            vbOKOnly, "Chapter 9 - Database Programming with ADO"

    Me.cmdRead.Caption = "Start Over"
    ResetForm
    Me.txtPage.Value = ""
    Me.lblQuestion.Caption = ""
    Me.cmdChoose.Visible = False

    'Call the GetPage procedure to display the
    'first page in the book.
    GetPage 1

End Sub
```

```
Private Sub Form_Load()

    'Perform some initial setup.
    ResetForm
    Me.txtPage.Value = ""
    Me.lblQuestion.Caption = ""
    Me.cmdChoose.Visible = False
    Me.cmdRead.Caption = "Read My Adventure"

    'Assign the current Access connection to my
    'Connection object variable.
    Set localConnection = CurrentProject.AccessConnection

End Sub
```

```
Private Sub Form_Unload(Cancel As Integer)

    On Error GoTo ErrorClosing

    'Close the connection.
    localConnection.Close

    Exit Sub

ErrorClosing:
    'Do nothing!

End Sub
```

```
Public Sub GetQuestion(pageID As Integer)

    Dim rsQuestion As New ADODB.Recordset
    Dim sql As String

    On Error GoTo BookError
```

```
'Using the incoming pageID, get and display
'the associated question (if one exists).
'This procedure calls the GetOutcome procedure.
sql = "select * from Questions where PageID = " & pageID

rsQuestion.Open sql, localConnection, adOpenForwardOnly, _
    adLockReadOnly, adCmdText

If rsQuestion.EOF = False Then

    Me.lblQuestion.Caption = rsQuestion!Question
    GetOutcome rsQuestion!questionID

Else

    ResetForm

End If

rsQuestion.Close

Exit Sub

BookError:

    ErrorMessage

End Sub
```

```
Public Sub GetOutcome(questionID As Integer)

    Dim rsOutcomes As New ADODB.Recordset
    Dim x As Integer

    Dim sql As String

    On Error GoTo BookError
```

```
'Using the incoming questionID, get all possible outcomes
'for the associated question.
sql = "select * from Outcomes where QuestionID = " & _
    questionID

rsOutcomes.Open sql, localConnection, adOpenForwardOnly, _
    adLockReadOnly, adCmdText

ResetForm

If rsOutcomes.EOF = False Then

    Me.lblOption1.Visible = True
    Me.optOption1.Visible = True
    Me.lblOption1.Caption = rsOutcomes!Outcome
    Me.optOption1.OptionValue = rsOutcomes!GoToPage
    rsOutcomes.MoveNext

End If

If rsOutcomes.EOF = False Then

    Me.lblOption2.Visible = True
    Me.optOption2.Visible = True
    Me.lblOption2.Caption = rsOutcomes!Outcome
    Me.optOption2.OptionValue = rsOutcomes!GoToPage
    rsOutcomes.MoveNext

End If

If rsOutcomes.EOF = False Then

    Me.lblOption3.Visible = True
    Me.optOption3.Visible = True
    Me.lblOption3.Caption = rsOutcomes!Outcome
    Me.optOption3.OptionValue = rsOutcomes!GoToPage

End If
```

```
    rsOutcomes.Close

    Exit Sub

BookError:

    ErrorMessage

End Sub
```

```
Public Function AnyMoreQuestions(pageID As Integer) As Boolean


    Dim rsAnyMoreQuestions As New ADODB.Recordset
    Dim returnValue As Boolean
    Dim sql As String

    On Error GoTo BookError

    'This procedure is called by the GetPage procedure.
    'It checks to see if there are any more questions
    'for the current page passed in.
    sql = "select * from Questions where PageID = " & pageID

    rsAnyMoreQuestions.Open sql, localConnection, _
        adOpenForwardOnly, adLockReadOnly, adCmdText

    If rsAnyMoreQuestions.EOF = False Then
        returnValue = True   'There are questions
    Else
        returnValue = False 'There are no questions
    End If

    rsAnyMoreQuestions.Close

    AnyMoreQuestions = returnValue

    Exit Function
```

```
BookError:

    ErrorMessage

End Function
```

```
Public Sub GetPage(pageID As Integer)

    Dim rsPage As New ADODB.Recordset
    Dim sql As String

    On Error GoTo BookError

    'Gets and displays the requested page. Calls GetQuestion
    'and AnyMoreQuestions procedures.
    sql = "select * from Pages where PageID = " & pageID

    rsPage.Open sql, localConnection, adOpenForwardOnly, _
        adLockReadOnly, adCmdText

    If rsPage.EOF = False Then
        Me.txtPage.Visible = True
        Me.txtPage.Value = rsPage!Content
    End If

    GetQuestion rsPage!pageID

    Me.txtPage.SetFocus

    If AnyMoreQuestions(rsPage!pageID) = False Then

        Me.cmdChoose.Visible = False
        Me.lblQuestion.Caption = ""

    Else
```

```
        Me.cmdChoose.Visible = True

    End If

    rsPage.Close

    Exit Sub

BookError:

    ErrorMessage

End Sub
```

```
Public Sub ErrorMessage()

    'A general error bin called by each error handler
    'in the form class.
    MsgBox "There was an error reading the book. " & Chr(13) _
        & Err.Number & ", " & Err.Description

End Sub
```

```
Public Sub ResetForm()

    Me.lblOption1.Visible = False
    Me.lblOption2.Visible = False
    Me.lblOption3.Visible = False
    Me.optOption1.Visible = False
    Me.optOption2.Visible = False
    Me.optOption3.Visible = False

End Sub
```

CHAPTER SUMMARY

- ADO is Microsoft's popular programming vehicle for managing data in databases such as Microsoft Access, SQL Server, and non-Microsoft relational databases such as Oracle.
- ADO's application programming interface (API) is made up of many objects such as Connection and Recordset and collections such as the Fields collection.
- It is good programming practice to use error handling whenever accessing a database through ADO.
- Connections to databases are established through ADO's Connection object.
- A result set is the set of rows retrieved by a command or SQL query.
- The Recordset object is used to work with rows in a database table.
- Database locking prevents multiple users (or processes) from updating the same row at the same time.
- A cursor is a structure that names and manages a storage area in memory. Programmers use cursors to point to one row of data at a time in a result set.
- The Recordset object methods MoveFirst, MoveLast, MoveNext, and MovePrevious are used to browse through records in a result set.
- Use the Recordset object properties AbsolutePosition and RecordCount to determine if the cursor position is at the end or beginning of a recordset.
- The Recordset object method Update is synonymous with saving a record.
- The Recordset object method AddNew is used to add a row to a table.
- The Recordset object method Delete is used to delete a row from a table.

PROGRAMMING CHALLENGES

1. Create a new Microsoft Access database application. Use the ADO `Connection` object to connect to a remote `Northwind.mdb` database. Display a successful confirmation in a message box. Use error handling to catch any connection errors.

2. Add controls to a form that mimics fields contained in Microsoft's `Northwind` `Products` table. Use ADO programming techniques to retrieve and fully browse the `Products` table. See Figure 9.2 for an example graphical user interface.

3. Update your application from Challenge 2 to allow a user to update records in the `Products` table.

4. Update your application from Challenge 2 to allow a user to add records to the `Products` table.

5. Update your application from Challenge 2 to allow a user to delete records from the `Products` table.

6. Build your own `Choose My Adventure` program with a unique story, questions, and outcomes.

OBJECT-ORIENTED PROGRAMMING WITH ACCESS VBA

H ave you ever wondered how VBA objects, methods, properties, and collections are created? Well, this chapter shows you how to leverage the power of *object-oriented programming* (also known as *OOP*) in Access VBA to create your very own custom objects, methods, properties, and collections!

INTRODUCTION TO OBJECT-ORIENTED PROGRAMMING

Object-oriented programming (OOP) is not a language unto itself, but rather a programming practice. OOP is seemingly easy at the surface, but can be quite challenging to master. In fact, many programmers coming from the procedural world of languages such as C or COBOL find they need to make a paradigm shift in how they think about programming. Even programmers who work with object-based languages such as VBA find the same paradigm shift inevitable. The paradigm shift I refer to is that of relating data, structures, and business requirements to objects.

OOP contains five core concepts, which are objects, classes, encapsulation, inheritance, and polymorphism:

- **Objects** represent a real-world thing such as person, place, or thing. Objects have behaviors and attributes.

- **Classes** are the blueprint for objects. They define how objects behave and how they expose attributes.

- **Encapsulation** hides implementation details from a user.
- **Inheritance** allows one class to inherit the features of another class.
- **Polymorphism** allows a class to implement the same operation in a number of different ways.

Unfortunately, VBA does not support inheritance or polymorphism in OOP's truest sense. Nevertheless, object-oriented programming in VBA allows the implementation of one of the most important benefits of OOP development known as encapsulation. In OOP terms, *encapsulation* allows programmers to reduce code complexity by hiding data and complex structures in classes. You and other programmers simply *instantiate* (create an object from a class) these classes as objects and access the object's methods and properties. Encapsulating implementation details is a wonderful benefit of OOP. Not only are complex details hidden, but code reuse is promoted. In VBA, OOP development is achieved through custom objects that are defined in class modules. Once built, custom objects don't necessarily add new functionality to your code. In fact, the same code you write in class modules could be written in event procedures, subprocedures, and function procedures. The purpose of using class modules is to provide encapsulation, code-reuse, and self-documenting code. Programmers using your custom objects work with them just as they would with other built-in VBA objects such as the ones found in the ADO library (Connection and Recordset objects).

Development with OOP generally requires more planning up front than in other programming paradigms. This design phase is crucial to OOP and your system's success.

At the very minimum, OOP design includes the following tasks:

- Identify and map objects to programming and business requirements.
- Identify the *actions* (methods) and *attributes* (properties) of each object. This action is commonly referred to as *identifying the responsibilities* of each object.
- Identify the relationships between objects.
- Determine the scope of objects and their methods and properties.

CREATING CUSTOM OBJECTS

You begin your investigation into object-oriented programming by creating custom objects that encapsulate implementation details. To create custom objects, VBA programmers use OOP techniques and class modules. You specially learn how to build class modules that contain member variables and property and method procedures. After learning how to build custom objects with class modules, you see how to instantiate custom objects and access custom object methods and properties.

Working with Class Modules

Classes are the blueprints for an object. They contain the implementation details, which are hidden from *users* (programmers who use your custom objects). In object-oriented programming with VBA, classes are implemented as class modules.

Class modules do not exist in memory. Rather, the instance of the class known as the object does. Multiple instances of a single class can be created. Each *instance* (object) created from a class shares the same access to the class's methods and properties. Even though multiple objects created from one class share the same characteristics, they are different in two ways. First, objects instantiated from the same class can have different property values. For example, an object called Bob instantiated from the Person class may have its hairColor property value set to brown, whereas an object called Sue, also instantiated from the Person class, could have its hairColor property value set to blond. Second, objects instantiated from the same class have unique memory addresses.

TRICK

In OOP terms, an *instance* refers to the object that was created from a class. The term *instantiate* means to create an object from a class.

To create a class module in Access VBA, simply open a Visual Basic window (VBE) and select the Class Module menu item from the Insert menu. Microsoft VBA automatically creates the class module for you as depicted in Figure 10.1.

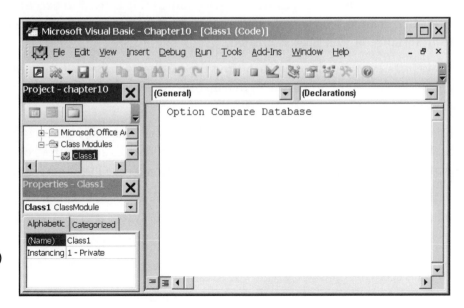

FIGURE 10.1

A newly created class module.

By default, VBA class modules contain two events called Initialize and Terminate. These events can be accessed through the Code window shown in Figure 10.2.

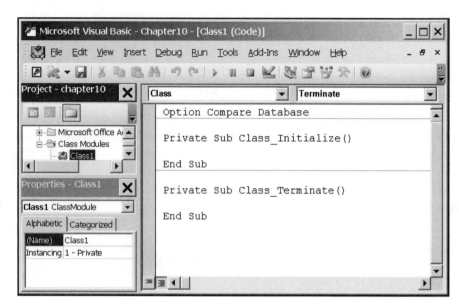

FIGURE 10.2

The Initialize and Terminate events are accessed through the VBE Code window.

The Initialize event for a class module is triggered each time the class is instantiated (created) using the New or Set keywords. The class module's Initialize event is similar to that of a constructor in OOP languages such as Java and C++. It is used to execute code when the object is first created. For example, you may wish to initialize certain member variables each time an instance of your class is created.

The Terminate event is triggered each time the instance is removed from memory. You can place code in this event procedure to free up other objects from memory or finalize any necessary transactions.

Another common use of the Initialize and Terminate events is in debugging your applications. If you'd like to know each time your application creates and destroys one of your custom objects, simply use the Initialize and Terminate events, like I've done here.

```
Private Sub Class_Initialize()

    Debug.Print "Object created."

End Sub
```

```
Private Sub Class_Terminate()

    Debug.Print "Object destroyed."

End Sub
```

 TRAP Microsoft recommends *not* using message boxes in the Initialize and Terminate events, which requires Windows messages to be processed.

Property Procedures

VBA provides property procedures for managing the attributes of a class, which are exposed internally for the class to use or exposed externally as object properties. Simply put, properties are just variables. You could simply declare variables in your class modules for your procedures to use, but that would defeat the purpose of object-oriented programming.

To work with properties in VBA, you create variables of various scopes and use a combination of property procedures to manage them. VBA provides three types of property procedures:

* Property Get. Returns the value of a property.
* Property Let. Assigns a value to the property.
* Property Set. Sets the value of an object property.

Property Get procedures are often used in conjunction with both Property Let and Property Set procedures. When used together, a Property Let procedure with a Property Get procedure or a Property Set procedure with a Property Get procedure must share the same name. Property Let and Property Set procedures, however, cannot be used together. They perform distinctly different roles in VBA object-oriented programming. Simply put, Property Let procedures are used for assigning data to scalar variables such as String, Integer, Double, or Date data types. Property Set procedures are used for assigning a reference to an object.

To add property procedures to your class module, select the Add Procedure dialog window from the VBE Insert menu to add property procedures as demonstrated in Figure 10.3.

VBA automatically adds a matching set of Property Get and Property Let procedures for you, as shown next:

```
Public Property Get Something() As Variant

End Property
```

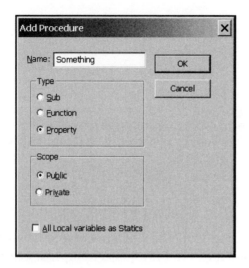

FIGURE 10.3

Use the Add Procedure dialog window to create property procedures.

```
Public Property Let Something(ByVal vNewValue As Variant)

End Property
```

The code required in each property procedure is short. You simply add a line to each respective procedure to assign a value and return a value.

Before adding code to your property procedures, you must first have a property (sometimes referred to as *member variables*) to manage. When working with property procedures, your properties are generally declared as Private in the general declarations area. By declaring the variable (property) in the general declarations area, you provide access to the property from any procedure in the class module. Declaring the variable (property) as Private provides encapsulation. Specifically, it forces your object's users to use the property procedures to access the member variable instead of accessing the member variable directly.

The concept of private properties and procedures is very important in OOP. Any procedure or property declared as Private is only accessible to the class module (not instances of your class module). Examine this concept further by studying the next block of VBA code.

```
Option Compare Database

Private privateSomething As Variant
```

```
Public Property Get something() As Variant

    something = privateSomething

End Property
```

```
Public Property Let something(ByVal vNewValue As Variant)

    privateSomething = vNewValue

End Property
```

Notice that the `Property Get` procedure behaves much like a `Function` procedure in that a value is assigned to the procedure's name. This type of assignment statement returns the property's value to the calling procedure. The `Property Let` procedure takes a single argument as a parameter and assigns its value to the `Private` property. This is how instantiated objects of this class access the `privateSomething` property without knowing how it's declared or what its name is.

The previous code blocks typify a *read/write property*. In other words, instantiated objects of this class can read this property and write data to it. It's common, however, to require read-only properties in OOP. To do so, simply use a single `Property Get` procedure by removing the corresponding `Property Let` procedure.

```
Option Compare Database

Private readOnlySomething As Variant
```

```
Public Property Get something() As Variant

    something = readOnlySomething

End Property
```

Using the `Private` property and a single `Property Get` procedure, instantiated objects of this class can only read the property.

You can also use the Add Procedure dialog window to create matching `Property Set` and `Property Get` procedures. After VBA has created the matching property procedures, simply change the keyword `Let` to `Set`.

```
Option Compare Database

Private employee As Employee
```

```
Public Property Get NewEmployee() As Variant

    NewEmployee = employee

End Property
```

```
Public Property Set NewEmployee(ByVal vNewValue As Employee)

    employee = vNewValue

End Property
```

Instead of a `Variant` data type (or any other data type, for that matter), the `Property Set` procedure called `NewEmployee` takes in a parameter of `Employee` type. The `Property Set` procedure then assigns the object reference from the argument to the property of the same object type. A matching `Property Get` procedure is used to return an object reference of the property.

You've probably noticed by now that these procedures are very simple. That's because they should be! The primary purpose of property procedures is to manage access to member variables. It may seem like overkill for what appears to be variable access, but in sections to come and through practice you see the power of property encapsulation through property procedures.

Method Procedures

Method procedures expose methods internally to the class module or externally to an instance of the class. They are the meat and potatoes of object-oriented programming!

Creating methods for custom objects is quite easy. Simply create and place `Sub` or `Function` procedures in your class modules to represent methods.

Remember from earlier in the book that function procedures return a value and subprocedures do not.

An example of each type of method is shown next.

```
Option Compare Database

Private result1 As Integer
Private result2 As Integer
```

```
Public Sub AddTwoNumbers(num1 As Integer, num2 As Integer)

    result1 = num1 + num2

End Sub
```

```
Public Function MultiplyTwoNumbers(num1 As Integer, num2 As Integer) As Double

    MultiplyTwoNumbers = num1 * num2

End Function
```

The first method, AddTwoNumbers, takes two parameters and sets a property. If it's necessary for instances of this class to access this result, you should create a Property Get procedure that returns the value of the result1 member variable.

The second method, MultiplyTwoNumbers, is a function that also takes two arguments and performs a simple calculation. The big difference is that this method is a function, which returns a value to the calling procedure by assigning a value to the method's name.

To get a better understanding of object methods, consider the Connection object from the ADO library. The Connection object has a method called Open. You and I both know that this method establishes a connection to a database. But do we know how that method is implemented? No, we don't. And believe it or not, that's a good thing. Think about all the programming that must be involved to implement the Open method of the Connection object. It's a sure bet that it contains complicated data structures and algorithms. This is encapsulation at its finest. Because the implementation detail is hidden, VBA programmers can simply call the method and pass it a few parameters to successfully open a database connection.

You can, of course, encapsulate the ADO library even further by writing your own classes to hide the dirty details of ADO programming. To demonstrate, imagine that a friend familiar with VBA but not with ADO asks for your expertise in developing database connectivity. You agree to help by creating a class that performs all details of ADO programming for connecting to a database. You start your program design by thinking about what would be easiest for your colleague to use. During design, you decide to create a new class called DbConnection that takes care of all facets of connecting to a database and providing connection objects. Your DbConnection class provides methods to connect and close the database connection and provides properties to access the ADO Connection object. After careful design, your class and its methods and properties look something like the following code.

```
Option Compare Database

Private cnn As New ADODB.Connection
```

```
Public Sub OpenConnection(dbPath_ As String)

    On Error GoTo ConnectionError

    'Assign OLEDB provider to the Provider property.
    'Use the Open method to establish a connection to the database.
    With cnn
        .Provider = "Microsoft.Jet.OLEDB.4.0"
        .Open dbPath_
    End With

    Exit Sub

ConnectionError:

    MsgBox "There was an error connecting to the database. " & Chr(13) _
            & Err.Number & ", " & Err.Description

End Sub
```

```
Public Sub CloseConnection()

    On Error GoTo ConnectionError:
```

```
    'Close the database connection.
    cnn.Close

    Exit Sub

ConnectionError:

    MsgBox "There was an error connecting to the database. " & Chr(13) _
        & Err.Number & ", " & Err.Description

End Sub
```

```
Public Property Get ConnectionObject () As Variant

    'Return an object reference of the Connection object.
    Set ConnectionObject = cnn

End Property
```

This simple class, which contains two methods (CloseConnection and OpenConnection) and one property (ConnectionObject), encapsulates the ADO programming required to manage a database connection. In the next section, you see how easy it is for your friend to use your class for managing a database connection.

Creating and Working with New Instances

Once you've created a new class module, it becomes an available object type for you to use when declaring variables. Using the DbConnection class from the preceding section, I can declare an object variable in a Form Class module of DbConnection type.

```
Private Sub Form_Load()

    'Declare object variable as DbConnection type.
    Dim db As New DbConnection

    'Open the database connection.
    db.OpenConnection ("C:\temp\myDatabase.mdb")

End Sub
```

You can easily see how little code it takes to open a connection with the ADO programming encapsulated in the DbConnection class. Users of the DbConnection class need only know what methods and properties to utilize rather than concern themselves with the specific ADO implementation details.

Working with object methods and properties is pretty straightforward. If you've been working with VBA even a little, you've already had exposure to objects and their properties and methods. When object methods or properties return an object reference, you need to decide how the returned object reference is to be used. For example, the DbConnection class contains a Property Get procedure called ConnectionObject that returns a reference of the current ADO Connection object.

```
Public Property Get ConnectionObject() As Variant

    'Return an object reference of the Connection object.
    Set ConnectionObject= cnn


End Property
```

This property procedure appears as a property of the object when an instance of the class is created. Because this property returns an object reference, I use a Set statement to retrieve and assign the object reference to another object.

```
Private Sub Form_Load()

    Dim db As New DbConnection
    Dim newConnection As New ADODB.Connection

    db.OpenConnection ("C:\temp\myDatabase.mdb")

    'Returns an object reference.
    Set newConnection = db.ConnectionObject


End Sub
```

Another example of using the DbConnection class's ConnectionObject property is to use it as an argument by passing it into methods for recordset processing. To demonstrate, I added a new method (function procedure) called ReturnAThing to my DbConnection class, which takes an ADO Connection object as an argument.

```
Public Function ReturnAThing(cnn_ As ADODB.Connection) As Variant

    Dim rs As New ADODB.Recordset
    Dim thing As Variant
    Dim sql As String

    On Error GoTo DbError

    'Generate SQL string.
    sql = "select thing from AThing"

    'Open the read only / forward only recordset using SQL and the
    'Connection object passed in.
    rs.Open sql, cnn_, adOpenForwardOnly, adLockReadOnly, _
        adCmdText

    If rs.EOF = False Then
        thing = rs!thing
    End If

    rs.Close

    'Return the thing back to the calling procedure.
    ReturnAThing = thing

    Exit Function

DbError:

    MsgBox "There was an error retrieving a thing from " & _
            " the database. " & Chr(13) _
            & Err.Number & ", " & Err.Description

End Function
```

I can now use this method and the ConnectionObject property in the form class module to return a thing.

```
Private Sub Form_Load()

    Dim db As New DbConnection
    Dim myThing As Variant
    Dim newConnection As New ADODB.connection

    db.OpenConnection ("C:\temp\myDatabase.mdb")

    myThing = db.ReturnAThing(db.ConnectionObject)

End Sub
```

Passing ADO Connection objects to methods allows me to be flexible in the type of connection (database) used in recordset processing. If users of my class are fluent in SQL or the database structure, I might add another parameter to the ReturnAThing method. This new parameter could be a SQL string or part of a SQL string, which allows users to define what they want from the database or from where they want it.

An important part of working with object instances is freeing and reclaiming resources when your objects are no longer required. When objects are instantiated, VBA reserves memory and resources for processing. To free these resources, simply set the object to Nothing.

```
Private Sub Form_Load()

    Dim db As New DbConnection
    Dim myThing As Variant
    Dim newConnection As New ADODB.connection

    db.OpenConnection ("C:\temp\myDatabase.mdb")

    myThing = db.ReturnAThing(db.ConnectionObject)

    'Reclaim object resources
    Set db = Nothing

End Sub
```

It's good programming practice to reclaim resources not only from custom objects but from built-in objects such as the ones found in the ADO library. If you neglect to free object resources, VBA does not remove them from memory until the application is terminated. If your application uses a lot of objects, this can certainly lead to performance problems.

WORKING WITH COLLECTIONS

Collections are a data structure similar to arrays in that they allow you to refer to a grouping of items as one entity. Collections, however, provide an ordered means for grouping not only strings and numbers, but objects as well. As demonstrated next, the Collection object is used to create a collection data structure.

```
Dim myCollection As New Collection
```

Collections are popular data structures in object-oriented programming because they allow the grouping of objects using an ordered name/value pair. In fact, collections are objects themselves!

Items in a collection are referred to as *members*. All collection objects have one property and three methods for managing members, as described in Table 10.1.

TABLE 10.1 COLLECTION OBJECT PROPERTIES AND METHODS

Type	Name	Description
Property	Count	Returns the number of members in the collection (beginning with 1).
Method	Add	Adds a member to the collection.
Method	Remove	Removes a member from the collection.
Method	Item	Returns a specific member in the collection.

Adding Members to a Collection

Use the Add method of the Collection object to add members to a collection. The Add method takes four parameters:

```
object.Add item, key, before, after
```

- item. A required expression that identifies the member to be added.
- key. An optional expression (string-based) that uniquely identifies the member.
- before. An optional expression that adds the member before the member position identified.
- after. An optional expression that adds the member after the member position identified.

When adding a member to a collection, only the before or after parameter can be used, not both.

The following VBA code creates a new collection and adds three string-based members.

```
Dim myColors As New Collection

myColors.Add "red"
myColors.Add "white"
myColors.Add "blue"
```

As mentioned, collections are useful for grouping objects. The next VBA code creates three ADO Recordset objects and adds them to a Collection object.

```
Dim books As New ADODB.Recordset
Dim authors As New ADODB.Recordset
Dim publishers As New ADODB.Recordset
Dim myRecordsets As New Collection

myRecordsets.Add books
myRecordsets.Add authors
myRecordsets.Add publishers
```

By grouping objects in a collection, I can simplify code by accessing all objects through one Collection object.

Removing Members from a Collection

Members are removed from a collection using the Collection object's Remove method. The Remove method takes a single parameter that identifies the index or key value of the member.

Removing a collection member using both the index value and key value is demonstrated here.

```
Dim myColors As New Collection

myColors.Add "red", "r"
myColors.Add "white", "w"
myColors.Add "blue", "b"

myColors.Remove 1 'using an index value
myColors.Remove "w" 'using a key value
```

Accessing a Member in a Collection

To access a member in a collection, use the Item method, which takes a single parameter that matches a member's index or key value.

```
Dim myColors As New Collection

myColors.Add "red", "r"
myColors.Add "white", "w"
myColors.Add "blue", "b"

MsgBox myColors.Item(1)
MsgBox myColors.Item("b")
MsgBox myColors.Item(4)   'Generates an error.
```

If the index or key value of the member is not found in the collection, an error like that in Figure 10.4 is generated.

FIGURE 10.4

An error is generated when trying to access a member's key value or index that does not exist.

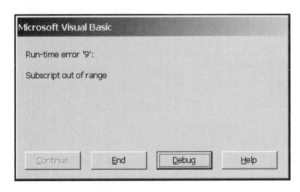

For Each Loops

VBA provides a looping structure specifically designed for iterating through members in a collection or an array. The For Each loop executes one or more statements inside the block so long as there is at least one member in the collection.

```
Dim myColors As New Collection
Dim vColor As Variant

myColors.Add "red", "r"
myColors.Add "white", "w"
myColors.Add "blue", "b"
```

```
For Each vColor In myColors

    MsgBox vColor

Next
```

Notice the syntax of the `For Each` statement. The statement basically says, "For every object in the collection, display the member name in a message box."

HINT

The variable used in the `For Each` statement (called `vColor` in the preceding example) is always of variant type regardless of the collection's content. This is an important note because `For Each` statements cannot be used with an array of user-defined types; variants can't contain a user-defined type.

The next program code loops through all control names on a form using the built-in VBA `Controls` collection.

```
Dim myControls As New Collection
Dim vControl As Variant

For Each vControl In Form_Form1.Controls

    MsgBox vControl.Name

Next
```

TRICK

If you need to exit the `For Each` loop early, VBA provides the `Exit For` statement.

CHAPTER PROGRAM: MONSTER DATING SERVICE

The `Monster Dating Service` program in Figure 10.5 uses chapter-based concepts to build a funny and simple application. Essentially, the program allows a user to find an available monster for a date by selecting character criteria.

Controls and properties of the `Monster Dating Service` program are shown in Table 10.2.

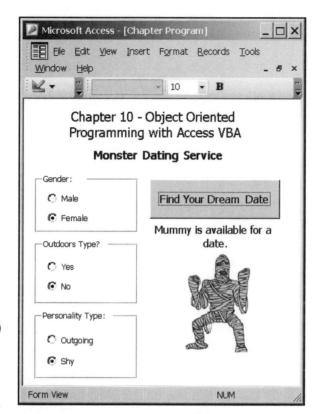

FIGURE 10.5

Using chapter-based concepts to build the Monster Dating Service program.

TABLE 10.2 CONTROLS AND PROPERTIES OF THE MONSTER DATING SERVICE PROGRAM

Control	Property	Property Value
Form	Name	Monsters
	Caption	Chapter Program
	Record Selectors	No
	Navigation Buttons	No
	Dividing Lines	No
Label	Name	lblHeading1
	Caption	Chapter 10

(continues)

TABLE 10.2 CONTROLS AND PROPERTIES OF THE MONSTER DATING SERVICE PROGRAM (CONTINUED)

Control	Property	Property Value
Label	Name	lblHeading2
	Caption	Monster Dating Service
Frame	Name	fraGender
Frame Label	Name	lblGender
	Caption	Gender:
Option Button	Name	optMale
Option Button Label	Name	lblMale
	Caption	Male
Option Button	Name	optFemale
Option Button Label	Name	lblFemale
	Caption	Female
Frame	Name	fraOutdoors
Frame Label	Name	lblOutdoors
	Caption	Outdoors Type?
Option Button	Name	optYes
Option Button Label	Name	lblYes
	Caption	Yes
Option Button	Name	optNo
Option Button Label	Name	lblNo
	Caption	No
Frame	Name	fraPersonality
Frame Label	Name	lblPersonality
	Caption	Personality Type:
Option Button	Name	optOutgoing
Option Button Label	Name	lblOutgoing
	Caption	Outgoing
Option Button	Name	optShy
Option Button Label	Name	lblShy
	Caption	Shy

<table>
<tr><td colspan="3">TABLE 10.2 CONTROLS AND PROPERTIES OF THE MONSTER DATING SERVICE PROGRAM (CONTINUED)</td></tr>
</table>

Control	Property	Property Value
Command Button	Name	cmdFindMonster
	Caption	Find Your Dream Date
Label	Name	lblMonsterName
	Caption	Mummy is available for a date.
Image	Name	imgPicture
	Picture	mummy.gif
	Size Mode	Stretch

The `Monster Dating Service` program uses object-oriented programming techniques split across two modules. The class module called `Monster` defines a `monster` object, which encapsulates all the functionality required to connect to the current database and retrieve monster attributes based on user input.

```
Option Compare Database
Option Explicit

Private name As String
Private picture As String
Private id As Integer
```

```
Public Sub FindMonster(sql_ As String)

    Dim rs As New ADODB.Recordset
    Dim sql As String

    'This method finds and sets all necessary monster details.
    'It does not return a value. User's of this method must use
    'the read-only property procedures to access the monster
    'attributes.
    On Error GoTo MonsterError
```

```vba
'Open the recordset based on the SQL string passed
'in as an argument.
rs.Open sql_, CurrentProject.AccessConnection, _
    adOpenForwardOnly, adLockReadOnly, adCmdText

If rs.EOF = False Then

    'Retrieve the monster's id, which will be used later.
    id = rs!monsterId

Else

    'No monster found with those attributes.
    'Raise a custom error.
    Err.Raise vbObjectError + 512, , "No monster found."

End If

rs.Close

'Generate a new SQL string to retrieve the monster's
'name and picture.
sql = "select * from Monsters where MonsterId = " & id

rs.Open sql, CurrentProject.AccessConnection, _
    adOpenForwardOnly, adLockReadOnly, adCmdText

If rs.EOF = False Then

    'Assign monster name and picture to properties.
    name = rs!MonsterName
    picture = Application.CurrentProject.Path & "\" & _
        rs!picture

End If

rs.Close

Exit Sub
```

```
MonsterError:

    MsgBox "Sorry, there was a problem finding the monster. " & _
        Chr(13) & Err.Number & ", " & Err.Description

End Sub
```

```
Public Property Get MonsterName() As Variant

    'This property procedure returns the monster's name.
    MonsterName = name

End Property
```

```
Public Property Get MonsterPicture() As String

    'This property procedure returns the path and file
    'name of the monster's picture.
    MonsterPicture = picture

End Property
```

The form class module instantiates Monster objects to find an available monster for a date:

```
Option Compare Database
Option Explicit
```

```
Private Sub cmdFindMonster_Click()

    Dim aMonster As New Monster
    Dim gender As String
    Dim personality As String
    Dim outdoors As Boolean
    Dim sql As String
```

```vba
'Generate a SQL string based on user selection criteria.
If Me.fraGender.Value = 1 Then
    gender = "Male"
Else
    gender = "Female"
End If

If Me.fraOutdoors.Value = 1 Then
    outdoors = True
Else
    outdoors = False
End If

If Me.fraPersonality = 1 Then
    personality = "Outgoing"
Else
    personality = "Shy"
End If

sql = "select * from MonsterAttributes where Outdoors = " & _
    outdoors & " and Gender = '" & gender & "'" & _
    " and Personality = '" & personality & "'"

'Try to find a monster based on the search criteria.
aMonster.FindMonster sql

'If a monster was found, display their name and picture.
If aMonster.MonsterName = "" Then

    Me.lblMonsterName.Caption = _
        "Sorry, no one is available with " & _
        "that search criteria."

    Me.imgPicture.picture = _
        Application.CurrentProject.Path & "\" & "logo.gif"

Else

    Me.lblMonsterName.Caption = aMonster.MonsterName & _
    " is available for a date."
```

```
        Me.imgPicture.picture = aMonster.MonsterPicture

    End If

End Sub
```

CHAPTER SUMMARY

- Object-oriented programming maps data, structures, and business requirements to objects.
- Encapsulation allows programmers to reduce code complexity by hiding data and complex data structures in classes.
- Class modules contain member variables as well as property and method procedures.
- Class modules do not exist in memory.
- Multiple instances of a single class can be created.
- By default, VBA class modules contain two events called Initialize and Terminate.
- The Initialize event for a class module is triggered each time the class is instantiated (created) using the New or Set keywords.
- The Terminate event is triggered each time the class's instance is removed from memory.
- VBA provides property procedures for managing the attributes of a class.
- VBA provides three types of property procedures: Property Get, Property Let, and Property Set.
- Property Get procedures return the value of a property.
- Property Let procedures assign a value to a property.
- Property Set procedures set the value of an object property.
- Use a single Property Get procedure to create a read-only property.
- Method procedures are created in class modules with Sub and Function procedures.
- Setting objects to Nothing frees system resources.
- Collections are objects that contain an ordered list of items.
- Items in a collection are called members.
- Members in a collection can be referenced with an index or key value.
- VBA provides the For Each loop to iterate through members in a collection or an array.

Programming Challenges

1. Create a new database called BookStore with one table called Books. Add the columns ISBN, Title, PublishDate, and Price to the Books table. Create a new connection class called CustomConnection that connects to your BookStore database. The new class should have two methods—one method for opening an ADO Connection object and a second method for closing the ADO Connection object. The method that opens a database connection should take a single string argument, which represents the path and filename of the database.

2. In the same database application from Challenge 1, create a new class called Books. This class should have a read-only property for each column in the Books table. Create a method in the Books class called FindBook. The FindBook method should take in an ISBN. Build a SQL string based on the ISBN and use ADO programming techniques to open a recordset and assign the recordset field values to the class's matching properties. You should use the CustomConnection class to create and retrieve any Connection objects.

3. Create a user interface in the database application from Challenge 1. Add form elements that allow a user to find a book by entering an ISBN. Use your Books class from Challenge 2 to find and retrieve book details.

4. Enhance the user interface from Challenge 3 to allow a user to add and remove books. To accomplish this, you need to modify the Books class from Challenge 2 by adding two methods called AddBook and RemoveBook.

5. In a new Access application, create a Collection object called Friends. Construct a user interface that allows a user to add and remove names of friends in the Friends collection.

6. Add a command button to Challenge 2's user interface that displays each friend in a message box. Hint: Use the For Each loop to iterate through members in the Friends collection.

MICROSOFT OFFICE OBJECTS

Microsoft Office Objects are an excellent example of what makes VBA such a powerful and popular object-based programming language. Specifically, Access VBA exposes the Microsoft Office Object Model, which allows you to leverage much of the Microsoft Office internal functionality and utilities such as the Microsoft assistant, command bars, and file dialogs. In this chapter I show you how to leverage each of these Microsoft Office Objects using VBA programming techniques.

INTRODUCTION TO MICROSOFT OFFICE OBJECTS

In addition to objects such as DoCmd, Err, Debug, as well as objects found in the ADODB library, VBA provides the Microsoft Office Object model for use in the suite of applications found in Microsoft Office. Most of the Microsoft Office Objects can be used across the Microsoft Office suite of applications such as Microsoft Word, Microsoft Excel, and Microsoft Access. Some office objects, however, are application specific.

To work with the examples in this chapter, ensure that your Access program has a reference set to the Microsoft Office Object library. Setting a reference allows you to work with other application objects in your code.

In older versions of Microsoft Access, the Microsoft Office Object references may not be set. You know if a reference is not set as soon as you try to access a property, constant, or method of an object that requires a reference. If references to

Microsoft Office Objects are not set, VBA notifies you with an error message asking if you want Access to set the reference for you.

You can verify references ahead of time by selecting Tools, References from the menu in the VBE. A sample References window with the Microsoft Office 11.0 Object library selected is seen in Figure 11.1.

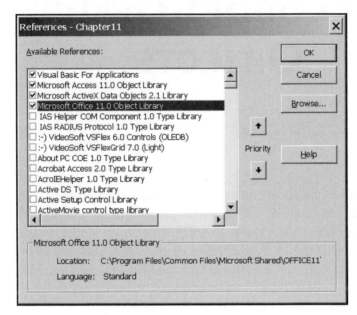

FIGURE 11.1

Using the References dialog window to set or verify Object library references.

The Microsoft Office 11.0 Object library may be a different version if you have a previous edition of Microsoft Office (earlier than Microsoft Office 2003) installed.

In VBA, the concept of setting a reference involves creating a link to another application's object or objects for use in your code.

ASSISTANT OBJECT

Because of its professional graphics and animation, the Assistant object is a popular Microsoft Office Object to work and learn with. More than likely, you have already seen the Assistant object with Microsoft applications such as Microsoft Word, Microsoft Excel, and Microsoft Access.

In a nutshell, the `Assistant` object exposes the animated Microsoft assistant. Depending on the version of Microsoft Office you have, there are up to eight Office assistant characters you can install.

To manually choose an assistant (see Figure 11.2), ensure the Microsoft assistant is visible by selecting Help, Show the Office Assistant item from the menu in Access. Once the assistant is displayed, right-click it and select the Choose Assistant menu option.

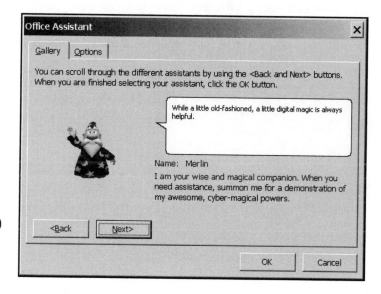

FIGURE 11.2

Choosing an Office assistant character.

Through VBA, you can choose which assistant character is displayed to the user by passing a Microsoft assistant filename to the `Assistant` object's `FileName` property. Filenames for Microsoft assistants, also known as Microsoft *agents*, end with an .ACS file extension, as seen in this list of filenames:

```
CLIPPIT.ACS
DOT.ACS
F1.ACS
LOGO.ACS
MERLIN.ACS
MNATURE.ACS
OFFCAT.ACS
ROCKY.ACS
```

VBA generates an error if you try to access an office assistant using the `Application` object's `FileName` property for an assistant that has not been installed.

To install an office assistant, select it using the Choose Assistant menu item as described earlier in this section. If the assistant is not installed, Microsoft Office prompts you to install it.

To display the Office assistant using VBA, you need to work with the `Application` object's `Assistant` property. The `Assistant` property returns an object of `Assistant` type. Once the `Assistant` object is returned, you can use its properties and methods as shown in the code example.

```
Private Sub cmdShowAssistant_Click()

    With Application.Assistant

        .On = True
        .FileName = "F1.ACS"
        .Animation = msoAnimationGestureDown
        .Visible = True

    End With


End Sub
```

In the preceding code example, I've used a minimal number of `Assistant` object properties to display the character. In short, the `On` property enables and disables the assistant, the `FileName` property takes a string which identifies the assistant character to be displayed, and the `Visible` property hides or shows the assistant character.

There are more than 30 different animations that can be assigned to the `Animation` property:

```
msoAnimationAppear
msoAnimationBeginSpeaking
msoAnimationCharacterSuccessMajor
msoAnimationCheckingSomething
msoAnimationDisappear
msoAnimationEmptyTrash
```

```
msoAnimationGestureDown
msoAnimationGestureLeft
msoAnimationGestureRight
msoAnimationGestureUp
msoAnimationGetArtsy
msoAnimationGetAttentionMajor
msoAnimationGetAttentionMinor
msoAnimationGetTechy
msoAnimationGetWizardy
msoAnimationGoodbye
msoAnimationGreeting
msoAnimationIdle
msoAnimationListensToComputer
msoAnimationLookDown
msoAnimationLookDownLeft
msoAnimationLookDownRight
msoAnimationLookLeft
msoAnimationLookRight
msoAnimationLookUp
msoAnimationLookUpLeft
msoAnimationLookUpRight
msoAnimationPrinting
msoAnimationRestPose
msoAnimationSaving
msoAnimationSearching
msoAnimationSendingMail
msoAnimationThinking
msoAnimationWorkingAtSomething
msoAnimationWritingNotingSomething
```

Note that not all animations produce the desired animation (that depends on the selected character) and that different animations produce the same action.

To further demonstrate the Assistant object, consider the following program code. It uses form controls to show, hide, and animate Office assistants using VBA. Output is seen in Figure 11.3.

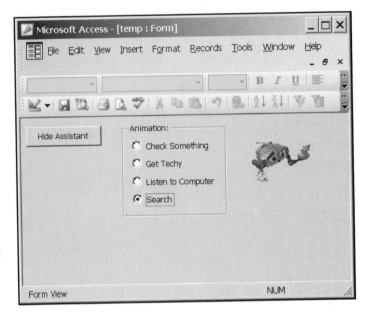

FIGURE 11.3

Using VBA to manage the Office assistant.

```
Private Sub cmdShowAssistant_Click()

    If cmdShowAssistant.Caption = "Show Assistant" Then

        With Application.Assistant

            .FileName = "F1.ACS"
            .Animation = msoAnimationGestureDown
            .Visible = True

        End With

        cmdShowAssistant.Caption = "Hide Assistant"

    Else
```

```
    With Application.Assistant

        .Visible = False

    End With

    cmdShowAssistant.Caption = "Show Assistant"

  End If

End Sub
```

```
Private Sub optCheckingSomething_GotFocus()

    With Application.Assistant

        .Animation = msoAnimationCheckingSomething

    End With

End Sub
```

```
Private Sub optGetTechy_GotFocus()

    With Application.Assistant

        .Animation = msoAnimationGetTechy

    End With

End Sub
```

```
Private Sub optListenToComputer_GotFocus()

    With Application.Assistant
```

```
        .Animation = msoAnimationListensToComputer

    End With

End Sub
```

```
Private Sub optSearching_GotFocus()

    With Application.Assistant

        .Animation = msoAnimationSearching

    End With

End Sub
```

Once the `Assistant` object is displayed in an Office application (Access, for example), the user can click it to use the assistant's help and search features or right-click the assistant character to display character options.

Balloon Object

With the help of the `Assistant` object, you can even create your own specialized balloons. *Balloons* are the graphical text area that the Office assistant uses to display information. To create custom balloons, simply access the `NewBalloon` property from the `Assistant` object.

```
Application.Assistant.NewBalloon
```

The `NewBalloon` property returns a new `Balloon` object that contains its own methods and properties for managing custom balloons. You can customize your balloons to include labels, check boxes, icons, and various button and balloon types. In the following program I create a new balloon that provides information as a tip of the day. Sample output is seen in Figure 11.4.

```
Private Sub cmdTip_Click()

    With Application.Assistant.NewBalloon
        .BalloonType = msoBalloonTypeBullets
        .Icon = msoIconTip
        .Button = msoButtonSetOK
```

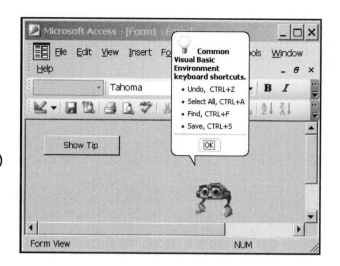

FIGURE 11.4

Using the
`Assistant` and
`Balloon` objects
to create and
display custom
balloons.

```
        .Heading = "Common Visual Basic Environment " & _
            "keyboard shortcuts."
        .Labels(1).Text = "Undo,   CTRL+Z"
        .Labels(2).Text = "Select All, CTRL+A"
        .Labels(3).Text = "Find, CTRL+F"
        .Labels(4).Text = "Save, CTRL+S"
        .Show
    End With

End Sub
```

Properties of the `NewBalloon` object with common uses are described next.

- Use built-in Office Object constants in the `BalloonType`, `Icon`, and `Button` properties to change the appearance of your custom balloon.
- The `Heading` property displays information in the balloon's heading.
- The `Labels` property contains a collection of `BalloonLabels`. The `Labels` property can be used in conjunction with the `BalloonType` property to display labels with different types of bulleted lists.
- The `Show` method displays the balloon and returns a constant that contains the value of the button or label clicked by the user.

To determine what label or button the user has clicked in a balloon, assign a `Variant` variable to the result of the `Show` method. The next program demonstrates this using a more informative balloon with different `Label` types (clickable). Output is seen in Figure 11.5.

FIGURE 11.5

Using the result of the Show method to determine what label or button has been clicked in a balloon.

```
Private Sub cmdTip_Click()

    Dim choice
    Dim heading As String
    Dim txt As String

    With Application.Assistant.NewBalloon
        .heading = "Common Visual Basic Environment " & _
            "keyboard shortcuts."
        .Labels(1).Text = "Undo,   CTRL+Z"
        .Labels(2).Text = "Select All, CTRL+A"
        .Labels(3).Text = "Find, CTRL+F"
        .Labels(4).Text = "Save, CTRL+S"
        choice = .Show
    End With

    Select Case choice

        Case 1
            heading = "Undo, CTRL+Z"
            txt = "Undoes the most recent change."
        Case 2
            heading = "Select All, CTRL+A"
            txt = "Selects all text in the current window."
        Case 3
            heading = "Undo, CTRL+F"
```

```
        txt = "Opens the Find and Replace window " & _
            "to search for text."
     Case 4
        heading = "Undo, CTRL+S"
        txt = "Saves current work."

  End Select

  If choice <> -1 Then

     With Application.Assistant.NewBalloon
        .BalloonType = msoBalloonTypeBullets
        .Icon = msoIconTip
        .heading = heading
        .Labels(1).Text = txt
        .Show
     End With

End If

     End Sub
```

By assigning the result of the Show method to the choice variable, I can easily determine what the user clicked. Based on the user's selection, I customize variables that are used later. If the value of the choice variable is -1, I know the user has clicked the OK button and that it's unnecessary to show any other balloons. If the value of the choice variable is anything other than -1, I show a new balloon with a custom header and label.

COMMAND BARS

In VBA, *command bars* represent a number of user interface entities such as toolbars, menu bars, and shortcut menus (via right-click). You can declare variables in VBA as a CommandBar object type. To demonstrate, the next program code declares a CommandBar object variable and uses a For Each loop to iterate through each CommandBar object found in the CommandBars collection. Each command bar's name is printed to the Immediate window. Output is seen in Figure 11.6.

```
Private Sub cmdFindCommandBars_Click()

  Dim myCommandBar As CommandBar
```

```
For Each myCommandBar In CommandBars

    Debug.Print myCommandBar.Name

Next myCommandBar

End Sub
```

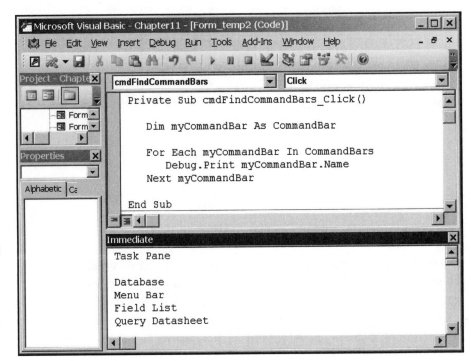

FIGURE 11.6

Using the CommandBar object to iterate through each command bar in a CommandBars collection.

The CommandBars collection contains all command bar objects in the current application.

CommandBarControl Object

The CommandBarControl object represents controls found in menus and toolbars. Command bar controls can be buttons, boxes, and pop-up controls. Using the CommandBars collection, you can identify each command bar control found in a command bar. This concept is revealed in the next program code, which outputs the Caption property for each control found in the Database command bar.

```
Private Sub cmdFindCommandBarControls_Click()

    Dim myControl As CommandBarControl

    For Each myControl In CommandBars("Database").Controls
        Debug.Print myControl.Caption
    Next myControl

End Sub
```

The CommandBarControl is a general object for working with built-in command bar controls. Its properties and methods are common among more specialized command bar control objects such as the CommandBarButton, CommandBarComboBox, and CommandBarPopUp objects.

CommandBarButton Object

The CommandBarButton object is a specialized command bar control that represents a button on a toolbar or menu that the user can click. You can use the CommandBarButton object in conjunction with the CommandBar object to build your own custom toolbars, which is demonstrated in the next procedure.

```
Private Sub cmdAddCustomCommandBar_Click()

    Dim customBar As CommandBar
    Dim newButton As CommandBarButton

    Set customBar = CommandBars.Add("Sheila")

    Set newButton = customBar.Controls _
        .Add(msoControlButton, CommandBars("Insert") _
        .Controls("Table").ID)

    Set newButton = customBar.Controls _
        .Add(msoControlButton, CommandBars("Insert") _
        .Controls("Query").ID)

    Set newButton = customBar.Controls _
        .Add(msoControlButton, CommandBars("Insert") _
        .Controls("Form").ID)

    customBar.Visible = True

End Sub
```

Using the Add method of the CommandBar object, I can create a new custom command bar called MyCommandBar. Then I can use Add methods of new CommandBarButton objects to create buttons on my custom command bar. Note that the Controls property of the CommandBar object returns a CommandBarsControls collection. I use this collection's Add method to add a new button to the command bar. The Add method takes five optional parameters. In my example, the first parameter determines the type of control to be added. The options for this parameter are MsoControlType constants:

msoControlButton

msoControlEdit

msoControlDropdown

msoControlComboBox

msoControlPopup

The next parameter in the Add method requires an Integer value, which represents a built-in control. In my example, I use the ID property of the Controls collection to return an Integer value representing a known control.

 TRICK You can pass a string into the Controls collection, which identifies a specific control name. The control name, however, must match a control name found in the CommandBars collection. Note that control and command bar names are found in Access command bars, not in VBE command bars.

Once a custom command bar has been created, it is added to your current application. To manage the newly added custom command bar, simply right-click a toolbar and select Customize or select Customize from the View/Toolbars menu group. Custom command bars can be removed from the same Customize Toolbars window.

FILEDIALOG OBJECT

The FileDialog object is a very useful Microsoft Office Object. Believe it or not, you've already seen the FileDialog object in action. Almost all Microsoft Windows applications use some variation of it. In a nutshell, the FileDialog object allows you to display and manage standard Open and Save file dialog windows. An example of the Windows Open dialog window is seen in Figure 11.7.

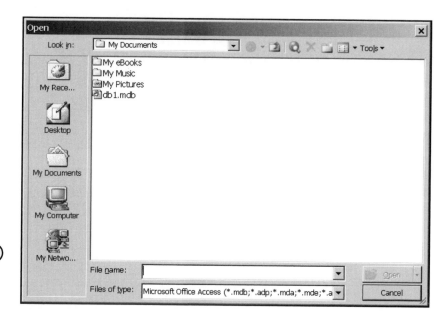

FIGURE II.7

A Microsoft
Windows Open
dialog window.

To work with the FileDialog object, you also need to work with the Application object. More specifically, you access the Application object's FileDialog property, which takes a single dialog type parameter. Valid FileDialog property parameters are one of four MsoFileDialogType types:

- msoFileDialogFilePicker. Allows users to select one or more files. Selected files are saved in the FileDialogSelectedItems collection.

- msoFileDialogFolderPicker. Allows the user to select a path. Selected items are saved in the FileDialogSelectedItems collection.

- msoFileDialogOpen. Allows the user to select one or more files to open. Files are opened in the application using the Execute method.

- msoFileDialogSaveAs. Allows the user to select only one file for saving using the Execute method.

The return value of the Application object's FileDialog property should be assigned to your FileDialog object variable.

```
Set myFileDialog = Application.FileDialog(msoFileDialogOpen)
```

After doing this, you can use the FileDialog object's Show method to display the specified dialog window. Use a For Each loop and the FileDialog object's SelectedItems property to iterate through each of the user's selections. An example program that uses the FileDialog object is shown next.

```
Private Sub cmdAddFiles_Click()

    'Declare a FileDialog object variable.
    Dim myFileDialog As FileDialog

    'Declare a variant to hold each file selected.
    Dim vFileSelected As Variant

    'Create a FileDialog object as an Open dialog window.
    Set myFileDialog = Application.FileDialog(msoFileDialogOpen)

    'If the user didn't press Cancel, process each selection.
    If myFileDialog.Show = -1 Then

        For Each vFileSelected In myFileDialog.SelectedItems

            lstFiles.AddItem vFileSelected

        Next vFileSelected

    Else

        'The user pressed Cancel.
        MsgBox "No files selected."

    End If

    'Set the myFileDialog object variable to Nothing.
    Set myFileDialog = Nothing


End Sub
```

I use the FileDialog object to show an Open dialog window from which the user can select one or more files. Files selected by the user are added to the list box. If the user elects to press Cancel, a message is displayed instead. After finishing with the FileDialog object variable, I set it to Nothing, freeing memory.

CHAPTER PROGRAM: ANIMATED MATH

The Animated Math game in Figure 11.8 uses chapter-based concepts to make simple math problems fun. Specifically, I used the Assistant object to present and guide users through simple addition problems.

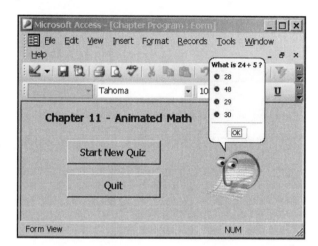

FIGURE 11.8

The Animated Math program uses the Assistant object to make math fun.

Controls and properties of the Animated Math program can be seen in Table 11.1.

TABLE 11.1 CONTROLS AND PROPERTIES OF THE ANIMATED MATH PROGRAM

Control	Property	Property Value
Form	Name	Chapter Program
	Caption	Chapter Program
	Record Selectors	No
	Navigation Buttons	No
	Dividing Lines	No
Label	Name	lblHeading
	Caption	Chapter 11-Animated Math
Command Button	Name	cmdStartNewQuiz
	Caption	Start New Quiz
Command Button	Name	cmdQuit
	Caption	Quit

All of the VBA code required to build the Animated Math program is seen next.

```vba
Option Compare Database
Option Explicit
```

```vba
Private Sub Form_Load()
    Randomize
End Sub
```

```vba
Private Sub cmdQuit_Click()
    DoCmd.Quit
End Sub
```

```vba
Private Sub cmdStartNewQuiz_Click()

    Dim choice
    Dim myAssistant As Assistant
    Dim question As String
    Dim txt As String
    Dim loopNumber As Integer
    Dim iNumber1 As Integer
    Dim iNumber2 As Integer
    Dim randomAnswerOrder As Integer

    'Display the Assistant and prompt the user
    'for number of questions to ask.
    Application.Assistant.On = True
    Application.Assistant.Visible = True
    With Application.Assistant.NewBalloon
        .Icon = msoIconNone
        .heading = "How many math questions would you like?"
        .Labels(1).Text = "1"
        .Labels(2).Text = "2"
        .Labels(3).Text = "3"
        .Labels(4).Text = "4"
        choice = .Show
    End With
```

```
'Prompt the user with math questions, based on their
'initial response.
If choice <> -1 Then

    For loopNumber = 1 To choice

            'Generate random numbers for math problems.
            iNumber1 = Int((100 * Rnd) + 1)
            iNumber2 = Int((100 * Rnd) + 1)

            'Generate a random number that will be used for
            'placing the correct answer in a random order
            'for each question.
            randomAnswerOrder = Int((4 * Rnd) + 1)

        With Application.Assistant.NewBalloon

                .Animation = msoAnimationThinking
                .Icon = msoIconNone
                .heading = "What is " & iNumber1 & "+ " & _
                    iNumber2 & " ?"

                'Based on the random location of the answer,
                'populate four labels with possible answers.
                Select Case randomAnswerOrder
                    Case 1
                        'correct answer
                        .Labels(1).Text = iNumber1 + iNumber2
                        'wrong answer
                        .Labels(2).Text = iNumber1 + iNumber1
                        'wrong answer
                        .Labels(3).Text = (iNumber1 + iNumber2) - 1
                        'wrong answer
                        .Labels(4).Text = (iNumber1 + iNumber2) + 1
                    Case 2
                        'wrong answer
                        .Labels(1).Text = iNumber1 + iNumber1
```

```
                      'correct answer
                      .Labels(2).Text = iNumber1 + iNumber2
                      'wrong answer
                      .Labels(3).Text = (iNumber1 + iNumber2) - 1
                      'wrong answer
                      .Labels(4).Text = (iNumber1 + iNumber2) + 1
              Case 3
                      'wrong answer
                      .Labels(1).Text = (iNumber1 + iNumber2) - 1
                      'wrong answer
                      .Labels(2).Text = iNumber1 + iNumber1
                      'correct answer
                      .Labels(3).Text = iNumber1 + iNumber2
                      'wrong answer
                      .Labels(4).Text = (iNumber1 + iNumber2) + 1

              Case 4
                      'wrong answer
                      .Labels(1).Text = (iNumber1 + iNumber2) + 1
                      'wrong answer
                      .Labels(2).Text = iNumber1 + iNumber1
                      'wrong answer
                      .Labels(3).Text = (iNumber1 + iNumber2) - 1
                      'correct answer
                      .Labels(4).Text = iNumber1 + iNumber2
        End Select

        choice = .Show

    End With

    If choice = -1 Then
        'user canceled
        Exit For
    End If

    If choice = randomAnswerOrder Then
        MsgBox "That's right!"
```

```
        Else
            MsgBox "Sorry, incorrect answer."
        End If

    Next loopNumber

    End If

End Sub
```

CHAPTER SUMMARY

- Access VBA exposes the Microsoft Office Object Model, which allows you to leverage much of the Microsoft Office internal functionality and utilities.

- Most Microsoft Office Objects are available to the suite of Microsoft Office applications. Some Microsoft Office Objects, however, are available only to specific suite applications.

- Sometimes Microsoft Office Object references are not set automatically. To set object references in VBA, use the References window.

- Setting an object reference sets a link to another application's objects for use in your code.

- The Assistant object exposes an animated Microsoft assistant character.

- With the Balloon object, you can create customized balloons to work with the assistant character.

- Command bars represent a number of user-interface entities such as toolbars, menu bars, and shortcut menus.

- The CommandBars collection contains all command bar objects in the current application.

- The CommandBarControl object represents controls found in menus and toolbars.

- Command bar controls can be buttons, boxes, and pop-up controls.

- The CommandBarButton object is a specialized command bar control that represents a button on a toolbar or menu that the user can click.

- Use the Customize dialog window to remove a custom command bar.

- The FileDialog object allows you to display and manage standard Open and Save file dialog windows.

PROGRAMMING CHALLENGES

1. Using the `Assistant` object, build a custom balloon that displays three useful Access VBA tips you've learned about in this book.

2. Build a custom command bar named after you. Your custom command bar should have four controls. Use existing controls found in the Access File menu (`CommandBar`).

3. Use the `FileDialog` object to show a file picker dialog window. Output to a message box each file the user selects.

INTRODUCTION TO DATA ACCESS PAGES AND ACCESS SECURITY

H ave you ever thought about creating Web-based front ends to your Access databases? If you have and shied away because of Web programming and script complexities, you may be pleasantly surprised to learn about Access's easy-to-use interface for creating Web forms. This chapter specifically shows you how to create Web forms connected to your Access databases using data access pages. In addition, you learn how to secure both your Access database and data access pages using Access security essentials.

INTRODUCTION TO DATA ACCESS PAGES

Data access pages are Web pages you create in Access that allow users to view and work with a database over the Internet or an intranet. Sources for a data access page can be Microsoft Access, Microsoft SQL Server 6.5 or later, and others such as Microsoft Excel.

Microsoft Access stores data access pages in an Internet file format using the .htm extension. The .htm file contains HTML forms to view and work with data and script information to connect to your data source.

You can open data access pages in either Access or via Internet Explorer. To open an existing data access page in Access, select the Pages object from the main Access window and double-click an available data access page like that in Figure 12.1.

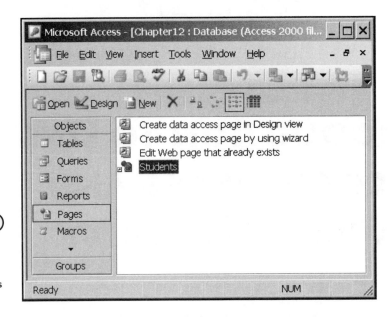

FIGURE 12.1

Finding and opening a data access page in Microsoft Access page view.

As mentioned, data access pages are stored with the Internet extension .htm, which Access creates for you when a data access page is saved. While saving the data access page, Access allows you to select where to save the Internet file. As you can see from Figure 12.2, I've saved a sample data access page to the same directory location as my Access database file.

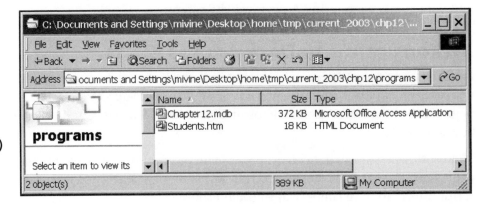

FIGURE 12.2

A saved data access page in .htm format.

To open and work with data access pages stored in .htm format, you must have Microsoft Internet Explorer 5.01 with Service Pack 2 (SP2) or later. Figure 12.3 depicts a sample data access page opened in .htm format using Microsoft Internet Explorer.

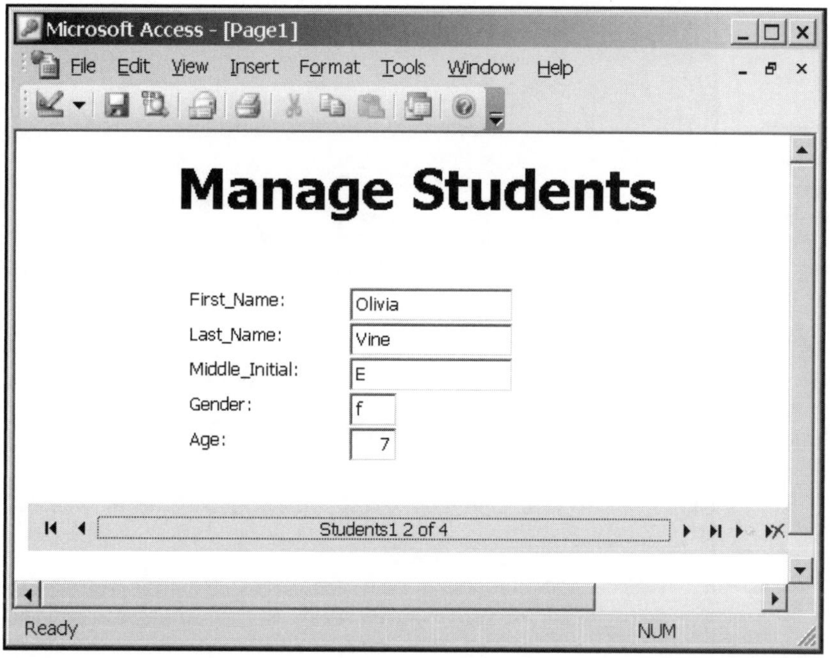

Microsoft Access - [Page1]
File Edit View Insert Format Tools Window Help
Manage Students
First_Name:
Olivia
Last_Name:
Vine
Middle_Initial:
E
Gender:
f
Age:
7
Students1 2 of 4
Ready
NUM

FIGURE 12.3

A sample data access page opened in `.htm` format using Internet Explorer.

As you will see in sections to come, Microsoft Access allows you to create data access pages and deploy them to locations other than your PC, such as file and Web servers.

Creating Data Access Pages

You can create data access pages with either the Access Data Access Page wizard or by yourself in Design view. To create a data access page in design view, simply double-click the Create Data Access Page in Design View link from the Pages window in Figure 12.1.

TRAP

Data access pages created in Microsoft Access 2003 cannot be opened in Design view in older versions of Access. In other words, Access 2003 data access pages are not backward-compatible. When creating a new Access 2003 data access page, Access warns you with the message seen in Figure 12.4.

A new data access page created in Design view looks similar to the one seen in Figure 12.5.

Creating a data access page in Design view allows you to manage the data access page's connection to a data source through the page connection properties link seen in Figure 12.5.

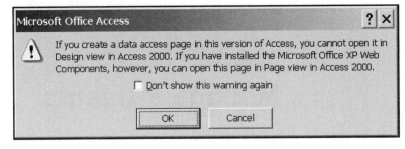

FIGURE 12.4

Data access page
backward-
compatibility
warning.

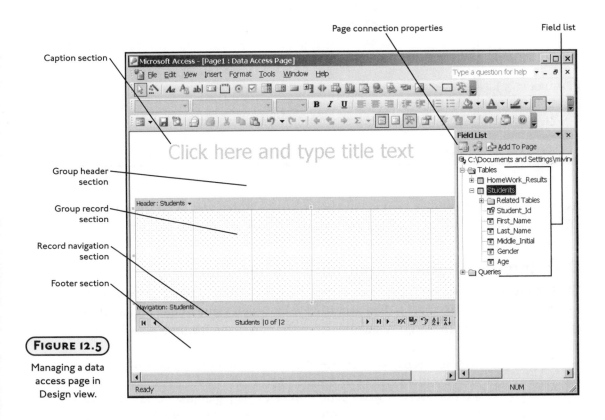

FIGURE 12.5

Managing a data
access page in
Design view.

The page connection properties links open the Data Link Properties window, seen in Figure 12.6, which allows you to specify the type and location of your data source. Since data access pages are directly connected to a data source such as Access, careful consideration should be given to your database's location.

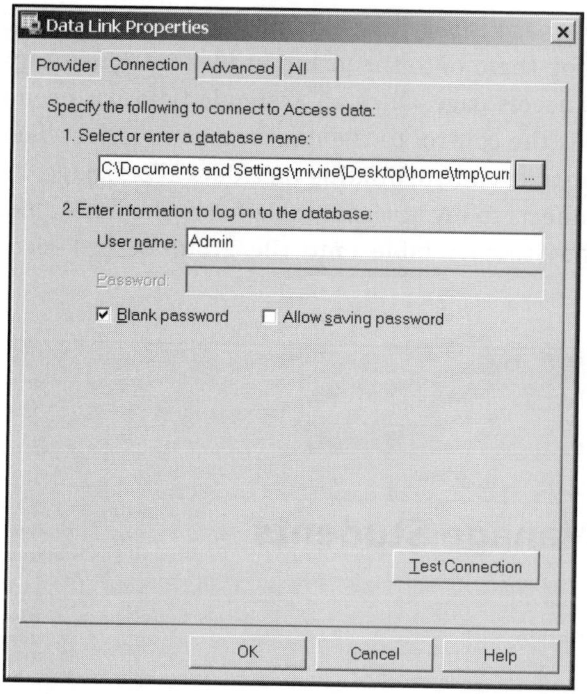

FIGURE 12.6

Specifying a data
access page's
connection
properties.

If your data access page will be accessed from a file or HTTP (Web) server and connected to an Access database, use a *universal naming convention (UNC)* path when specifying the database name:

```
\\server_name\share_name\database_name.mdb
```

Use the Data Link Properties window's Provider tab to specify other data source providers, such as Microsoft SQL Server 6.5 or higher.

Database fields can be added to your data access page from either tables or queries using the Field List window seen in Figure 12.5.

Parts of a data access page are typically broken into sections, with the most common of these sections listed next:

- Caption section
- Group header section
- Group record section
- Record navigation section
- Footer section

Adding fields to a data access page is very easy—simply drag one or more data fields from the Field List window and drop them onto the group header section, group record section, or footer section of the data access page. Once an available field has been placed onto the data access page, Access binds the control to the data source field just like bound controls on an Access form. To demonstrate control binding on a data access page, I've created a simple data access page that connects to my Students table from Chapter 1, "Access Essentials." I placed five fields from the Students table onto the group record section of the page depicted in Figure 12.7.

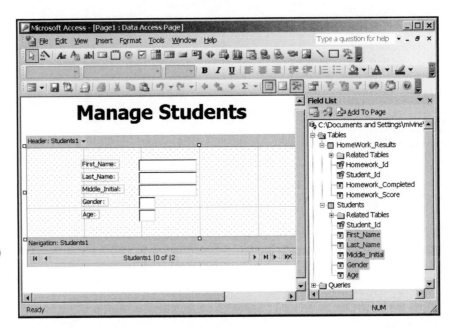

(**FIGURE 12.7**)

Adding fields to
the group record
section of a data
access page.

The built-in record navigation toolbars are a great feature that allow a user to scroll through records, add, update, filter, and delete records, and even get help using a data access page. The record navigation toolbar is shown in detail in Figure 12.8.

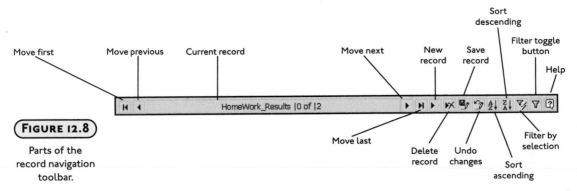

(**FIGURE 12.8**)

Parts of the
record navigation
toolbar.

Creating a simple but useful data access page is that easy! In the next section I show you how to create a more robust data access page by adding group levels.

Adding Group Levels

Consider the Students database from Chapter 1, which has two tables: Students and HomeWork _Results. The Students table has a one-to-many relationship with the HomeWork_Results table, meaning for every one record in the Students table, one or more records are in the HomeWork _Results table. Access allows you to graphically display the one-to-many relationship in a data access page by grouping like records and linking one group to another.

Grouping and linking in a data access page is accomplished in group levels by promoting one field from a table or query or grouping by table:

- To group by one field from a table or query, click the Promote icon on the Access toolbar. See Figure 12.9.
- To group by table, click the Group by Table icon on the Access toolbar. See Figure 12.10.

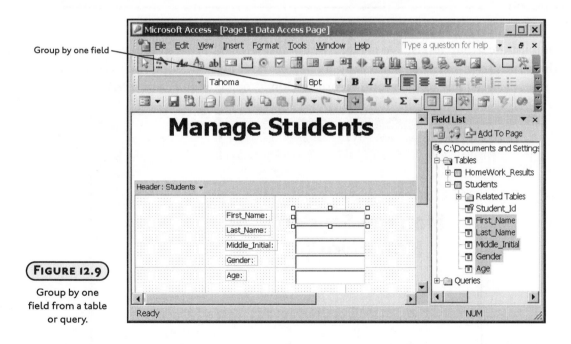

Group by one field

FIGURE 12.9

Group by one field from a table or query.

TRICK

Grouping by one field is typically used on fields that are primary keys in a table.

Group by table

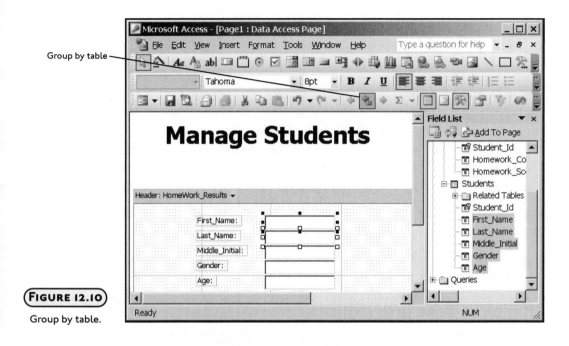

FIGURE 12.10

Group by table.

To demonstrate group levels, I've created a new data access page that allows users to manage the results from students' homework. To begin, I add the First_Name and Last_Name fields from the Students table to the group record section as depicted in Figure 12.11.

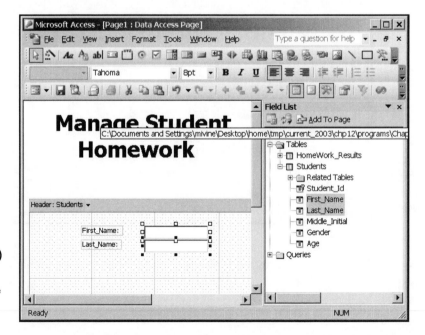

FIGURE 12.11

Adding Student table fields to the group record section.

Next, I add Homework_Id, Homework_Completed, and Homework_Score fields from the HomeWork_Results table to the same group record section seen in Figure 12.12.

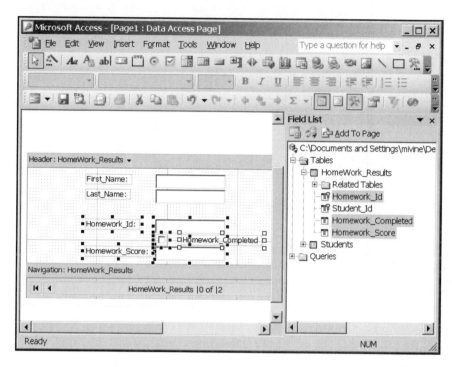

FIGURE 12.12

Adding
HomeWork_Results
table fields to the
group record
section.

I now create a new group level using the Students table. I can accomplish this with two non-primary key Students table fields using the Group by Table option.

To create the new group level, I select both First_Name and Last_Name (from the Students table) fields in the record group section and click the Group by Table icon in the Access toolbar.

TRAP Access creates group levels by selecting bound controls in the group record section. If you select unbound controls such as labels, neither the Promote nor Group by Table icons is available in the Access toolbar.

When a new group level is added to a data access page, Access adds a new group header that contains an expand control, which displays or hides record details, and a record navigation section that allows you to scroll through the group records as depicted in Figure 12.13.

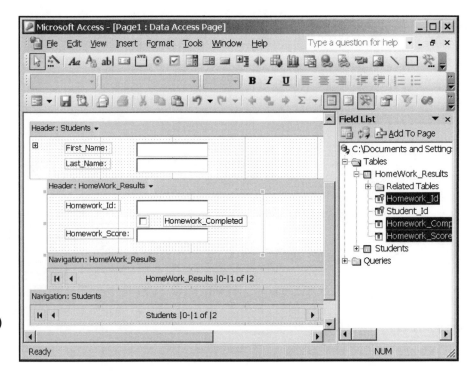

FIGURE 12.13

Adding a new
group level.

Before using your new group levels, it's a good idea to consider how many records will be
displayed in each group. You can control how many records display in a group by right-clicking
each group record section and selecting the GroupLevel properties menu item (seen in Figure 12.14) and changing the DataPageSize property.

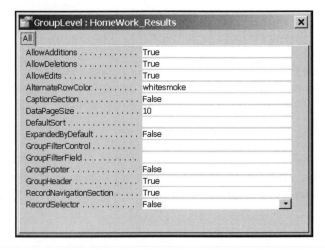

FIGURE 12.14

Viewing group
level properties.

I changed each group's `DataPageSize` property from 10 to 1, which means users leverage the record navigation tool bar in each group to scroll through records in a group.

Figure 12.15 reveals the final `Manage Student Homework` data access page in Page view with two group levels.

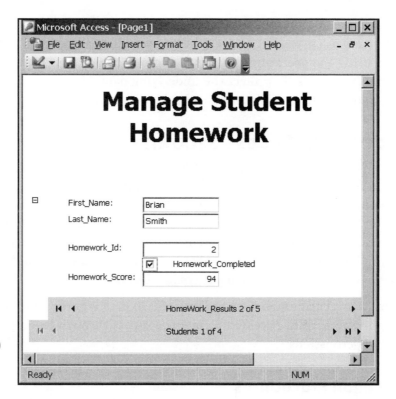

FIGURE 12.15

Two group levels in Page view.

In the next section I show you how to publish, secure, and share your data access pages.

Publishing Data Access Pages

Publishing a data access page is straightforward. Simply open a data access page in Design view and click the Save or Save As item from the File menu. Access then prompts you to provide a name for the .htm file and a location for storing your .htm (data access page) file. You may recall that data access pages are not stored or saved in the Access file (.mdb). Instead, they are typically saved or published to either a file server, such as Microsoft Windows 2000, or a Web server, such as Microsoft IIS.

Keep two things in mind when considering where to publish a data access page:

- Users must have access to the .htm file created by Access.
- The connection properties in the .htm file must have access to the data source (such as Microsoft SQL Server or Microsoft Access).

Anyone who has access to your data access page by default can access your underlying data presented in the data access page. To properly secure your data access page, modify the .htm file permissions using the operating system's (Windows 2000 Server, for example) or Web server's (IIS) security features. To protect the underlying data, leverage security functionality provided by your data source. I discuss this in the next section.

INTRODUCTION TO ACCESS SECURITY

A huge benefit of moving from data sources such as spreadsheets to a database management system such as Access is the database's ability to have multiple and concurrent users working on your system. In a multiuser environment, however, one of your concerns should be security and the varying roles your users fill. For example, some of your users may simply need to view data, whereas other users may need to alter data or create objects such as tables, queries, and forms. The users who only need to view data should not have the same security privileges as those who alter data or create objects.

Access implements a security model that allows you to create groups and users with specialized privileges. Specifically, Access implements security through logon procedures and user-level security permissions.

Activating Logon Procedures

Logon procedures for an Access database must be enabled before you work with user-level security permissions. To initialize Access logon procedures, select Tools, Security, User and Group Accounts (seen in Figure 12.16) from the menu.

By default, Access 2003 databases come with two groups, Users and Admins. Also by default, one user account called Admin belongs to the Admins group.

From the Users and Groups Account window, select the Admin user account in the Name drop-down list box, then click the Change Logon Password tab and enter a new password. See Figure 12.17.

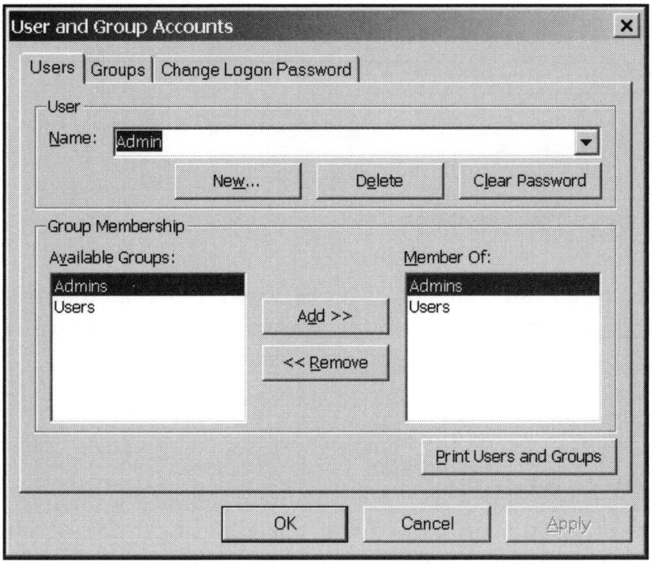

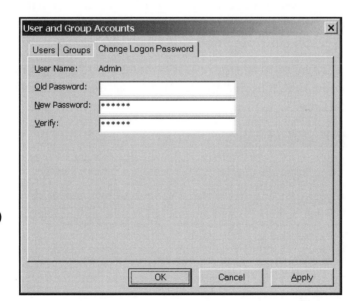

FIGURE 12.16

Viewing the User
and Group
Accounts security
window.

FIGURE 12.17

Changing the
Admin account's
password to
enable logon
procedures.

By default, the Admin user account's password is clear, which also disables the logon procedures for an Access database. Creating or changing the Admin account's password enables logon procedures. Once the Admin account's password has been created, close the Access program and reopen it. Access prompts you to enter your user name and password via the security dialog window seen in Figure 12.18.

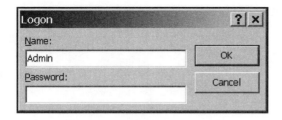

FIGURE 12.18

Logon procedures
enabled.

TRAP Make sure you carefully note the password you created for the Admin account. If you forget the Admin account password and have no other users created in the database, you cannot open your Access database!

Enabling User-Level Security

With logon procedures enabled, you can create user-level security mechanisms through Access's one-stop-shop for enabling and managing user-level security. Accessed from the Tools, Security menus, the User-Level Security wizard is a robust security mechanism for protecting your Access databases. The wizard does a good job of logically grouping security enablement and management activities into a nine-step process:

1. The User-Level Security wizard in Figure 12.19 creates a workgroup information file (stored in an .MDW file) that contains group and user account information, which Access reads at startup.

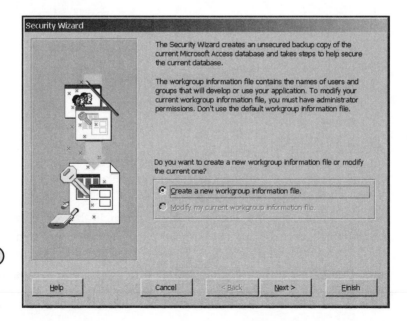

FIGURE 12.19

Creating a new
workgroup
information file.

2. The wizard allows you to make your new workgroup information file the default for all Access databases (see Figure 12.20) or simply enable your current Access database with security-enhanced features.

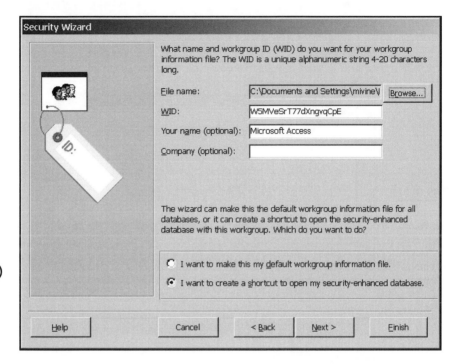

FIGURE 12.20

Specifying the workgroup information file as default or as a shortcut.

3. You can prevent Access from applying security mechanisms to one or more objects by deselecting the items in Figure 12.21.

4. Using the wizard, you can select one or more optional security group accounts for inclusion in your security-enhanced database. In Figure 12.22, I've opted to include the Read-Only Users and Update Data Users groups.

5. By default, all users belong to the Users group in all workgroup information files. The User-Level Security wizard assigns no permissions to the Users group, but you can override this, as seen in Figure 12.23.

6. You can manage users, their passwords, and the unique alphanumeric string property called PID, which generates a unique encoded value to identify each user. See Figure 12.24.

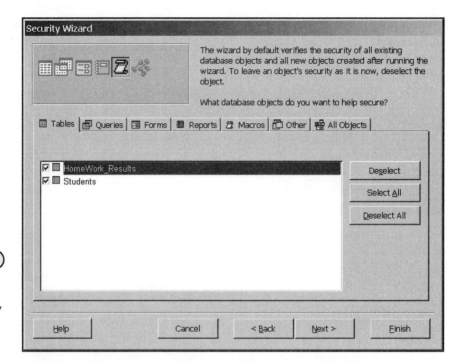

FIGURE 12.21

Preventing
Access from
applying security
mechanisms to
one or more
objects.

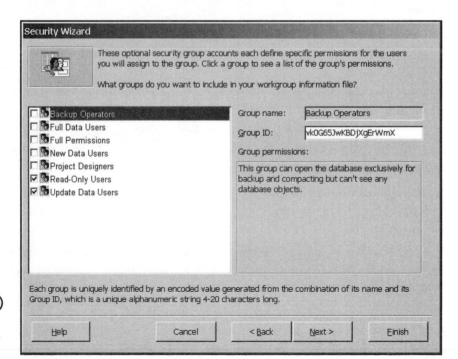

FIGURE 12.22

Selecting
optional security
group accounts.

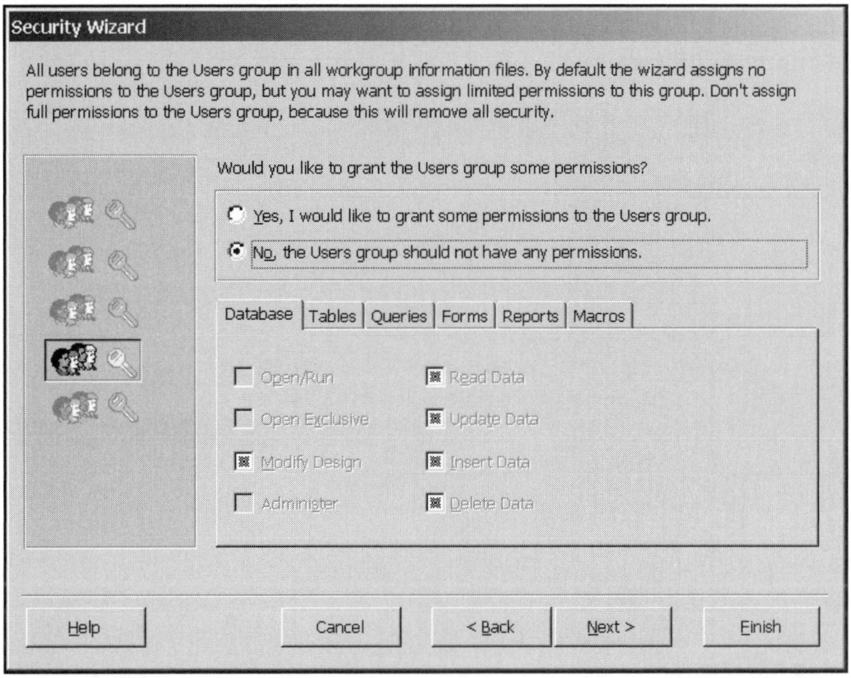

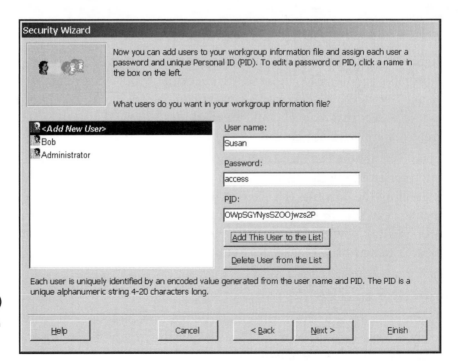

FIGURE 12.23

Modifying default
Users group
permissions.

FIGURE 12.24

Managing users in
the User-Level
Security wizard.

7. The User-Level Security wizard allows you to assign users to one or more groups. In Figure 12.25 I assign the user Bob to the Read-Only Users group.

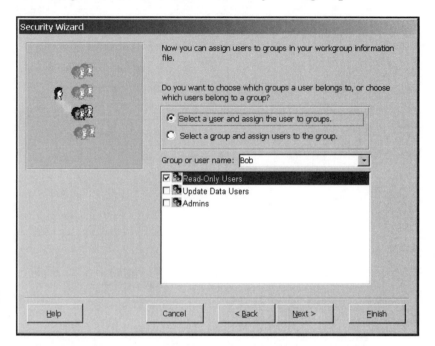

8. Before the wizard completes your security-enhanced database (see Figure 12.26), it prompts you to create an unsecured backup of your Access database, which essentially means Access creates a backup of your database as it is currently without user-level security enabled. This is a great idea in case the security mechanisms you created don't work as planned.

9. Upon completion, the User-Level Security wizard creates and saves the workgroup information file in the same location as the current Access database. In addition to generating the .MDW file, the security wizard generates and displays a security report that you can save to a file and later use to recreate your security-enhanced database. After saving the wizard's security report, Access must close the current database before the new user-level security-enhanced features take effect.

Connecting to a Workgroup

With logon procedures and security-enhanced features (user-level security) enabled, you're now ready to log back into your database. When the Access file is reopened, you receive a log-in window similar to the one in Figure 12.27.

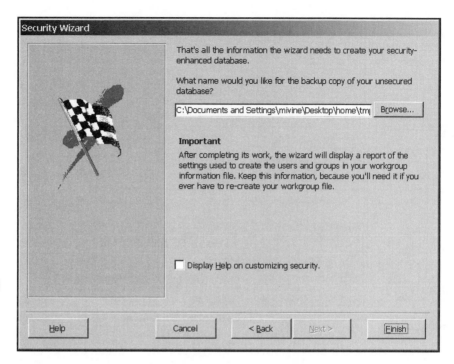

FIGURE 12.26

Creating an unsecured backup of your database.

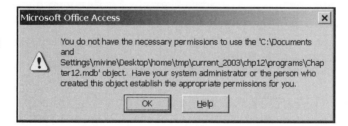

FIGURE 12.27

Opening a security-enhanced database without permissions.

Access gives an error when a user attempts to log into a security-enhanced database without the necessary permissions. To correct this problem, you or your users must connect to the workgroup information file created by the User-Level Security wizard (discussed in the previous section). To connect to a workgroup, select the Workgroup Administrator item from the Tools, Security menus.

As you can see from Figure 12.28, my security-enhanced database is still pointing to the default Access workgroup information file and not the one created in the previous section using the User-Level Security wizard. I can change this by clicking the Join command button and selecting the workgroup information file created by the wizard. Access notifies me of a successful workgroup connection (join) with the message in Figure 12.29.

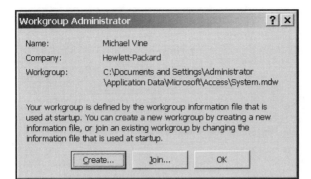

FIGURE 12.28

Viewing your current workgroup membership.

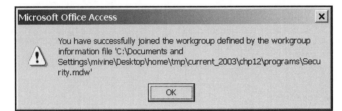

FIGURE 12.29

Joining a workgroup.

After successfully joining my newly created workgroup, I can reopen my security-enhanced database and log in with one of my new user accounts. To disable user-level security, simply clear the Admin user password and rejoin the default workgroup information file that is installed with Microsoft Access.

Securing Access from Data Access Pages

As mentioned, data access pages are not stored in the Access .mdb file and therefore do not automatically protect you from rogue users accessing your database via the Internet or intranet.

TRAP After enabling logon procedures and user-level security in an Access database, users cannot access your underlying data without implementing the data link property settings discussed in this section.

Access allows you to link a data access page to a workgroup information file, which helps secure Access from data access pages. Once a data access page is linked to a workgroup, Internet and intranet users are prompted for a user name and password when opening a data access page. To enable data access page security at the workgroup level, follow these steps:

1. Open the data access page in Design view and click the Page connection properties icon.

2. Once the Data Link Properties window is open, click the All tab and double-click the `OLEDB:System database` property.

3. Enter the path and filename of your workgroup information file into the property value section depicted in Figure 12.30.

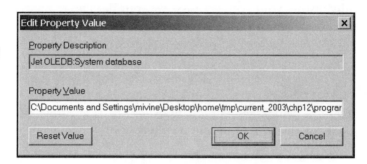

FIGURE 12.30

Assigning a workgroup information file path to the `OLEDB:System database` property.

4. Go back to the Connection tab; enter a user name and password that have appropriate database permissions.

5. Test the connection (as seen in Figure 12.31).

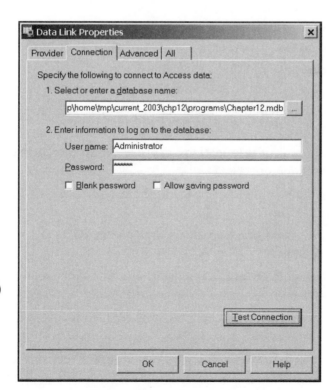

FIGURE 12.31

Testing a page's data source connection after assigning a workgroup information file.

TRAP

It is not advisable to select the Allow Saving Password option in Figure 12.31, which allows any user to access data in the Web page. In other words, this option defeats the purpose of user-level security.

6. After successfully testing your connection, save your data access page and test the user-level security by opening the Web page in Internet Explorer. Users should now be prompted to enter a user name and password before accessing the underlying data.

CHAPTER SUMMARY

- Data access pages are Web pages you create in Access. They allow users to view and work with a database over the Internet or an intranet.
- Sources for a data access page can be Microsoft Access, Microsoft SQL Server 6.5 or later, and Microsoft Excel.
- Microsoft Access stores data access pages in an Internet file format using the .htm extension.
- You can open data access pages in either Access or via Internet Explorer 5.01 with Service Pack 2 (SP2) or later.
- Data access pages created in Microsoft Access 2003 cannot be opened in Design view in older versions of Access.
- Creating a data access page in Design view allows you to manage the data access page's connection to a data source through the page connection properties link.
- Database fields can be added to your data access page from either tables or queries using the field list.
- Data access pages are broken into sections: caption, group header, group record, record navigation, and footer.
- Access binds controls on a data access page to the data source field (just like bound controls on an Access form).
- You can graphically display a one-to-many relationship in a data access page by creating additional group sections.
- Data access pages are typically published to either a file server such as Microsoft Windows 2000 or a Web server such as Microsoft IIS.
- Logon procedures for an Access database must be enabled before you can implement user-level security permissions.
- By default, Access 2003 databases come with two groups, Users and Admins. Also by default, Access comes with one user account called Admin belonging to the Admins group.

- Clearing the Admin user account's password disables logon procedures for an Access database.

- Creating or changing the Admin account's password enables logon procedures.

- The User-Level Security wizard is a robust security mechanism for protecting your Access databases.

- The User-Level Security wizard allows you to make a new workgroup information file to enable your Access database with security-enhanced features.

- Users can join a workgroup that has security-enhanced features created by the User-Level Security wizard.

- To disable user-level security, clear the Admin user password and rejoin the default workgroup information file installed with Microsoft Access.

- Access allows you to link a data access page to a workgroup information file, which helps secure Access from data access pages.

PROGRAMMING CHALLENGES

1. Create a new Access database with two tables named Books and Authors. The Books table should have the following fields and properties:

   - Book_Id: **AutoNumber**
   - Author_Id: **Number (Long Integer)**
   - Book_Title: **Text**
   - Page_Count: **Number (Long Integer)**
   - Publisher: **Text**
   - Publish_Date: **Date/Time**
   - Sales_Price: **Currency**

   The Authors table should have the following fields and properties:

   - Author_Id: **AutoNumber**
   - Author_LastName: **Text**
   - Author_FirstName: **Text**

   Create a one-to-many relationship between the Books and Authors tables using the Author_Id field. Insert records into both tables and save the database.

(continues)

PROGRAMMING CHALLENGES (CONTINUED)

2. Using the same database from Challenge 1, create a new data access page that allows a user to manage book information only.

3. Using the same database from Challenge 1, create a new data access page that uses groups to manage both books and authors. Users should be able to select an author from the top group and view the author's books in a separate group.

4. Activate logon procedures for the database created in Challenge 1. Remember to note the password created for the Admin user!

5. Enable user-level security for the database created in Challenge 1 by creating a new workgroup information file for this database only (security-enhanced database). Create two new user accounts, assigning one to the Update group and the other to the Read-Only group. Test your new security-enhanced database by connecting to the new workgroup and logging into the database with both users. Verify that one user can update table data and that the other user cannot.

6. Link the data access page from Challenge 3 to the workgroup information file created in Challenge 5. Save your data access page and open it using Internet Explorer. When opening the Web page, you should be prompted with an Access login window. Verify that each user created in Challenge 5 can log into the data access page successfully with the appropriate security privileges.

Common Character Codes

The items in this table represent the most common characters and associated character codes used in conjunction with the Chr and Asc functions.

Code	Character	Code	Character
8	Backspace	46	.
9	Tab	47	/
10	Line feed	48	0
13	Carriage return	49	1
32	Spacebar	50	2
33	!	51	3
34	"	52	4
35	#	53	5
36	$	54	6
37	%	55	7
38	&	56	8
39	'	57	9
40	(	58	:
41	)	59	;
42	*	60	<
43	+	61	=
44	,	62	>
45	–	63	?

(continues)

Code	Character
64	@
65	A
66	B
67	C
68	D
69	E
70	F
71	G
72	H
73	I
74	J
75	K
76	L
77	M
78	N
79	O
80	P
81	Q
82	R
83	S
84	T
85	U
86	V
87	W
88	X
89	Y
90	Z
91	[
92	\
93	]
94	^
95	_
96	`
97	a

Code	Character
98	b
99	c
100	d
101	e
102	f
103	g
104	h
105	i
106	j
107	k
108	l
109	m
110	n
111	o
112	p
113	q
114	r
115	s
116	t
117	u
118	v
119	w
120	x
121	y
122	z
123	{
124	|
125	}
126	~
127	Del (Delete key)

KEYBOARD SHORTCUTS
FOR THE CODE WINDOW

The items in the following table represent common keyboard shortcuts that can be used in the Visual Basic Environment's (VBE) code window.

Task	Shortcut
Beginning of module	Ctrl+Home
Clear all breakpoints	Ctrl+Shift+F9
Delete current line	Ctrl+Y
Delete to end of word	Ctrl+Delete
End of module	Ctrl+End
Find	Ctrl+F
Find next	F3
Find previous	Shift+F3
Go to last position	Ctrl+Shift+F2
Indent	Tab
Move one word to left	Ctrl+Left Arrow
Move one word to right	Ctrl+Right Arrow
Move to beginning of line	Home

(continues)

Task	Shortcut
Move to end of line	End
Next procedure	Ctrl+Down Arrow
Outdent	Shift+Tab
Previous procedure	Ctrl+Up Arrow
Replace	Ctrl+H
Shift one screen down	Ctrl+Page Down
Shift one screen up	Ctrl+Page Up
Undo	Ctrl+Z
View code window (control selected in Design View)	F7
View definition	Shift+F2
View Object Browser	F2
View shortcut menu	Shift+F10

TRAPPABLE ERRORS

Microsoft provides a comprehensive list of trappable errors that you can catch, display, and troubleshoot during runtime, development, or compile time.

Error Code	Error Description
3	Return without GoSub
5	Invalid procedure call
6	Overflow
7	Out of memory
9	Subscript out of range
10	This array is fixed or temporarily locked
11	Division by 0
13	Type mismatch
14	Out of string space
16	Expression too complex
17	Can't perform requested operation
18	User interruption (Ctrl + Break) occurred
20	Resume without error
28	Out of stack space

(continues)

Error Code	Error Description
35	Sub, Function, or Property not defined
47	Too many code resource or DLL application clients
48	Error in loading code resource or DLL
49	Bad code resource or DLL calling convention
51	Internal error
52	Bad filename or number
53	File not found
54	Bad file mode
55	File already open
57	Device I/O error
58	File already exists
59	Bad record length
61	Disk full
62	Input past end of file
63	Bad record number
67	Too many files
68	Device unavailable
70	Permission denied
71	Disk not ready
74	Can't rename with different drive
75	Path/file access error
76	Path not found
91	Object variable or With block variable not set
92	For loop not initialized
93	Invalid pattern string
94	Invalid use of Null
97	Can't call Friend procedure on an object that is not an instance of the defining class
98	A property or method call cannot include a reference to a private object, either as an argument or as a return value
298	System resource or DLL could not be loaded

(continues)

Error Code	Error Description
320	Can't use character device names in specified filenames
321	Invalid file format
322	Can't create necessary temporary file
325	Invalid format in resource file
327	Data value named not found
328	Illegal parameter; can't write arrays
335	Could not access system registry
336	Component not correctly registered
337	Component not found
338	Component did not run correctly
360	Object already loaded
361	Can't load or unload this object
363	Control specified not found
364	Object was unloaded
365	Unable to unload within this context
368	The specified file is out of date; this program requires a later version
371	The specified object can't be used as an owner form for Show
380	Invalid property value
381	Invalid property-array index
382	Property Set can't be executed at runtime
383	Property Set can't be used with a read-only property
385	Need property-array index
387	Property Set not permitted
393	Property Get can't be executed at runtime
394	Property Get can't be executed on write-only property
400	Form already displayed; can't show modally
402	Code must close topmost modal form first
419	Permission to use object denied
422	Property not found
423	Property or method not found

(continues)

Error Code	Error Description
424	Object required
425	Invalid object use
429	Component can't create object or return reference to this object
430	Class doesn't support Automation
432	File name or class name not found during Automation operation
438	Object doesn't support this property or method
440	Automation error
442	Connection to type library or object library for remote process has been lost
443	Automation object doesn't have a default value
445	Object doesn't support this action
446	Object doesn't support named arguments
447	Object doesn't support current locale setting
448	Named argument not found
449	Argument not optional or invalid property assignment
450	Wrong number of arguments or invalid property assignment
451	Object not a collection
452	Invalid ordinal
453	Specified code resource not found
454	Code resource not found
455	Code resource lock error
457	This key is already associated with an element of this collection
458	Variable uses a type not supported in Visual Basic
459	This component doesn't support the set of events
460	Invalid Clipboard format
461	Method or data member not found
462	The remote server machine does not exist or is unavailable
463	Class not registered on local machine
480	Can't create AutoRedraw image
481	Invalid picture
482	Printer error

(continues)

Error Code	Error Description
483	Printer driver does not support specified property
484	Problem getting printer information from the system; make sure printer is set up correctly
485	Invalid picture type
486	Can't print form image to this type of printer
520	Can't empty Clipboard
521	Can't open Clipboard
735	Can't save file to TEMP directory
744	Search text not found
746	Replacements too long
31001	Out of memory
31004	No object
31018	Class is not set
31027	Unable to activate object
31032	Unable to create embedded object
31036	Error saving to file
31037	Error loading from file

Index

License Agreement/Notice of Limited Warranty